SPLASH

ACROSS
TEXAS!

The Definitive Guide to Swimming in Central Texas

Chandra Moira Beal

La Luna Publishing
Austin, Texas 1999

Splash Across Texas!
The Definitive Guide to Swimming in Central Texas

By Chandra Moira Beal

Published by:
La Luna Publishing
Post Office Box 33189
Austin, Texas 78764-0189 USA
www.beal-net.com/chandra
laluna@onr.com

All photographs taken by the author unless otherwise noted. Logo of City of Austin Parks and Recreation reprinted by permission.

The information in this book is true and correct to the best of our knowledge. All recommendations are made without guarantee on the part of the author or La Luna Publishing. The author and publisher disclaim any liability in connection with the use of this information.

Copyright © 1999 by Chandra Moira Beal
First Printing 1999
Printed in the United States of America

Beal, Chandra Moira
Splash Across Texas! The Definitive Guide to Swimming in Central Texas/by Chandra Moira Beal.—1st edition
Includes bibliography and index
1. history
2. nature and natural history
3. sports and recreation
4. travel and travel guides

ISBN 0-9671604-0-5

ACKNOWLEDGMENTS

I am grateful for the support that enabled me to write this book, and wish to thank the following persons:

My family, first and foremost, for believing in me and my goal; my father, Richard Beal, and step mother, Kathy Beal, provided me with essential tools and guidance; my mother, Jorja Latham, answered numerous style questions and proofread; my extended family encouraged me from the outset; Maia, for her patience; the staff at the Austin Public Library and the Austin History Center for their guidance and expertise during my research; Jim Halbrook, the City of Austin Parks and Recreation Department Public Information Officer, for answering all of my questions; Susan Lish and Chris Karvelas in the Austin State School Community Relations Department for letting me borrow original photographs of Swimathon; Jim Collett at the Austin Nature Center who gave me a better understanding of the Edwards Aquifer; Ron Downing of the Kingsland Chamber of Commerce for loaning me pictures of 'the Slab'; Bob McCollough and Bob French of Sea World; Sherrie Brammall of Schlitterbahn; Michael Baxter of Splashtown Houston; Michele Melkerson-Granyrd at The Hills; Keith Kinney of Splashtown San Antonio; Scott Young of Adventure Bay; Anne Cook, the audio-visual librarian at the Texas Department of Transportation for assisting me with photographs; Jim Miller at the University of Texas for letting me photograph Gregory Gym, and Marsha Miller at the University of Texas for researching photographs of Gregory Gym; Signature Color and Holland Photo for photographic reproduction; Rex A. Maximilian for technical assistance and editing; the countless park and pool employees and lifeguards who gave me access to facilities for research; and to all the swimmers and water lovers in Central Texas who reminded me how relevant this book would be.

Very special thanks to F. Stan Gove and Presence of minD for technical support, moral support, cover design, and above all, love.

DEDICATION

This book is dedicated to Beverly Sheffield, former Director of Austin Parks and Recreation. We are indebted to Mr. Sheffield for developing Austin's aquatic resources and ensuring their success. He provided me with invaluable information, resources, and stories. I will always treasure the time he spent with me talking about Austin's good ol' days, and I simply could not have written this book without his input. Thank you, Beverly, for a lifetime of service. Your vision is a reality, and we are forever grateful.

TABLE OF CONTENTS

How High's The Water, Mama? Three Feet High and Rising!

CENTRAL TEXAS SPLENDOR
Municipal Pools Outside of Austin 199

OLD FASHIONED SWIMMIN' HOLES
Natural Springs & Rivers 219

PREFACE

Austin, Texas is often referred to as the 'live music capital of the world'. While that title is often debated, you will hear no argument whether Austin is the swimming pool capital of the world. In fact, Austin has more swimming pools per capita than any other city in the nation. We also sport the largest natural swimming pool located within an urban area (Barton Springs) and a multitude of swimming holes, creeks and lakes. Opportunities to get wet abound all over Central Texas.

I wish I could say that I grew up in and around the splendid pools of Central Texas, but I did not. Instead, I had the equally enviable fortune of growing up in Santa Cruz, a small, coastal resort town in central California. I spent summers bodysurfing with my brothers in the Pacific Ocean. The water was cold, salty and sandy. The beach was our babysitter, the warm sand our security blanket. We occasionally swam in the city's man-made pools, but considered the ocean to be our own backyard pool, free of lifeguards and imposed rules. On the coast, air conditioning was unheard of, and swimming pools were for the elite. Little did I know what was in store for me.

The author's passion for pools began at an early age.

The first time I saw Austin was from an airplane. As we flew over hundreds of miles of brown, flat earth in west Texas, my heart sank. Then suddenly the landscape turned a lush green, and large, finger-like lakes appeared below. I could make out houses as we descended, but one thing in particular stood out: there was water everywhere. From above, it seemed that it was requisite to have a swimming pool in your backyard. Kidney-shaped, square, round, oval. I suppose that it was inevitable that I discovered Barton Springs and Hamilton Pool on my first visit to this area. I was immediately enchanted, and when I returned to California, I began to yearn for those warm summer nights and blistering days spent swimming in Barton Springs. I dreamed about Central Texas, about wiggling my toes in the dirt and wading deep into the water for relief. The mild year-round climate seemed conducive to recreation, and there were plenty of opportunities to do so. So, I moved to Austin. It took me a while to discover that Austin had a multitude of swimming pools and springs. I began hanging out at Deep Eddy, Big Stacy, and Barton Springs. It was here that I learned the most about Austin, about its character and makeup, its traditions and history. My curiosity piqued, I began to explore other pools around Central Texas.

Swimming has become one of my favorite rituals. I love the aesthetics of water. The layers of paint on the sides of the pool tell the story of its history: little chips of robin's egg blue, mint green, vanilla white, and that institutional pink-beige color seen in old public buildings. The texture is rough in places where it has been painted over and over, and smooth in others. The black glossy numbers telling the depth on the side of the pool are fresh this year. Rust stains gradually appear around the metal spigots and drains. The water is glassy and clear. Refractions of light dance around the walls and cast shadows on the underside of the lifeguard's umbrella. Cicadas buzz in the pecan trees, grackles chase smaller birds around the base of an oak with their hysterical cry. Cotton tufts float downward from the towering cottonwood trees, and the leaves produce a tiny applause in a brief, soft breeze. Cumulus clouds drift across the big blue sky, sometimes obscuring the sun and providing relief for a minute or two. People are strewn all over the grass, hanging on the side of the pool, reading the Sunday paper, asleep under an open magazine, tapping their toes to their headphones, people-watching, browning in the sun like lizards, squinting, wiping sweat from their brows and the back of their necks. You can taste the chlorine, the suntan lotion, the coconut oil, the salt, and the sweat. The concrete sidewalk is too hot to stand on, even with wet feet. There are only two places to be: in the water or in the shade.

The children are everywhere, playing games that never go out of style. They are barely able to keep from breaking into a run, jumping into the water with a cannonball splash, diving for copper pennies that glint in the sun. Shouts of "Marco! Polo!" permeate the air. They are standing on their hands, floating on giant, inflatable alligators, counting change for sodas. When the lifeguard blows his whistle at the top of each hour, everyone must exit the water while the guards do a safety check. The silence is noticeable, and suddenly the only sound is coming from the buzzing cicadas. The water becomes still and calm. Five minutes later, the whistle sounds again and people rush back toward the water, splashing and shouting.

I prefer the outdoor pool so I can watch the moon rising as I backstroke. Birds dart overhead, and planes soar high above. I like to make shapes out of the clouds and daydream. I think people go to the pool to relax, to refresh, to renew, and to re-create. Some people don't ever get in the water, but they come every day because they want to be near it. In the water you can let go, flow, float, and relax. Being under water is like being in a totally different world. Sounds carry through the water like nothing else. You can hear children shrieking and water splashing and plunging. Birds are chirping and a plane is roaring overhead.

Water has a protective, healing quality about it. Springs are about hope, rebirth and rejuvenation. They frequently support life in an area where water is scarce. Springs are sacred places, considered the meeting place between the surface and the underworld, the conscious and the unconscious.

Austin's neighborhood pools are aptly named. They have the feeling of a neighborhood bar, a source of community and friendship. You recognize people by their bathing suits, even if you don't talk to them. Parading around in a bathing suit with wet hair somehow equalizes people. Year after year, tan lines change, bodies change. You spread your blanket out in the same spot every year.

This is summer in Central Texas, and it is heaven on earth.

BATHING THROUGHOUT HISTORY

The pleasure of swimming is as old as the history of man. Evidence of five thousand year-old swimming pools and baths is still evident in Egypt and India, while in Rome two thousand year-old baths are still in use. Bathing was an absolute passion with the Romans. At the height of the Roman Empire, Rome itself had more than eight hundred pools, some large enough to accommodate thousands of people. The Roman baths were quite luxurious, even as the empire crumbled around them. Surrounded by statuary and warmly lit by torches and refracted light from the water, some baths had secret alcoves hiding dens of vice. Large marble columns and ornate paintings of water nymphs decorated the walls. Romans also swam in the Tiber River where they developed the breaststroke to keep the mouth above water and particles away by sweeping with the arms in response to deteriorating waterways. The Romans not only swam for pleasure but built elaborate aqueducts and filled their amphitheaters with water to re-enact naval battles.

The Greeks were less obsessed about swimming, but they wanted water to surround them everywhere, flowing in public fountains and through channels throughout the city. The Greeks believed that water was a source of renewal and built places of worship around springs and pools. Water was considered magical, mysterious, and sometimes dangerous. Some springs were thought to cause insanity, while others made you drunk. The Greeks held Olympian diving championships and swam for sport, revering the athlete as a hero.

Native Americans, too, bathed regularly in springs and rivers. Pocahontas was an accomplished diver and swimmer.

With the rise of Christianity, swimming and bathing declined. The Church spread tales of horrible sea monsters who dwelled in the water and mermaids who would seduce you into a terrible fate. The swimmer was no longer deemed a hero but rather a lost soul in need of saving in a vast sea, adrift from faith. Swimming also became associated with sensual pleasure and was discouraged. In fact, during the Victorian age, it was considered indecent for women to learn to swim. Many women drowned in shipwrecks weighted by their clothing and lack of swimming skills. It did not become popular again until the early nineteenth century, but a few people continued to take the waters.

For example, Benjamin Franklin jumped naked as a blue jay into the Thames River for a swim in 1726. Before the Victorian Age, most people swam naked, a practice perhaps we should have never given up. Today, Hippie Hollow at Lake Travis is the only place in Texas where you can legally swim without clothing. Controversy still rages over women going topless at Barton Springs.

When Pompeii was rediscovered by English archeologists in the middle of the eighteenth century, they found massive fountains and numerous pools. This finding, coinciding with the height of Romanticism, sparked a renewed interest in Classicism, which considered swimming a noble sport. In 1828 the first Swimming Society of England was formed.

At the turn of the century, the English experienced a sea-bathing fad. Sea water was touted as therapeutic and a cure-all, healing everything from cancer to gout. Men wore calceons—one-piece bathing suits that came down to the knees and resembled an undershirt above. The women were required to wear long bloomer skirts which billowed up over their heads when they entered the water and became transparent when wet, a costume which must have been defeating and uncomfortable. As bathing resorts popped up all over England's coast, so did underwater spectacles. 'Lurline' was one such entertainer who performed for the

A calceon

Royal Family and the thousands of people who gathered to watch. In 1881 she remained underwater for nearly three minutes, while her counterpart, Elise Wallenda, stayed underwater for almost five minutes sewing, undressing, writing, eating and drinking all the while. These kinds of stunts became more and more dramatic and dangerous and were eventually banned.

Typical women's bathing attire at the turn of the century

From the 1870s to the mid-twentieth century, America had its own bathing craze. Hundreds of resorts and hot springs attracted thousands of people from all over the country seeking to 'take the waters'. Reminiscent of ancient Rome, some springs had elaborate resorts built around them with entertainment and recreation provided.

Towns such as Hot Springs in Arkansas, Sulphur Springs in West Virginia, Saratoga Springs in New York and Mineral Wells in Texas earned fame for their 'magic water curatives'. People wanted to drink it, bathe in it, bottle it and take it home, and they were willing to pay any price. The mineral springs and hot wells were a naturally occurring phenomenon. Many contained lithium, among
other chemicals and minerals, such as sulfur, sodium, and magnesium; naturally, people felt better after their baths. In fact, sanitariums were often built around the wells as insane people were seemingly 'cured' by the bath water.

Texas was definitely in on the bathing fad. Sam Houston attended Sour Lake Resort in East Texas in 1863 to minister to his war injuries. Numerous bathhouses were built in Central Texas, some around hot springs and others around chilly rivers. Remember, this was during an era without indoor plumbing, and baths were considered a luxury. Baths were places to get a good scrubbing, a shave and a haircut, and a good meal.

The toilet barbershop, Harry Hawkins proprietor, has just been handsomely repainted and refitted in modern style. Its bathrooms have also been refurbished and altogether it is a model establishment--in fact, the best place in town to get a good shave and a cool bath. The barbers are very attentive and efficient. Don't forget to call on Harry Hawkins when you wish anything in this line, as he will take pleasure in attending to your wants.

July 20, 1881 Austin Democratic Statesman

The only mineral water health resort still operating in Texas is Stovall Wells in South Bend. Bathhouses have been replaced by spas and health clubs, but natural springs continue to abound. Many springs continue to operate by reputation of their medicinal benefits.

Early swimming strokes were modeled after animals such as frogs and dogs. The Australian crawl or freestyle stroke did not become popular until the turn of the century when an American won the event at the 1904 Olympics. Americans then began building lavish and glamorous pools, usually symbols of affluence. Swimming was popularized and glamorized for several decades, and Americans choose swimming as a favorite pastime to this day.

One person responsible for thousands of young girls getting started in swimming is Esther Williams, a professional swimmer turned aquatic actress, famous for her roles in the 1930s 'Aquacade' musicals of Busby Berkeley. Synchronized swimming in waterproof makeup and a perfect smile were her trademarks.

3

Annette Kellermann also popularized swimming. Originally from Australia, Kellermann overcame polio as a child to become a world-renowned championship swimmer covering long stretches in rivers such as the Thames, Seine and Danube. Her act was a graceful underwater ballet.

Today, swimming is as popular as it has ever been. Summertime rituals of frequenting the pool, lake, river or spring are almost universal. Perhaps in the future when the remains of Central Texas are unearthed by archeologists, our reputation for bathing will rival that of ancient Rome.

> *Swimming cultivates imagination; the man with the most is he who can swim his solitary course day or night and can forget a black earth full of people. This love of the unknown is the greatest of all the joys which swimming has for me. I am still looking for my chest of gold in a cool, dripping sea cave, or mermaid combing long green hair.*
>
> Annette Kellerman

LAND OF 1,100 SPRINGS

The old slogan for Pearl Beer claimed Central Texas is the 'Land of 1,100 Springs'. That number is probably a gross underestimate. Central Texas is simply swimming in natural springs and rivers. Add to that the abundance of man-made pools, water parks, and old-fashioned swimming holes, and the opportunities for getting wet are staggering. People caught on to this notion a long, long time ago. Numerous arrowheads and Native American artifacts have been found around our springs, evidence that Indian tribes used them for centuries as a natural form of air conditioning. Although modern urbanization and pollution have reduced the number of flowing springs, the Pearl Beer slogan is, at least, still accurate.

The first humans to live in what is now known as Travis County probably came here at the end of the Ice Age eleven thousand years ago. Archeological sites in the area have turned up evidence and relics of human presence since prehistoric times. People have continued to live in this area since that time because of the abundance of water. Tonkawa, Comanche, Apache, and Jumano Indians resided in this area or migrated through it, and Spanish explorer and missionaries later encountered these tribes when they settled the area in the 1700s. Between 1680 and 1800 the Colorado River was their lifeline. Missions and forts were established along the banks, including one at Barton Springs in Austin.

Anglos did not settle here until Texas became independent from Mexico in 1837. The areas now known as Austin and Bastrop supported some of the first settlements along the Colorado River. Jake Harrell, a friend of Texas Vice-President Mirabeau B. Lamar, founded a camp on the Colorado River about where the Congress Avenue Bridge in Austin is now located and named it Waterloo. Lamar was out buffalo hunting one day when he came across the Waterloo camp. An officer of the Republic of Texas had earlier described it to Lamar as "The most beautiful and at the same time the most sublime scene I ever saw... The atmosphere was charged with the most delightful perfume and every shrub and every hill and every flower seemed to extend a welcome to the weary traveler." Lamar must have agreed because he deemed it worthy as the site of the new Texas capital. Lamar and Sam Houston battled each other over which camp would host the new Republic's government, but in 1839 Austin was officially chosen. It was named after Stephen F. Austin, a prominent farmer who had settled here with his family. The area now known as Montopolis

5

was also considered as the future capital site, as was Bastrop, then known as Mina (say 'Mee-nah'). Travis County and the City of Austin were both incorporated in 1839. The capital was officially moved from Houston in 1840 and the first permanent building in Austin was erected. Edwin Waller, for whom Waller Creek is named, surveyed the area near Waterloo and sold 320 lots, dividing up the forty thousand square-miles that originally made up Travis County. In 1842 the capital temporarily moved back to Houston when the Mexican Army captured San Antonio. In 1845 the government relocated permanently back to Austin and the capitol building was completed in 1850. It was then destroyed in 1860 by fire, and the present building was completed in 1888. The Colorado River played an integral part in the building of the capitol and the city of Austin. Building materials and workmen were transported on the water by boat, limestone was excavated out of the riverbed, and the flow of the water powered early mills and tools.

Central Texas is at the convergence point of several distinct geological features, making it a unique place in the world. The Edwards Plateau to the west is characterized by limestone caves, deep aquifers and granite beds, which house many varieties of animals, some endangered or rare. The Edwards Plateau is covered by the western Hill Country and the Highland Lakes. Plant and animal life are abundant and varied. This area is strewn with hundreds of springs, streams, creeks and natural pools. The Balcones Fault bisects Austin with a 600-foot uplift, and is the source of many springs, one of the largest being the San Marcos River. The Blackland Prairies lie to the east of the fault with abundant wildflowers and native plants and deep, rich soil. The Colorado River weaves through it all. In the northernmost part of Travis County the Crosstimbers region of rolling, woody Savannah just grazes the boundary. Post oaks and blackjack oak can be found there. Since the Colorado River was dammed in the 1940s, residents in this area have been enjoying a plenitude of recreational opportunities.

The Edwards Aquifer formed as the result of a shallow sea that covered Texas during the Cretaceous period, about 100 million years ago. Austin was part of a reef system littered with seashell creatures. Over the years, beds of limestone formed from the shells of these animals, and water has dissolved tiny holes throughout that act like a porous filter. Earthquakes then ripped open sections of the limestone along fault lines allowing the water to rise as springs. About 300,000 acre-feet of water are stored in this underground maze. The Aquifer curves from Bell to Kinney County and provides drinking water to Austin, San Antonio, Salado, Georgetown, and Round Rock. It is recharged from six creeks: Barton, Williamson, Slaughter, Bear, Little Bear and Onion.

Well discharge of the Edwards Aquifer increased substantially from the late 1800s as it was used extensively for public water supply and agriculture. A continuous increase in well discharge has had an effect on natural spring discharge, and San Pedro, San Antonio and Comal Springs have become intermittent instead of flowing. Water conservation plans are now *de rigueur* and the Texas Natural Resources Conservation Commission monitors the flow of springs to make sure they are not jeopardized.

The climate in Central Texas is ideal for water-oriented recreation. With mild winters and just a few days below freezing, and summer temperatures soaring in excess of 100 degrees, water sports are enjoyed year-round. Average rainfall is thirty-two inches per year.

To the lovers of athletics and aquatics: Austin certainly enjoys facilities on the Colorado River for aquatic sport that any other city would indeed be justly proud of. The apathy of your citizens must of a surety be quite apparent in this mater when only just now the question is mooted as to the practicality of utilizing these natural resources. Mr. G.H. Hammersley, a gentleman of experience and indefatigable exertion, is again included to inaugurate an event for the benefit of our suffering community, a panacea for all the afflictions these are heir to. He proposes to raise by joint stock cooperation of 150 shares at $25 a share, to build and equip a floating boat house, gymnasium and swimming school combined, etc. The plan is quite feasible and self-supported by catering to the public taste at a mere nominal rate of charge besides realizing the agreeable and healthy stimulus accruing from bodily exertion in all its varied forms. This school is certainly a good one, therefore heartily recommend its expediency and all who can not hesitate a moment in favoring so praiseworthy an object, remembering its two-fold influences for pleasure and profit. We therefore reiterate in the strongest terms, not to neglect so glaring an opportunity to advance a cause so beneficial to the public welfare and assist Mr. Hammersley in his laudable endeavor.

Austin Democratic Statesman, date unknown

CITY OF AUSTIN

Austin has a climate which allows outdoor recreation throughout the year, and the city enjoys excellent natural resources for swimming and all water sports. One of the reasons that the city has so many outdoor swimming pools is that Austin has its own water system with a large supply of water; and of course, the beautiful Barton Springs is incomparable.

-from Planning Ahead: Recreation in Austin

CITY OF AUSTIN PARKS AND RECREATION

901 West Riverside Drive
Austin, Texas 78704
(512) 499-6700
http://www.ci.austin.tx.us/parks/pkpools.htm

Among the many delightful features which Austin possesses over any other city in Texas as a Home City is the comfort and luxury of inviting surroundings. It matters not how unpleasant the weather may be in other parts of Texas, it is never muddy in Austin. The red bugs and the mosquitoes have never invaded these precincts. The air is always tempered by cooling breezes from the river and lake, while the encircling semi-mountains protect the inhabitants of the city from storms. In Austin the individual who does not possess an automobile can find comfort on the Lake, at Deep Eddy, or on the cedar-clad hills in the cool of the evening when the day's work is over. Or he may ride on the river or Lake for pleasure or profit—the profit coming from splendid fish which can be caught all the year around. The individual who owns an automobile can add still other pleasures to his home life by a tour among the hills that present views unparalleled by any country short of Colorado. We will tell you more about this wonderful section and help you to make splendid investments here for your home life if you are interested.

-from a 1918 Chamber of Commerce tourism brochure

T he tourism brochure may have been laying it on a bit thick but Austin has plenty of reasons to be proud of its recreational resources. Austin has over two hundred parks, twenty-three greenbelts, thirty miles of hike and bike trails, and forty-four swimming pools— more per capita than any other city in the United States. From the inception of the Parks and Recreation department there existed a grand vision for Austin's future. Leaders envisioned a swimming pool within walking distance of every Austinite, a goal which has been effectively reached. Foresight in planning and systematic distribution have made this program successful. Today, participants in swimming still outnumber all other local sports activities. Austin's pools and parks were developed and promoted with objectives such as increasing health and safety, decreasing juvenile delinquency, and encouraging education, citizenship, and the enjoyment of leisure time. Recreation has always been recognized by this city as a valuable and essential aspect of our quality of life. Combined with an abundance of natural resources and an ideal climate for outdoor recreation, the vision was bound to succeed. The department is justly proud that they are well above the national standard for swimming pools per capita.

Before 1928, the city did not have any organized facilities, although people enjoyed boating excursions on the Colorado River and swimming at Barton Springs and Deep Eddy Resort, both privately owned at the time. In 1917 the city bought Barton Springs; the bathhouse came later in 1947. Rosewood was one of the earliest pools that the city constructed. Opened in 1929 it was segregated 'for Negroes only'. Doris Miller Auditorium, named for a young African-American seaman who was killed at Pearl Harbor, was added to the park in 1944. In the 1930s, Andrew Zilker donated the land adjacent to Barton Springs for a public park. This was quickly followed by the purchase of Deep Eddy and A.J. Eilers's park. Shortly after the city completed improvements at Deep Eddy, a flood on the Colorado River destroyed the bathhouse and caused major damage to the pool.

Boating on the Colorado River

Like most cities, the Great Depression was in some ways a boon to Austin's growth. The heyday of the Parks and Recreation department was between 1928 and 1937 when the city increased its facilities exponentially in an effort to boost the spirits of its citizens. Workforces such as the Works Progress Administration and the Civilian Conservation Corps built over two thousand pools across the nation during this period, including Pease, Eastwoods, Shipe, Metz, Rosewood, Palm, Big Stacy, Westenfield, and Parque Zaragosa here in Austin. The city and the WPA joined forces to rebuild Deep Eddy after the flood and developed Emma Long Park on Lake Austin in 1939. Emma Long Park is still the city's largest park with nearly twelve hundred acres.

By 1937, the city had completed East Avenue (no longer in existence), Ramsey and Bailey pools. Pan American Park followed in 1946. The department combined forces with public schools for the first time in 1939, when they built a pool at Metz

Elementary School. The pool benefited the students and the public community at the same time. The City of Austin continues this arrangement with many other schools to this day. By 1953 Gillis, Brentwood, Govalle and Patterson were added to the department, and in 1960 the city expanded to include West Austin. The 1970s saw the construction of Mabel Davis, Dottie Jordan, Kennemer, Montopolis and other pools; the growth didn't end in the 1980s when the city built Dittmar and Walnut Creek, among others. By 1988 the city had 190 parks in its system. Dick Nichols Pool is the newest, built in 1997. The national average is ten acres of park land per one thousand people, whereas in Austin we average twenty-two acres per one thousand people. Today Austin has over 140 parks and recreation centers. The system is one of the largest in the nation.

Friends at Deep Eddy

Austin's pools are much more than just places to splash around; neighborhood pools are places of community gathering, socializing and family fun. During the 1920s through the 1950s, beauty pageants were held at the pool. Carnivals were held at the pools in August to raise money for pool and playground equipment. Rosewood held an annual Juneteenth celebration and beauty revue. Water pageants were a regular part of the pools' season opening. There was ongoing entertainment such as beach and sports fashion revues, music, food, and swimming demonstrations. The city grew up with its population through Learn-to-Swim programs, lessons that have been ongoing since the department's inception. The city also held swim meets against other pools and cities, and taught life-saving and diving skills.

Miss Stacy Pool, 1953

In 1962 a city ordinance was passed requiring children under the age of 12 to demonstrate an ability to swim thirty yards if not accompanied by a guardian. Apparently, this was fine with the general public as more parents accompanied their children to the pools: *"There was no argument from a youngster if the guard ordered him out of the pool because he couldn't manage the required thirty-yard swim."-from the 1961-1962 Annual Report.*

13

Learning to swim at Westenfield Pool

The city has an excellent safety history. There has never been a single drowning in any of the city pools due to negligence, though there have been numerous accidents in the area's lakes and rivers throughout history.

The city now has a free 'Summer Playground Program' for kids aged 6-12. They meet at many of the parks and pools and provide learning and environmental fun. They also have a similar program for teens to keep them occupied during the summer.

The Parks and Recreation Department is part of the quality of life that makes Austin what it is, a unique and beautiful community that everyone loves. Austin symbolizes what other Texas cities wish to be. If you have suggestions on how to improve the parks and pools, or want to volunteer, Parks and Recreation welcomes your input.

Beverly Sheffield

The hand that guided the development of Austin's parks and pools deserves a few words. Mr. Beverly Sheffield was Director of Parks and Recreation from 1946 until 1973. Born in 1913 and raised in Alamo Heights, he first swam in Barton Springs when he was 10 years old, an event he still remembers vividly ("Cold!"). He became a lifeguard when he was 21 and served at Westenfield Pool. He then became a playground leader and gave swimming lessons, organized water pageants, and promoted aquatics for the city. In 1940, Director Jim Garrison took a leave of absence to work for the Department of Defense, and an ad was placed for a replacement:

Recreation Genius Needed by March 15, 1941: Are you an authority on art, music, drama? Do you know athletics and recreation? Are you an administrator of the first rank, and do you understand finance? Have you a pleasing personality and the patience and tact of a canonized saint and the firm determination of an insurance salesman? If the answer is "yes," the city has a job for you in the recreation department. Beverly Sheffield has been carrying on in the absence of Garrison, but Sheffield is but one man, not triplets.

Austin American Statesman, March 6, 1941

Beverly Sheffield fit the description so well he continued as the acting Director of Parks and Recreation until 1946, when he decided he'd stay on permanently. Sheffield refers to himself as 'Austin's most prolific liar'; he'd often tell people that he couldn't attend a meeting because he had a conflicting appointment, and that 'appointment' was usually with Barton Springs! For a time, he had the only key to Barton Springs and would let himself in to cool off on summer nights while the rest of Austin sweated out the days before air conditioning. Friends would remark how he always seemed so comfortable and refreshed, and Sheffield would smile inwardly with guilty pleasure.

There have been six directors since Sheffield left, which attests to his towering reputation. In addition to his passion for swimming pools and park land, he helped guide the development of the Zilker Botanical Gardens and the Town Lake hike and bike trail, among other things. Thanks to Sheffield, much of the history of Austin has been recorded for posterity.

Although he has always been interested in swimming, he didn't get serious about it until his friend, Charlie Morrison, swam a mile on his 80th birthday. This wake-up call prompted him to take better care of his body and start logging his swims. Since he began keeping records in 1963, Sheffield estimates he has swum all the way to the West Coast and about halfway across the Pacific Ocean to Hawaii. Sheffield still swims as often as he can in Barton Springs, but can occasionally be found at Deep Eddy. He is a regular Polar Bear (see page 33) and swims year-round.

A Few Details

In terms of municipal pools, Bartholomew, Garrison, and Mabel Davis are generally open from Memorial Day to Labor Day, with hours varying from pool to pool. It is always best to call ahead. Sometimes hours are posted at the entrance gate. Deep Eddy opens in April and stays open until the end of October. Northwest opens in mid-May and closes in mid-September. Walnut Creek opens mid-May and closes Labor Day weekend. Municipal pools dedicate certain hours to swim team practice sessions and lessons.

The neighborhood and wading pools generally open on Memorial Day, or the first week of June. Most of the neighborhood pools close when Austin schools resume in mid-August. People often ask why the city's pools are not open year-round. The answer is understaffing. Of the 400 or so lifeguards, about 350 are high school and college students who are unable to continue working when school resumes in the fall. The city used to keep all pools open from Memorial Day to Labor Day, but to continue that practice the aquatics department would need fifty permanent lifeguards for just ten of the system's pools. As of this writing the city is considering allocating staff to keep a handful of pools open through early October. Generally, the municipal and neighborhood pools have lifeguards on duty at all times; the wading pools do not. Barton Springs does; Emma Long does not. If you are interested in becoming a lifeguard, see the following chapter.

Parks are generally open 5:00 A.M. to 10:00 P.M. Alcohol and glass are not allowed. Dogs must be on a leash, with the exception of Pease Park where dogs can run free.

All city pools are fenced by at least a four-foot fence, by ordinance of 1988. There are no high diving boards at any of the city pools, but there are low and medium diving boards.

Pools are built with funds from bond elections, state grants, and the Capital Improvement Program, plus interest on the CIP program. One percent of all CIP funds is set aside for the Art in Public Places program, as seen in the Dick Nichols and Dove Springs murals. Some private donations come in. For example, Dove Springs and Dick Nichols pools were built with funds donated from the Lumberman's Association ($425,000). Each of these brand new pools cost $2.5 million to build. Some of the older pools were built with federal funding by the CCC and WPA. The city relies on community input when deciding where to put a pool. Neighborhood demand

and areas which may not have access to any other recreation facility have priority. In the future the city will focus on larger pools, and the older neighborhood pools will be phased out. They simply are not cost- effective.

Barton Springs and Big Stacy are the only year-round pools, and therefore have the highest attendance. Barton Springs attendance peaks in the summer at about 80,000 people monthly or over 250,000 per year. Big Stacy also peaks in the summer at 8,000 people, but 3,000 still swim there every month year-round. Palm, Citivan, Gillis, Kealing, Patterson, Montopolis, and St. John's are the least used neighborhood pools, so if you're looking to avoid the crowds, try one of them. Of the municipal pools, Bartholomew and Mabel Davis are the least used, while Deep Eddy is the most popular pool with Northwest coming in a close second. The most popular wading pool is Shipe, although Little Stacy is a close second. Bailey and Clarksville wading pools have very low attendance.

Which pool is right for me?

Municipal pools are large and charge admission to cover the costs of operating the bathhouse. Lap lanes are three to four feet minimally, and divers will have their own depth needs. Neighborhood pools have an average size of one hundred by forty feet, and have a park and playground. Wading pools are no more than three to four feet deep, and are designed for kids up to age 12. They are also free.

How's the Water?

None of the outdoor city pools are heated. Fourteen pools in the city system are 'draw and fill' pools. These pools do not use filtration and are comparable to sinks which are filled and drained every day. The draw and fill pools use 72,000-145,000 gallons of water every day during operation; each night the water is dumped into area creeks or the city's wastewater system. Needless to say, this is an expensive way to run a pool. In the past, the majority of Austin's pools were draw and fill, but as the costs of water rose the city began converting to filtered pools at a cost of $100-250,000 per pool. Big Stacy Pool just underwent such a conversion. At present, the remaining draw and fill pools are not scheduled for conversion.

FEE STRUCTURE AND PASS OPTIONS

Most of the City of Austin pools are free, but municipal pools will charge a fee.

> Seniors: 62 and over
> Adults: 17-62
> Juniors: 12-17
> Children: 11 and under

Daily Fees:

All Municipal Pools: Adult $2.00, Junior 75¢, Child 50¢

Barton Springs:

Adult $2.50, $2.75 on weekends, Junior 75¢, Child 50¢

40-Visit Swim Ticket:

Adult $66, Junior $22.50, Child $15, Senior $30

I find this pass option to be the most versatile. For an affordable price you can gain forty admissions to municipal pools. This works out to be about a twenty-five percent discount. It has no expiration date so you can use it over several seasons. If you primarily swim at neighborhood pools but like to occasion municipal pools, this is a good option. The pass comes printed on durable Tyvek, making it water-proof, a very handy quality! I've left my ticket in my shorts pocket and then put it through the washing machine on several occasions, and it still came out fine. When you've used up all forty admissions, it makes a nice souvenir of your efforts. The forty-ticket swim pass can be purchased at any municipal pool, at Barton Springs, and at the Parks and Recreation office on Riverside Drive.

Season Pass:

Adult $200, Junior $50, Child $25, Senior $75
Family of four $325 (Additional family members are required to purchase an individual pass for their age group.)

This pass allows you to swim from mid-March through October at any municipal pool with unlimited admissions. While there are exceptions, most municipal pools do not open until mid-May and stay open only through Labor Day. Check the season dates for your favorite pool before choosing this option.

Summer Pass:

Adult $120, Junior $45, Child $30, Senior $60, Family of four $225
(Additional family members are required to purchase an individual pass for their age group.)

This option allows you to swim at any municipal pool from Memorial Day through Labor Day with unlimited admissions. I believe that this is a better option than the seasonal pass for the average pool patron, since most municipal pools are only open during this period. A current wallet-sized photo of each pass holder must be presented at the time of purchase. Your pass will then be ready at the pool of purchase within 48 hours. A $2.00 replacement fee is charged for summer passes.

Adaptive Swim Ticket (Forty Visits):

Adult $35, Junior $17.50, Child $10, Senior $25

Adaptive Swim Tickets may be purchased Monday through Friday, 8:00 A.M. through 5:00 P.M. at the McBeth Recreation Center, 2401-A Columbus Drive (in Zilker Park). Proof of eligibility must be provided by physician or other certified professional to qualify.

Pool Rentals:

All municipal and neighborhood pools can be rented. Call the Aquatics Office for more information (476-4521). Pools can be rented before and after regular operating hours, but must be rented between 5:00 A.M. and 10:00 P.M. Request reservations in writing. You must reserve the pool and make a deposit on it seventy-two hours in advance of your event. Pool rental is also subject to lifeguard availability. Rates are $100 per hour for municipal pools, and $50 per hour for neighborhood pools.

JUNIOR LIFEGUARD PROGRAM

Have you ever wondered what it would be like to be a lifeguard? They always look so cool, calm and collected. Lifeguards are the silent sentries of the swimming pool They are most often young, but completely authoritative. If you want the real scoop about a pool, talk to the lifeguards. The most dedicated ones can be found at Barton Springs and Big Stacy Pool during the winter, all bundled up under coats and blankets, valiant and steadfast for those folks who are crazy enough to swim all winter. At Barton Springs the guards take forty-minute watches. At most other pools they have thirty-minute shifts. They are constantly aware and at Barton Springs they talk to each other via two-way radios, pointing out weak swimmers and problems. Between shifts they nap, study, listen to the radio, talk to patrons, and swim. The City of Austin's safety record is outstanding, and there has never been a drowning to my knowledge, although there have been a few pull-outs over the years. Considering that at Barton Springs during the peak of summer the swimmer-lifeguard ratio is 200 to 1, they're doing an awesome job.

Keeping watch at
Big Stacy Pool

The City of Austin offers water safety training for 13 to 15 year-olds. It's the perfect summer job for teenagers as they spend the day outside amongst their peers, they learn responsibility, and they can earn money for their efforts. Participants learn rescue techniques, CPR, and first aid skills. They also improve their physical condition through swimming, learn customer service skills, and have a chance to apprentice with current lifeguards at area pools. Upon completion of the course participants are ready to go on to become swim instructors or full-fledged lifeguards. Sessions are offered at five different pools and are limited to ten people per class. The cost is $60 which gets you a cool T-shirt and whistle, plus books and other materials. The group takes a field trip at the end of the class. Scholarships are available. Contact the City of Austin for more details and to register at 476-4521. Registration forms are also available at any recreation center.

The University of Texas also offers lifeguarding courses beginning in the late spring. The course is a week-long intensive training, and costs $85. Call 471-1535 for more information.

The Red Cross offers a similar course. Call them at 928-4271 for more information. The cities of Georgetown and Round Rock also have junior lifeguarding programs.

ADAPTIVE AQUATICS PROGRAM

Disability lift

The City of Austin offers an instructional swim program for people with disabilities. The lessons are geared toward the individual and his or her particular needs. All swim instructors are certified in first aid, CPR and water safety. Participants will learn how to overcome fear of being in the water, floating, breathing, strokes and exercises. Classes are held at St. Edward's University, Austin State School, Mabel Davis and Walnut Creek Pools. Teacher-student ratios are 1:4 for swim classes, ages 3 and up. Children under 6 must be accompanied by an adult in the water. Classes last forty minutes each. Classes vary from once, twice or three times per week in blocks of four, eight or twelve sessions, and are held in the mornings and evenings. Contact the City of Austin for more details and to register.

SWIM INSTRUCTION

Parks and Recreation Department Instructional Swim Program
901 West Riverside Drive
Austin, Texas 78704
451-8494 TDD line

The City of Austin offers affordable, highly effective swim lessons to anyone who is interested in learning. You must register in person or by mail (no phone calls) through the Parks and Recreation Department Instructional Swim Program. The cost is $32 for a two-week session; $36 for two lessons per week; $54 for three lessons per week; and $30 for the summer

summer swim team and for the Special Olympics swim team. Patrons are first come, first served. Classes for infants and preschoolers are thirty minutes long; upper-level classes are forty minutes each. Registration begins in late April through July, and several different sessions are offered. Each session has six lessons spread over two weeks. Registration forms can be picked up from the Parks and Recreation office.

Classes range from infants and toddlers, preschoolers, school-aged children, and adult beginners. The city follows the American Red Cross Swim Lesson guidelines. Classes are taught by certified instructors and lifeguards and are held at a variety of different pools.

If you are uncertain what ability level you or your child falls within, you can go to any of the municipal pools (Bartholomew, Deep Eddy, Garrison, Mabel Davis, Northwest and Walnut Creek) during their normal operating hours and ask for an ability level test. The participant will complete a water skills test for proper placement.

SWIM TEAMS

Swim teams are designed for children aged 5-17 who can swim at least twenty-five meters. Teams practice five days a week at selected pools for approximately six weeks, then they have a city-wide meet in mid-July, and a state meet the following week. The cost is $32 per participant, and you can register through the Parks and Recreation office. Swim teams are an excellent way for kids to hone their swimming skills in a supportive environment, make new friends, and have fun.

WATER

FRONTS

BARTON SPRINGS AND ZILKER PARK

Austin's Crown Jewel

2100-2200 Barton Springs Road
Austin, Texas 78704
(512) 476-9044 Pool
(512) 867-3080 Hotline
(512) 478-0905 Park
(512) 477-8672 Botanical Garden
(512) 327-8180 Nature Center
(512) 327-6498 McBeth Recreation Center
(512) 327-6662 TDD
(512) 478-8167 Zephyr Train
(512) 397-1464 Hillside Theatre
http://www.tec.org/bartonsprings

STATISTICS

Operating Schedule: Barton Springs is open year-round. Hours vary with the weather and cleaning schedule, so always call the hotline before heading out. March through October it generally opens at 5:00 A.M. and close at 10:00 P.M.; November through February it opens at 10:00 A.M. and closes at dusk.

Admission is $2.75 for adults. A $2.00 parking fee is charged for the city lot on weekends and holidays. Another unpaved lot is located on the east side of the pool off of Robert E. Lee Road. It is free, and has a second entrance to the pool.

Barton Springs Pool is 997 feet from dam to dam and 145 feet at the widest point. It is the fourth largest spring in Texas. The pool has a surface area of three acres. Record keeping of the spring's flow began in 1894. Six million gallons of water per day was recorded in 1956 and 166 million gallons in 1961. The maximum-recorded rate per twenty-four hours was 107 million in May, 1940, and the minimum was 6,200,000 in March, 1956. Average flow is 26 million gallons per day. An average of 250,000 people visit Barton Springs every year.

Barton Springs *is* Austin. It is the largest natural swimming pool in the United States located within an urban area, setting Austin apart from other metropolitan cities. Barton Springs is Austin's soul and sums up everything that Austin stands for. A chilly swimming hole, the center of a political and environmental debate, a meeting place… Barton Springs is all of these things. Here you can swim with politicians, musicians, ducks and salamanders. If you're lucky, you might catch a glimpse of 'Leonard', a giant fish reputed to patrol the waters. Barton Springs has been used by people inhabiting this area for tens of thousands of years. In the days before air conditioning Austinites used the springs to stay cool. Barton Springs has powered several mills, cooled many Native American tribes, hosted Spanish missionaries, provided a community meeting place for early settlers, and soothed millions of people over the years.

Half a billion years ago what was to become Austin was covered by an ocean on the edge of an ancient continent which would become North America. One-third of a billion years ago, the ocean closed in as massive plates of earth moved in from the southeast and crushed against the North American Plate, creating mountains from Arkansas to Uvalde, Texas. One-quarter of a billion years ago the mountains eroded into plains. 150 million years ago plates pulled away from North America and the sea rushed back in. Layered deposits of sediment, rich in fossils and dinosaur tracks, formed the limestone rocks and caves of the Edwards Aquifer. Water probably sprang from the rocks about 7,000 BC. Barton Springs, actually a series of springs, emerges from fissures in the limestone at a rate of 26 million gallons per day. People who have witnessed the water surging out of the mouth of the main spring, Parthenia, say it resembles a pulsating heartbeat. Parthenia is just to the right of the diving board. If you swim down to it you can see the mouth of a cave about three feet wide and five to seven feet deep. Water from Barton Creek no longer enters the pool; it is kept full from the springs alone, so the water is clearer and a constant temperature of 68°F. Eliza Springs issues from a cave-like sinkhole on the north bank near the lower end of the pool, and Walsh Springs comes from a sinkhole on the south bank below the pool. Deep Eddy Springs is actually somewhat connected but is covered by Town Lake.

Barton Springs remained about the same until nine thousand years ago. We know that humans have been using Barton Springs for at least eleven thousand years. About 5,500 BC the Olmecs were known in the Western Hemisphere and probably used the springs. Wild horses, too, were once bountiful at the springs. Native American tribes such as the Lipan Apache, Jumano and Tonkawa gathered here to cool off and camp. A Comanche trail made a stop at Barton Springs, and the tribes left numerous artifacts around the area.

In the 1600s and 1700s Spanish explorers looking for gold came through Travis County, and some say that Cabeza de Vaca and Coronado stopped at Barton Springs on their quests. Franciscan friars built the Mission San Jose de los Nazonis in 1730 at Barton Springs. Later, San Francisco de los Neches and Nuestra Senora de la Purisma Concepcion d'Hanis were moved from East Texas to Barton Springs because French troops were pushing them westward. The missionaries thought that the land was worthless for growing crops or settling and moved on to San Antonio. In 1835 the Governor of Coahuila y Tejas granted Barton Springs to Henry P. Hill, and Anglo colonists began settling the area.

'Uncle Billy Barton' was one of these early settlers and he settled on what was then called Spring Creek with his three daughters, Parthenia, Eliza and Zenobia. Spring Creek was Barton's link to the outside world, a camp called Waterloo on the Colorado River which was developing into the new Texas capital. He built a cabin there and kept two tame buffalo which apparently attracted many sightseers. Barton started to charge admission to the springs and hired W.C. Walsh and Henry Steussy to build a gristmill. The mill was three stories high and located on the south side of the creek near the main dam. Barton's place was a stage stop and quickly became popular as a favorite swimming hole. When Waterloo was officially selected as the new Texas capital in 1839, Barton deeded the springs to the city to furnish power for a sawmill. William Barton died on April 11, 1840. He was buried at the springs but his body was later moved to Round Rock. There are actually six different Barton Springs in Texas, some that are named after our William Barton. He certainly got around! There are apparently a few other William Bartons but we all know there's only one Barton Springs.

Barton Springs was still very primitive in 1842. Sam Houston, who was bitter about Austin becoming the new capital, said that he wouldn't risk his scalp in that #&?! hole called Austin. Houston feared Indians, and since some people had been scalped on their way to Barton Springs, he was somewhat justified. In the 1850s, peaceful tribes of Lipan Apaches and Tonkawas were still living near Barton Springs, but were driven out by Comanches during an attack on white settlers at the springs.

In 1860, John Rabb bought the Barton property, then deeded it to his son, Gail T. Rabb. G.T. Rabb sold five acres of the property, not including the springs, to Jacob Stern. Stern built another gristmill and allowed Confederate troops to camp there during 1861. W.C. Walsh, who had built Barton's original gristmill, built a rock quarry in 1866 and moved his family there. Quarrying was done by hand and uncovered many fossils which were preserved. G.T. Rabb opened a gristmill and ice factory in 1871 and built a two-story rock house on the south side of the creek. He also built a dam out of logs and a merry-go-round, and rented swimsuits to men only! In 1879, Rabb constructed a new three-story mill but it was destroyed by fire in 1886. In 1889 he completed a footbridge across the shallow end of the pool but it was wiped out in the 1900 flood. An entrepreneur soon began renting bathing suits to people to swim in Barton Springs. People could also camp there. On Saturdays and Sundays the whole family would pack a picnic, pay ten cents admission, and spend the day at the springs enjoying sing-a-long concerts, plays and dances. Swimming societies and clubs are nothing new in Austin. A ladies' swimming club was formed in 1884 and only one man was allowed within hearing distance as a safeguard. He was under oath to keep his eyes shut and his face turned away from the river. The first bathhouse was just four walls painted white and open to the sky. The walls didn't extend all the way to the ground because of the moisture and potential for rot. Baptisms took place in the springs, sometimes hundreds at a time. In 1875 the Riverboat Sunbeam shuttled swimmers up and down what is now Town Lake and Barton Creek for fifty cents per person. Barton Springs was still very much 'out in the country' at the time and getting there was an ordeal.

In 1907 Rabb sold more of his property to Andrew Jackson Zilker, who then bought the other five acres from Stern. Zilker's story is a classic rags to riches tale. When he was just 18 he moved from Indiana to Austin in 1876 with fifty cents in his pocket. The first night he got a job washing dishes and doubled his money. He then got a job constructing the Congress Avenue Bridge and befriended the owner of an ice plant who gave him a job there. Zilker also found the time to be a volunteer fireman, Director of the First National Bank, Water and Light Commissioner, and head of the Travis County School Board. He quickly became the engineer of the ice plant and in 1901 began buying land between the Colorado River and Barton Creek. Zilker had soon acquired 350 acres surrounding Barton Springs and used the land to pasture the horses and mules that pulled his ice wagons.

During the first World War Austin attempted to establish military schools near Barton Springs. In order to do so they had to provide water, so the Military Affairs Committee suggested that the city buy Barton Springs and route the water to the soldiers for bathing. Droughts in the years 1910 and 1917 also prompted the city to seek alternative sources of water. In 1918 Zilker deeded the springs and a surrounding thirty-five acres to the city with the provision that it be used for education. The city also tore down the ruins of the old flour mill. In 1920, the Chamber of Commerce and Lions Club raised $8,000 to build a new bathhouse, completed in 1922. The new bathhouse was a two-story pavilion with a dance hall upstairs and dressing rooms downstairs. People recall it as quite romantic, with wood paneling and open-air screens. Schools of fish were visible in the springs, and water pageants and carnivals were held there annually. In 1932 Zilker donated another 330 acres to the military schools on the condition that the city would buy them for $200,000 from the schools. A bond election approved the information center and souvenir shop.

The Sunken Gardens, enclosed by circular stones, was built between 1935-38 on the south side of the creek by the National Youth Administration. This spring originally powered a mill, then an ice factory. The state's first fish hatchery was established at Sunken Gardens. Most of the walls have washed away and are in need of repair, but the spring still flows. As of this writing, Sunken Gardens will probably be fenced off to protect the Barton Springs salamanders.

A flood in 1935 left four inches of mud in the Barton Springs bathhouse and washed away the Lake Austin Dam. Zilker Park was left under water for days. A new bathhouse was built in 1947 for $180,000. It was designed by Groos and Driscool, the same firm that designed the Deep Eddy bathhouse. The 1947 bathhouse still stands and has large open-air dressing rooms and grassy areas.

During World War II, soldiers wrote to their families about fighting for Barton Springs. It was an Austin treasure. Little did they imagine that the land around Barton Springs would develop rapidly after the war. An environmental debate over the springs has been raging since the late 1950s when the Parks and Recreation staff noticed trash and dead animals in the runoff coming from the Barton Hills subdivision, or what used to be the Rabb land, and high levels of fecal coliform. In the 1960s, an environmental group formed and began addressing these concerns with the Parks Department. A plan for a greenbelt was drawn up but not built, yet the public showed an interest in extending Zilker Park up Barton Creek. However, the city didn't respond and valuable recharge areas in the aquifer were rapidly developed. Robert Mueller was a locker boy and cashier at Barton Springs. He offered to sell a portion of his land, about forty to fifty acres on the south side of the

Barton Springs today

31

creek from the pool up to Campbell's Hole, but the city declined to buy it. The city passed up several opportunities to buy and protect the land surrounding Barton Springs, and today it is an endangered natural resource.

Barton Springs does not use chlorine. Between 1929 and 1962, the pool was drained twice per week and cleaned with copper sulfate to remove the algae, which turned some of the rocks blue-green. In 1962, the city stopped using chlorine; instead workers scrubbed it with giant steel brushes pulled by tractors, then flushed it with water from a fire hose. It takes forty-five minutes to drain the pool, and about two hours to refill it. This practice continues today. The endangered Barton Springs salamander survived the entire time that copper sulfate was used to clean the pool. Beverly Sheffield has witnessed floods that completely encircled the bathhouse, yet the vegetation always grew back and helped make the water clear because it kept the silt from being disturbed by swimmers. It is unlikely that the salamanders are endangered by chemicals used in Barton Springs. More likely, fecal coliform running off from development all around the springs is the culprit. If fecal coliform counts are above 200 colonies per 100 milliliters of water, and visibility is impaired by more than four feet, the pool closes. The pool also closes as a precaution when there is thunder and lightning, and if more than one inch of rain has fallen over the Barton Creek watershed within twenty-four hours. Folks in Dripping Springs at the headwaters will call ahead to warn us if flooding is imminent. For more information, see the chapter on Organizations (page 337).

The 1950s also saw the development of Philosopher's Rock. Roy Bedicheck, a naturalist, J. Frank Dobie, a folklorist, and Walter Prescott Webb, a historian, would gather on a flat rock near the diving board and talk about an infinite number of things. John Henry Faulk, Walter Bremond, and Skinny Pryor were known to drop in. A statue by Santa Fe artist Glenna Goodacre at the main entrance to Barton Springs honors these men. *"If I have to fight for this country, I will not fight for the flag, or the American 'way of life', or democracy, or private enterprise or for any other abstractions, which seem cold as kraut to me. But I will fight to the last ditch for Barton Creek, Boggy Creek, cedar-covered limestone hills, blazing star and bluebonnets, golden- cheeked warblers and black-capped vireos... This love of your native land is basic."* -Roy Bedicheck.

People often ask about the pecan tree directly across from the diving board on the west side of the pool. No one knows exactly but it is probably several hundred years old. In 1970 people feared it would die so a backup tree was planted behind it. Support poles were built around the original tree and the trunk gutted and rebuilt. The older pecan tree finally succumbed but the stump was saved as a lifeguard throne.

The floor of the pool is made of limestone and Buda gravel mixed with clay, which acts like cement. There are three general sections to the pool. The wading area extends from the upper dam all the way to Bedicheck's rock where it drops off steeply to sixteen feet. This is where the diving board is located over the main spring. The area between the diving board and the lower dam is deep, from ten to sixteen feet. There used to be a high dive in this section but it was removed in the 1970s. The strip on the north side of the pool from the lower dam to the lifeguard stand near the entrance is about four feet and has a gravel bottom. It was once used as a lap lane. Lap lanes are not designated at Barton Springs but lap swimming is very popular. Serious swimmers hit the pool early in the morning to avoid the crowd and have an unspoken agreement about how to divide up the lanes. Some swim between the sidewalks, while others prefer to swim the whole length. Since the 1930s there has been an informal policy of leaving the front gate closed but accessible to early bird swimmers, but recently an iron fence with a lock was put in to keep children from entering unattended and to comply with city codes.

Large pecan and cottonwood trees provide plenty of shade and either side of the pool is surrounded by grassy slopes. During the peak summer hours it can get very crowded, with the teenagers hanging out on the east slope and everyone else on the flatter west bank. Floats are allowed only in the deepest section near the dam. You can still sunbathe nude inside the women's dressing area on a few grassy areas that are open to the sky, but it is an unwritten policy.

The Polar Bear Club at Barton Springs, which has over one hundred members, swims year-round. One member, Jill Carr, swam in such cold weather that her hair froze when she exited the water!

The Barton Creek Greenbelt officially opened in 1985. It is a 7.8-mile trail for hiking and bicycling. Several swimming holes dot the trail. Rock climbers also practice on the limestone cliffs. The trail is rocky and semi-primitive and cuts through scenic wildflowers, trees, limestone cliffs, caves, meadows, swimming holes and waterfalls. The trail varies from narrow ledges to wide walkways. Wildlife is abundant in the park. Hiking in the Greenbelt will really give you the feeling of being far away in the wilderness, not in the middle of the city, which it really is. The trail extends from Zilker Park to Lost Creek, with a trailhead at Zilker Park just west of the pool. You can also access the trail where Spyglass intersects with Barton Skyway; behind Barton Hills Elementary School on 2010 Homedale Drive; at the Gus Fruh Access at 2642 Barton Hills Drive; at Loop 360 near the office buildings behind Brodie Oaks; and at Camp Craft Road at the

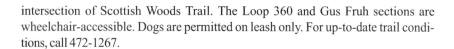

intersection of Scottish Woods Trail. The Loop 360 and Gus Fruh sections are wheelchair-accessible. Dogs are permitted on leash only. For up-to-date trail conditions, call 472-1267.

A new trail is being built that will connect Southwest Parkway with the Greenbelt at the MoPac Bridge. This 1.5-mile dirt trail will parallel Gaines Creek. Construction will be performed by thirteen members of the National Civilian Community Corps, which was created by Congress in 1993. No public funding will be used.

When enjoying the Greenbelt, remember to pack your trash and leave the trail better than you found it. The trail is open 5:00 A.M.-10:00 P.M.

Barton Creek flows forty-one miles from its headwaters in Dripping Springs to the Colorado River, wandering through Hays and Travis counties. It averages more than thirty feet in width at times which designates it as a navigable creek by the Texas Constitution. While Barton Springs flows year-round, Barton Creek responds more to spring and fall rains. During times of drought, the creek may dry up and leave only a few swimming holes. When it is dry, you can still see wagon ruts in the limestone bed that were carved out when the creek bed was used as a route into town.

Floating Barton Creek in an inner tube, canoe, kayak or boat is a favorite local pastime. Keep safety in mind and always wear a lifejacket, even if you are an experienced swimmer. The creek is shallow and dotted with trees and rocks which can easily upset your boat. Other hazards to watch out for are fire ants, water and land snakes, poison ivy and prickly plants. Wear sunscreen and river shoes or tennis shoes to protect your feet. Never float during rain or thunderstorms or during periods of flooding as the water can become muddy and hide hazards. Drink lots of water. Never boat or tube alone.

A number of swimming holes dot Barton Creek and are accessible from the Greenbelt. Catfish Pool is just below the junction of Barton Creek and Hebbingston Hollow. A small footbridge traverses the north side. Sculpture Falls has rapids and secluded sunbathing, just below Dam #7. Campbell's Hole has a small pebble beach and is a reliable pool. It's located about one mile upstream from Barton Springs. Legend has it that Robert E. Lee made numerous trips here while stationed at a camp to the west; Sam Bass, Bonnie and Clyde, and Jesse James also used the small cave above the pool as hideouts. Gus Fruh Pool is another reliable swimming hole even during droughts. It's located near 2632 Barton Hills Drive (respect private property). Triple Falls and Gus Fruh Park are at the three-mile mark on the trail and have large boulders and deep water. Twin Falls can be accessed at Loop 360 across from the entrance to Barton Creek Mall. You will find a rope swing and good swimming under two small waterfalls. Most access points have rest rooms and picnic tables. Of interest is Airman's Cave, a 2.1-mile long cave. It is the longest cave in the country with an average height of only three feet. Only five percent of the cave is tall enough to stand up in, and usually one person gets stuck every year and has to be rescued. For experienced spelunkers only!

COURTESY OF TEXAS DEPARTMENT OF TRANSPORTATION

Barton Creek

The Austin Chronicle published an excellent guide to hiking in the Barton Creek Greenbelt and floating Barton Creek in their April 17, 1992 issue, reprinted in April 18, 1997.

Zilker Park is often called 'the Central Park of Texas'. It is less than half the size of Central Park but has more acres per person. New York's Central Park is 843 acres but 20 million people use it ever year. Zilker Park is 485 acres and only onemillion people use it annually. Zilker Park was recently added to the National Register of Historic Places in recognition of its architecture and historical significance. The park has a playground, nine soccer fields (which used to be spinach fields), one rugby field, two multiuse fields, and a nine-hole disc golf course. Numerous picnic areas dot the park. Two historic log structures, the Esperanza Schoolhouse and a Swedish Cabin, can be seen in the Botanical Garden. Both structures were moved from outside of Austin. Zilker Park even has a fallout shelter, a relic from the 1950s. The park is the site of numerous baptisms, weddings, and memorial services. The Zilker Clubhouse was originally the Boy Scout lodge and is now used for community functions.

Campbell's Hole

The sixty-acre Botanical Garden has a series of trails of flowers and succulents, a Japanese garden, a butterfly garden, and the Mabel Davis Rose Garden. The Garden is home to many indigenous plants and animals. Tours of the Garden are offered every Saturday between May and Thanksgiving.

For some old-fashioned fun take a ride on the Zilker Zephyr, a three-mile miniature train ride. For almost fifty years the Zephyr, formerly known as the Eagle, has been chugging around the park. The train was privately owned for much of its history by attorney Charlie Beall and wife Carlene. They contract with the city but own the tracks, train, and ticket booth. There has been only one accident in all these years when the brakes failed and a passenger jumped out in fear. The train only goes eight miles per hour. Rides are available year-round, weather permitting, from 10:00 A.M. to dusk. Souvenirs are available.

The Zilker Hillside Theatre was developed by Beverly Sheffield, who selected the site. The theater has recently been renamed for him. Originally, the theater was just a tiny stage with a trellis of moonflowers blooming at night. Today, it thrives and hosts Shakespearean plays, jazz concerts, and Broadway musicals during the summer. Attendees are encouraged to bring a picnic.

The eighty-acre Austin Nature Center is a sanctuary for raccoons, foxes, deer, and many other animals. Located within Zilker Park at 301 Nature Center Drive, the Nature Center features exhibits on science, natural history and botany. The most interesting feature is over one hundred dinosaur tracks which are estimated to be 99 million years old. Open Tuesday through Saturday, 9:00 A.M. to 5:00 P.M.

The McBeth Recreation Center is especially designed to serve individuals with disabilities. The center has programs throughout the year, and visitors can use the multipurpose room, kitchen, computers, and picnic areas, or take part in crafts and games.

The Beverly Sheffield Education Center/Splash! Into the Edwards Aquifer is an interactive exhibit about the geology and biology of the Edwards Aquifer. Learn about the habitat of the Barton Springs salamander, how watersheds and aquifers work, and more.

Of historical interest is the story of the Butler Brick Company whose history is intertwined with Barton Springs. The Butler Brick Company was founded by Michael Butler in 1873 when he came from Limerick, Ireland to join his brother Patrick in Austin. The first plant was located between Congress Avenue and East Avenue (now IH 35) but was washed out by repeated floods. Butler built another plant south of the river along Barton Springs Road. Butler and Andrew Zilker had land that bordered each other where the fence line met at the old rock bridge over Barton Creek. If one built a fence, the other did, too. When one planted alfalfa, the other soon followed. One fenced in Robert E. Lee Road, so the other told city council to take it down. The Colorado River filled with deposits of red clay which were eventually used by Butler to construct bricks for the Paggi House. Bricks were hauled across the river on a cable (some of the support towers can still be seen on the shores of Town Lake). Eventually, a city dump was built on the old brick quarry and then Zilker Park was developed over it. The pit is still visible along the hike and bike trail and is marshy and sulfurous. The Butler family finally moved their plant to Sandy Creek near Elgin because the soil had more clay. Butler's bricks were used in the construction of City Hall, the capitol building of 1888, the train depot on Congress Avenue, and the Board of Trade building.

For more information about Barton Springs, I highly recommend *Barton Springs Eternal*, by Turk Pipkin and Marshall Frech; Softshoe Publishing, The Hill Country Foundation, Austin, Texas, 1993.

EMMA LONG METROPOLITAN PARK

1600 City Park Road
Austin, Texas 78730
(512) 346-1831

STATISTICS

Open May through September
Park day use 7:00 A.M.-10:00 P.M.
Swimming Beach on weekends 12:00-6:00 P.M.
and Holidays 12:00-7:00 P.M.

Fees are collected year-round.
$5.00 per vehicle per day Monday-Thursday
$8.00 per vehicle per day (Friday, Saturday, Sunday & holidays)
Pedestrians and bicycles no charge

This park is named for Emma Long, the first woman to be a full-time member of the Texas Statehouse Press Corps, and a writer for the Austin American Statesman. Ms. Long also became the first female city council member in Texas in 1948. During her stint as councilwoman, she reactivated the Parks and Recreation Board. Later she became the first woman mayor pro tem, appointed by President Johnson to the United Nations Population Commission. Contrary to popular belief, Emma was not related to Walter Long (see Decker Lake, page 169), and was actually his liberal antagonist on the council.

In 1933 the National Parks Service prepared plans to develop Emma Long Park, then known as Lake Austin Park. In 1939 fifty Civilian Conservation Corps enlistees moved to the Lake Austin area and began clearing a site to house another 200 workers. Barracks were constructed and a well was dug. After completion of the park, the bathhouse and concession stand were built of wood. Unfortunately, they burned but were replaced by the stone structures which stand today.

Emma Long Park is the largest city-owned park at almost 1,200 acres. There you can enjoy swimming, water-skiing, picnicking and camping. Commons Ford is an adjacent undeveloped area giving the park that 'away from it all' feeling. An endangered species of plant, the bracted twistflower, has been planted throughout the park in an effort to preserve it.

The swimming beach is a nice straight length of sandy shore on Lake Austin with a rope boundary to contain swimmers in their own section. There are two wooden docks on either side with swimming allowed in between. The lake has a sandy bottom. Lifeguards are on duty 12:00 to 6:00 P.M. on weekends only from Memorial Day to Labor Day. Children under 12 must be supervised by adults when a lifeguard is not on duty. Boats are not allowed in the swimming area or along the swimming docks. By city ordinance, there is no swimming allowed past fifty feet from the shoreline. Swimming under the docks is also prohibited. There is a bathhouse with hot showers and a concession stand which is open Memorial Day through Labor Day.

The park has numerous picnic tables with grills. Group picnic facilities which accommodate 100-300 people must be reserved by calling (512) 480-3036. Camping is popular at Emma Long and is the only park in Austin's city limits which allows overnight camping. There are ballfields; a paved entrance road and parking; two sand volleyball courts; an archery range; motorcycle, three-wheeler and mountain bike areas (one mile down Oak Shores Drive off City Park Road); and four miles of nature and equestrian trails.

Emma Long Beach

MUNICIPAL POOLS

BARTHOLOMEW POOL

The Alderman's Pool

1800 East 51st Street (at the corner of Berkman Drive)
Austin, Texas 78723
(512) 928-0014

STATISTICS

Open Memorial Day-Labor Day
Length: 50 yards
Minimum Depth: 1 foot, 10 inches
Maximum Depth: 13 feet

Bartholomew was an alderman, as was his father and grandfather. Acquired in the late 1950s, Bartholomew consists of a municipal pool and two wading pools. It is located just north of Robert Mueller Airport, so as you sunbathe on your back you can watch the bellies of the planes descending just overhead. Lap swimmers have three designated lanes. There is one diving board. Two separate wading pools for toddlers and splashers ease the crowd. Swim lessons are available at Bartholomew through the City of Austin. The bathhouse has hot showers, a dressing area, and rest rooms. Shade is provided by a vine-covered arbor, and covered picnic tables are situated near the wading pools. Bartholomew Park sports a recently renovated play apparatus with toddler swings, lighted ballfields and tennis courts, and picnic areas with grills. The park also has an eighteen-hole disc golf course. Tannehill Creek meanders through the park, which has fifty-one acres of wide, open grassy areas. There is plenty of off-street parking and access to the hike and bike trail. Wheelchair-accessible.

Above: Bartholomew Main Pool
Below: Bartholomew Wading Pool

DEEP EDDY SWIMMING POOL
A Texas First

401 Deep Eddy Drive
Austin, Texas 78703
(512) 472-8546

STATISTICS

Open Mid-April through October
Length: 100 x 204 feet
Minimum Depth: 9 inches
Maximum Depth: 8 feet

Deep Eddy Pool has the most colorful history of any pool I have come across. It began as a natural swimming hole on the Colorado River, thrived as a resort during the 1920s, and endured flooding by the Colorado River many times. Today it is a very popular swimming pool operated by the City of Austin. It is Texas's oldest swimming pool and one of Austin's first publicly owned parks. Deep Eddy Resort was the first tourist stop in Austin, sponsored the very first river parade on the Colorado, and was the first Works Progress Administration project in Austin.

Barney Bowling, a University of Texas champion swimmer and lifeguard at Deep Eddy Pool in the 1920s, remembers when the area now known as Eilers's Park and Deep Eddy Pool was a meadow full of trees, grass and sunflowers. Horses grazed nearby. People swam in the Colorado River where a huge boulder sat over a hole in the limestone riverbed, forming a dangerous eddy. Cold Springs rose from the banks and formed a primitive bathing area surrounded by stones. Hence, people began calling it Deep Eddy. Couples floated by in rowboats, and children played on waterslides and a cable pulley which spanned the river. Steamboat excursions along the Colorado stopped at Cold Springs before heading to Bee Springs. Today, Deep Eddy Springs and Cold Springs are both submerged by Town Lake where it meets Lake Austin. Deep Eddy Pool is fed by one of seven Artesian wells nearby.

In 1857, Charles Johnson emigrated from Sweden with his German bride, Amelia Loeschman. They bought forty acres at $30 per acre at the Deep Eddy site and built their home there. Johnson operated a limestone quarry where the current parking lot is located and built his home with the stone. The American Legion bought the house in 1924 for Travis Post 76. It is still standing just west of the pool on Veteran's Drive, above the community gardens. The quarry eventually closed because the rock was so hard that it wore out numerous rock saws. The Johnsons had eleven children. In 1902, two of those children, Henry and Mary Johnson, opened Austin's very first public park which included camping, picnicking, swimming, and boating.

COURTESY OF BEVERLY SHEFFIELD

Austin had four public squares at that time, including Woolridge Square next to the county courthouse. Pease Park was donated to the city in 1876 but was still undeveloped. Barton Springs was not within the city limits at that time, either. The boulder was dynamited by one of the Johnson boys and the resort became a very popular attraction for tourists and locals alike. Working men who couldn't take extended vacations would camp overnight near the river and its cool breeze. Gussie Lee Davenport, a great-granddaughter of the Johnsons born in 1906, recalls fond memories at Deep Eddy. Her family had leased the pool to a man named Joshua Merritt who managed it for a spell. Merritt had a strict rule about bathing attire: girls over age 12 had to wear stockings while they swam, and if they were the light colored variety then

Bathing Beauties at Deep Eddy.
Notice the stockings!

they had to show their seams in the back as proof. Another man, Mr. Petri, set up a merry-go-round in the summer season which was powered by a horse. A man known only as 'Dr. Lane' built a wooden deck for dancing near his tent and would crank phonographs for all who would gather.

Deep Eddy-1916

COURTESY OF BEVERLY SHEFFIELD

Deep Eddy as it appeared in 1916

In 1915, Mary Johnson sold the park to A.J. Eilers, Sr. and his two partners, Mr. Tolherst and Roy Mather, Sr. Not much is really known about Tolherst and Mather, and Eilers was the senior partner. Eilers contracted Max Brueggerman and William Maufrais, Sr. to build the concrete pool, which was completed in 1916. It was the very first outdoor pool in Texas. Nineteen rental cottages were built nearby for summer guests along with concession stands and five acres filled with all sorts of entertainment, such as Charleston contests and shooting galleries. At the time Deep Eddy was considered to be 'out in the country' and a summer resort so people would stay for the entire summer, including mayor-to-be Lester Palmer. The original bathhouses were made of wood with wooden boardwalks connecting them. Children used to hunt for small change which had fallen through the slats. On the Fourth of July Eilers would throw a sack of pennies into the pool so children could dive for them, and shot off sticks of dynamite and fireworks. A.J. Eilers changed the name to the Deep Eddy Bathing Beach and hired George A. Rowley, Sr., who bought Tolherst's twenty-five percent interest, to manage and promote the resort. Rowley had managed a carnival and had excellent showmanship skills.

Under George Rowley's direction, Deep Eddy Resort thrived. A trolley would take people from 6th Street and Congress Avenue to the Lake Austin Dam, which people sheepishly referred to as the 'dam trolley'. The pool became a circus-like amusement park, including a seventy-foot slide that ran down the hill toward the river and emptied into the pool. There were springboards, a flying trapeze, flying rings, horizontal bars and a forty-foot diving tower. There was also a Ferris wheel and carousel. Band concerts and dances were given twice a week and free silent movies, such as Rin Tin Tin and war pictures, were shown in the adjacent park every night except Sundays. Picnics on the beach were not uncommon, and political barbecues were held here. Deep Eddy attracted a variety of performers, such as Fred Lowery, the famous blind whistler, who got his start in show business right here. Jack Frieth, the human fish, ate while sitting on the bottom of the pool. In 1921, The World Champion Diving Baby from Fort Worth, Martha Burke, would dive from the high tower into the deep end. She was only 4 or 5 years old at the time.

COURTESY OF BEVERLY SHEFFIELD

Marcia Burke
World Famous Diving Baby

A very popular attraction was Lorena and Her Diving Horse. A deep hole to the east of the pool was dug and lined with canvas. A second diving platform 35-50 feet tall (accounts vary) was built over it. Every night at 8:45 Lorena would ride to the top of the diving ramp while the audience sat silent in suspense. Then she would dive into the water while sitting astride her horse. This stunt was extremely dangerous. Some of the other attractions such as the rings and slides were also quite hazardous and by today's standards seem crazy. In fact, it was not unusual for people to break bones!

The Rowley days were the era of the Deep Eddy River Rats, a group of teenagers who made the pool their home away from home. Sometimes they were called the Deep Eddy Roughnecks, the Damn Rats, and the Deep Eddy Hooters. Barney Bowling attributes the name to a rival gang in the Tenth Ward near Palm School, who were roughnecks that competed against the Deep Eddy area residents in football. The kids earned their nickname because they were so mischievous.

In 1928, Rowley resigned as manager and McKean Eilers, A.J.'s brother, took over. The same year, Austin's Parks and Recreation Department was formed. In 1935, people began to encourage the City of Austin to acquire Deep Eddy, and on May 31, 1935, the city council passed a resolution to buy the property for $10,000.

A.J. Eilers was glad the city bought his resort as he hoped the citizens of Austin would continue to enjoy the place for years to come. Eilers said, "I had cherished the idea of making the city a gift of the park, but financial conditions of the past few years prevented me from realizing that wish." He was referring to the Great Depression.

Two weeks after the city bought the property, the great Colorado River flood of June 15, 1935 inundated the entire city under fifty-two feet of water. Otto Ludwig, a city policeman at the time, remembers an elderly man named Zevoss who lived in a two-story house at Rainey and Cummings streets. The flood picked up his house and swept it along with several other neighbors down the river. Zevoss stayed on top of his house and as he approached the Montopolis Bridge people had to force him off for his own safety. The water washed away the Deep Eddy bathhouses, concession stands, and diving boards, leaving only the concrete pool which was filled with debris. Hopes of opening the park that summer were dashed, and workers even wondered if they could refurbish it before 1936.

The city began to clean out the pool by driving steam shovels in and were pleasantly surprised when the pool didn't buckle under the weight. It's a solidly built pool sitting on a bed of limestone so it's not going anywhere! The sidewalks were also rebuilt because the mighty cottonwood trees had caused them to buckle with their extensive roots. The city hired Driscoll and Groos Architects to design a new bathhouse and pool entrance. The city actually ran out of money when it came time to build the roof so they left it open. As it turned out, this was a smart move. Subsequent bathhouses were modeled after Deep Eddy because it offered great

COURTESY OF BEVERLY SHEFFIELD

Lorena and her Diving Horse
dove from this platform nightly.

ventilation. The plans were drawn up with speed and the construction was completed as part of the Works Progress Administration plan. In fact, it was the first WPA project in the City of Austin. The pool was re-opened on July 8, 1936 with four thousand people in attendance. The city council named the nine-acre park after Eilers, but it is still referred to as Deep Eddy.

Deep Eddy Pool remains much the way it was in 1936, although admission has increased from five cents to two dollars. The source of the water is a shallow

49

> *Austin people are at last waking up to the fact that the best camping places are not necessarily those at a distance. During the last year or two, Deep Eddy, that beautiful stretch of the river below the dam, has become a very popular camping ground and at present there are at least thirty tents on both sides of the river along the lake, or eddy. Businessmen, who are unable to secure vacations can reach these camps by a short walk from the end of the car line and spend nights in this delightful cool place.*
>
> Austin American Statesman, 1908

thirty-five-foot well dug by hand. It comes from the Colorado River and filters through sand and limestone to emerge pure and clear and cold. Another well on the eastern side of the pool was once used but caved in and is now only used as a backup. When the pool first opened, the water pumped so quickly that it didn't require any kind of treatment. These days, about 35,000 gallons are pumped through a chlorine filter every hour then pumped back into Town Lake. It is drained nightly, alternating shallow and deep ends that are divided by a wall.

Deep Eddy is famous for its swim team which went to the Texas Amateur Athletic Federation meet. Records were established by the 100-foot distance swimmers. The pool is actually 99 feet, 6 inches, not the regulation 100 feet, but who's counting?

Deep Eddy Today

A historical marker was dedicated on May 16, 1992. Beverly Sheffield was instrumental in researching and erecting the marker. You can view some of the photos included in this book, and others, on display at the entrance to the pool.

Deep Eddy Pool has some of the best lap swimming and the biggest wading area in Austin. The two sections are divided by a low concrete wall. You may not stand or walk on the dividing wall, but you can sit or lie on it. Eight lanes are designated for lap swimmers, and they are always busy. The water is a chilly 68-72°F. There are showers in the bathhouse and there is one outdoor shower near the pool. The bathhouses have rest rooms and changing rooms. Lockers are available for your possessions and have cute, memorable names like 'Superman'. Kickboards are usually available for free and have drawings and cartoons like turbo and cruise buttons to inspire you while working out.

Eilers Park has a playscape and picnic tables with grills. The park is at the very end of the Town Lake Hike and Bike Trail. There is a large parking lot but at the peak of summer it's packed tight. Tall cottonwood and pecan trees provide good shade. There is a flat grassy area near the lap lanes, and a hill at the shallow end. Vending machines provide concessions, and you can enjoy them from concrete bleachers which overlook the pool. Town Lake is just on the other side of the fence, although vegetation mostly hides it.

GARRISON POOL

6001 Manchaca Road (next to Crockett High School)
Austin, Texas 78745
(512) 442-4048

STATISTICS

Open Memorial Day-Labor Day
Length: 50 meters
Minimum Depth: 1 foot
Maximum Depth: 12 feet

Opened on May 27, 1967 with much fanfare, Garrison Pool was the sixth municipal pool in the city's system. The pool was named for James A. Garrison, the first director of Parks and Recreation.. When he took the position in 1928, he was a one-man department. Garrison was also a U.S. diplomatic and intelligence man, and Regional Defense Director for the National Defense Commission from 1946 until his retirement in 1966. Garrison organized the Parks and Recreation Department from its earliest beginnings. He recruited U.T. students as volunteers to oversee the playgrounds, organized amateur sports leagues, and sent Austin swim and diving teams to state competition.

Garrison Pool consists of a municipal pool and a separate wading pool. The main pool is wheelchair-accessible. There is one lane designated for lap swimming which is wide and meandering with a floating lane divider. It is not well defined; indeed the pool is not very lap swimmer-friendly because swim lessons are ongoing and children tend to wander in and out of the lane. It is, however, an excellent pool to learn to swim in because it has a shallow lane which stretches the entire length of the pool. For serious lap swimmers though, it is too shallow for flip turns. The pool accommodates up to eight lanes and has two diving boards, which are the same height. The open-air bathhouse has one partially enclosed shower, a dressing area, and rest rooms, which are decorated with brightly colored tile.

There is a huge parking area. The forty-acre park is full of post oaks which provide shade, and individual and group picnic tables with grills are scattered throughout the park, giving each one some privacy. The park is relatively flat and set back a little from busy Manchaca Road. A wildflower test patch fronts the street. Kids can play on the brightly colored, modern play apparatus that has a slide, a climbing structure, toddler and child swings, and spectator benches. A small hiking trial can be found within the park. The park also has lighted athletic fields and basketball courts. Concession machines are located inside the pool area, and food can be consumed at shaded, covered tables. The separate wading pool is partially fenced. Garrison is a popular pool with kids, who like to rush to the back fence and watch the train going by.

Garrison Pool dedication
June 1967

MABEL DAVIS POOL

Home of the Cholesterol-Free Swim

3427 Parker Lane
Austin, Texas 78741
(512) 441-5247

STATISTICS

Open May-September
Length: 25 meters
Minimum Depth: 2 feet, 10 inches
Maximum Depth: 12 feet

Mabel Davis Pool has recently become my favorite place to swim because of its accessibility and luxuriously late summer hours (9:00 P.M., second only to Barton Springs, which is open until 10:00 P.M.). The staff is exceedingly friendly, the patronage is mostly under 18, and lap swimmers can usually find a lane to themselves.

Mrs. Mabel Alden Davis was an Austin citizen who was actively involved in the beautification of the city for more than sixty years. Mrs. Davis had a hand in the development of many roadside parks and the rose garden in Zilker's Botanical Gardens. She was also a board member of Parks and Recreation, a position which she took quite seriously. Mrs. Davis worked quietly behind the scenes, but wielded a great deal of influence. In fact, politicians would often solicit her help, knowing she'd get on the phone and call 300 or 400 people to sway their opinion.

You'd never know it by looking at it, but Mabel Davis Pool is the site of a former landfill. It is a classic swimming pool, with clean white pavement and bright blue tile. It was built in 1979 but still looks brand-spanking new. A large wading area draws many children to Mabel Davis Pool, and four 25-meter lanes are reserved for lap swimmers. There are two diving boards. The Olympic-size pool accommodates many swimmers, and the bathhouse is spacious and open to the sky. There are dressing rooms and rest rooms with showers for men and women. Lockers are available for storing your valuables while you swim. There are a few benches for spectating, and lots of grassy areas. The only drawback at this pool is the lack of shade. Oak trees surround the park and play area, but very few trees surround the swimming pool itself. When you go, be prepared to protect yourself from the sun.

The surrounding park has plenty of parking, a playground, picnic tables with grills, and a basketball court. Concessions are available through vending machines with drinks and snacks. Swim teams and lessons are held at Mabel Davis Pool. Wheelchair-accessible.

Mabel Davis Pool

NORTHWEST POOL

7000 Ardath Street (corner of Ellise Street)
Austin, Texas 78757
(512) 453-0194

STATISTICS

Open Late April - Mid-September
Length: 50 meters
Minimum Depth: 1 foot
Maximum Depth: 11 feet

Northwest Pool is named simply for its location. This area used to be the far northwest boundary of Austin when it was developed in 1956. A municipal pool, Northwest consists of a large main pool and a separate wading pool. The pool is wheelchair-accessible. Northwest is popular with lap swimmers and two lanes are dedicated for lap swimming. There is also a diving board. Lessons are available through the City of Austin. The bathhouse has hot showers and rest rooms. The layout of Northwest Pool is similar to Garrison, with a long rectangular area and a diving well forming an L shape. Adjacent to the pool is a thirty-acre park with four double, lighted tennis courts, a volleyball court, a lighted baseball field, a play apparatus, and group and individual picnic areas with grills. Shoal Creek runs through the park, creating a pond, creek and natural wading area. There is plenty of parking, and the pool is nicely landscaped with native plants and flowers, and lots of grassy areas. Northwest is a quiet, albeit popular, pool which is tucked away in a suburban neighborhood.

Above: Northwest Wading Pool
Below: Northwest Municipal Pool

WALNUT CREEK

12138 North Lamar Boulevard (just south of Yager Lane)
Austin, Texas 78753
(512) 834-0824

STATISTICS

Open Mid-May through Labor Day
Length: 25 meters
Minimum Depth: 11 inches
Maximum Depth: 12 feet

A cquired by the city in 1964, this large park is still being developed. A scenic drive winding through groves of oak trees leads you from the entrance at North Lamar Boulevard to the pool. Named for the adjacent Walnut Creek, the modern pool complex (built in 1983) consists of a large municipal pool and a separate wading pool. Both pools are wheelchair-accessible. Lap swimmers have two dedicated lanes, and there are also two diving boards. Swim lessons are available at Walnut Creek through the City of Austin. The roomy bathhouse has hot showers, changing rooms, and rest rooms. The park is over 300 acres and has a playground, picnic tables, a hike and bike trail, three very modern baseball diamonds, and plenty of parking. The park is thick with oak, juniper and cypress trees, and has expansive grassy areas. The long drive from the main entrance places the pool far from the heavy traffic on Lamar, making it peaceful and giving you that 'away from it all' feeling.

A proposed 4.3-mile trail currently under consideration by the city would connect neighboring schools and parks (including Balcones and Walnut Creek) with major employers, such as Samsung, near Walnut Creek. The trail would also go through Jourdan Bachman Pioneer Farm and Big Walnut Creek Nature Preserve and then connect to the Colorado River and the Town Lake Trail. The Walnut

Creek Corridor is over fifteen miles long. The creek begins in Balcones Woods and flows eastward, crossing IH35, then continues south to the Colorado River. This new trail could potentially serve over 200,000 people living in north and east Austin. If you're interested in getting involved in the trail development, call the Austin Metropolitan Trails Council at (512) 478-4644 or the Austin Parks Foundation at (512) 477-1566.

Walnut Creek Municipal Pool

NEIGHBORHOOD POOLS

BALCONES POOL

12017 Amherst Drive (off of Duval)
Austin, Texas 78727

STATISTICS

Open May through August
25 yards
Minimum Depth: 2 feet, 1 inch
Maximum Depth: 4 feet

This nice little neighborhood pool provides summer fun for the Balcones area residents. The pool has two designated lap lanes but is only four feet at the deepest, making it suitable for wading, too. Lessons and swim teams practice here. There are indoor showers in a small bathhouse with rest rooms. The park is naturally landscaped with grassy areas and wildflowers. Live oaks provide shade. There is a modern playground, picnic tables with grills, and a three-mile hike and bike trail. You will also find volleyball and basketball courts. The park has plenty of parking and a soda machine for concessions. The pool is wheelchair-accessible.

Balcones Pool

BIG STACY POOL

800 East Live Oak Street
Austin, Texas 78704

STATISTICS

Open Year-round
100 feet
Minimum Depth: 3 feet, 3 inches
Maximum Depth: 10 feet

Closed some holidays. Big Stacy is open very early for
lap swimmers and swim team practice, and usually closes
about 8:00 P.M. in the summer. Hours change from season
to season, so check ahead.

Gillespie Stacy's Realty Company donated the 2.18 acres that became Big Stacy Pool in 1929. Stacy was on Austin's first Parks and Recreation Board of Directors and developed the Travis Heights neighborhood. The pool was built by the Works Progress Administration in 1933-1937, and someone's initials dated 1936 are still carved into the concrete in the northeast corner. The pool is called Big Stacy to differentiate it from the wading pool, Little Stacy (see page 108), a few miles away.

Big Stacy competes in popularity with Deep Eddy, according to lap swimmers, or maybe the lap swimmers compete for it! Big Stacy is extremely popular with lap swimmers because it is open year-round, it's warm, it's free, and it has dedicated lap lanes. In fact, you will probably find this author there on any given day. The pool has few amenities, yet it is always crowded. Perhaps part of the draw is that the water comes from an Artesian well 2,000 feet

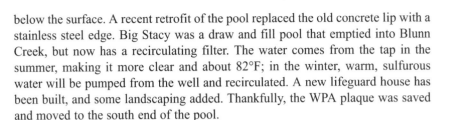

below the surface. A recent retrofit of the pool replaced the old concrete lip with a stainless steel edge. Big Stacy was a draw and fill pool that emptied into Blunn Creek, but now has a recirculating filter. The water comes from the tap in the summer, making it more clear and about 82°F; in the winter, warm, sulfurous water will be pumped from the well and recirculated. A new lifeguard house has been built, and some landscaping added. Thankfully, the WPA plaque was saved and moved to the south end of the pool.

Parking is scarce at Big Stacy in late afternoon when the lap swimmers get off work, but one can usually find a space. The pool is wheelchair-accessible and has a lift. There are usually three lap lanes during the summer and six in the winter. There are small bathhouses for men and women with one indoor shower each and rest rooms. There is minimal shade but lots of grassy areas. Kickboards and other equipment are available. Join the pool's swim team, the Stacy Sharks.

One of Austin's Moontowers can be seen from the pool, and is especially beautiful in the winter when the warm Artesian water steams above the pool.

Hike the 6.7-mile gravel trail along Blunn Creek through a twenty-acre greenbelt. The trail begins at Big Stacy Park and follows Blunn Creek north toward the Colorado River to Riverside Drive. Parking is available along the trail, and   rest rooms are located at both Little and Big Stacy Parks. Picnic tables with grills dot the park; or enjoy baseball, tennis, and a playground. By the time you reach the other pool, you'll be ready to get wet again.

Improvements to this trail are currently being proposed which would extend it under Riverside Drive and connect to the Town Lake Trail. For more information, contact the Austin Metropolitan Trails Council at (512) 478-4644.

Big Stacy Pool before the pool's edge was retrofitted

BRENTWOOD POOL

6710 Arroyo Seco Street
Austin, Texas 78757

STATISTICS

Open June through August
60 feet
Minimum Depth: 2 feet, 7 inches
Maximum Depth: 4 feet, 9 inches

Brentwood Pool is identical in design to Patterson Pool (see page 91). The main pool is rectangular, while the wading pool is a separate octagon with a fountain in the center, wooden deck and gazebo.

This spacious sixteen-acre park has wide-open grassy areas, a playground, picnic areas, plenty of oak and cottonwood trees for shade, baseball fields, and basketball and tennis courts. Concessions are available in the form of a vending machine. Parking is allowed on the street.

CANYON VISTA POOL

8455 Spicewood Springs Road
Austin, Texas 78759

STATISTICS
May through August
25 yards
Minimum Depth: 3 feet, 8 inches
Maximum Depth: 12 feet, 6 inch

Canyon Vista isn't a very big pool, but there is a sweeping view from the poolside. It is wheelchair accessible. There is one diving board and a shallow wading area. There are no bathhouses, but there is an outdoor

shower and rest room. There is plenty of parking but zero shade. Some grassy areas can be found outside the fence, but concrete surrounds the pool. A soda machine provides concessions. Swim lessons and swim teams are offered at Canyon Vista.

CITIVAN POOL

513 Vargas Road
Austin, Texas 78741

STATISTICS

Open June through August
60 feet
Minimum Depth: 11 inches
Maximum Depth: 4 feet, 7 inches

Citivan Pool is named for a public service club that contributed to the develop-ment of this park, acquired in 1953. Citivan Park is inte-grated into Citivan School and consists of two pools, one a small neighborhood pool and another for wading. The facilities are somewhat dilapidated. East Austin pools are often overlooked and under-financed, but in my opinion are jewels. They are usually less crowded than West Austin pools and have the same sorts of amenities. It should be noted that in the early days of Austin everyone wanted to live in East Austin, especially the fine families who built some magnificent homes there. Nobody wanted to live in West Austin because Indian raids happened too often, and they always had the sun in their eyes on the way to work and back. Citivan Pool has one outdoor shower and rest rooms, but no bathhouse.

DICK NICHOLS POOL

8011 Beckett Road
Austin, Texas 78749

STATISTICS

Open May through August
135 feet
Minimum Depth: 1 foot
Maximum Depth: 8 feet

Dick Nichols Pool is the newest, largest free pool in Austin. It opened on May 24, 1997, and is named for a city council member of the late 1960s. Nichols supported the needs of East Austin, and considered himself 'the voice of South Austin'. Nichols played a role in developing the Renaissance Market near UT, and he helped facilitate the construction of Garrison Park and the South Austin Recreation Center. He died in 1979.

Oak Hill was settled in the 1840s and was originally called Live Oak Springs, then Shiloh, then Oatmanville, and finally, Oak Hill since about 1900. A bounty of limestone excavated from this area was furnished for the building of the state

Entrance to Dick Nichols Pool
Mural by Dale Whistler

capitol and a railroad line was extended here in 1882 to transport the stone. Convict labor was used to quarry the stone, and three of these men died, hence the name Convict Hill. The markers are long gone.

The 150 acres of land for Dick Nichols Pool was purchased in 1980. In 1992, Texas Parks and Wildlife granted the City of Austin $457,000 toward construction of the pool, and the city matched that. Construction began in 1993 and the facility cost $1.2 million to build.

Dick Nichols Pool is identical in design to Dove Springs (see page 73). A colorful mural by Dale Whistler depicting tropical fish welcomes swimmers. Another mural demonstrates the phases of the moon. The murals are part of the Art in Public Places project, a division of the Capital Improvements Projects. The facility is painted bright blue, pink, purple, green, and yellow, giving it a festive feel.

There is plenty of parking, a huge new playground, basketball courts, baseball and soccer fields, tennis courts, volleyball courts, picnic areas and grills. A large, airy bathhouse surrounds the pool. There isn't much shade around the pool but there are other picnic areas throughout the park that do have shade. A 1.1-mile hike and bike trail encircles the park.

Dick Nichols Park also has a cave with stalactites, stalagmites and soda straw formations.

Dick Nichols Pool

DITTMAR POOL

1009 West Dittmar Road
Austin, Texas 78745
(512) 441-4777

STATISTICS

Open May through August
25 yards
Minimum Depth: 2 feet
Maximum Depth: 11 feet

The land that is now Dittmar Park was once a thriving dairy farm operated by A.B. Dittmar. Dittmar's farm was purchased in 1985 for $800,000 by the City of Austin with bond election funds.

The pool is an ample twenty-five yards and irregularly shaped. It is one of the nicer neighborhood pools. Five or six lap lanes are usually marked off, and divers can take advantage of a mid-height board. There is a separate wading pool. Swim lessons and teams are popular at Dittmar. A large bathhouse has two indoor showers, rest rooms and changing rooms. There are no shade trees near the pool, but tents have been erected over picnic tables, and there are nice grassy areas next to the pool.

Twelve-acre Dittmar Park is spacious and offers a variety of activities. Boggy Creek runs along the southeastern boundary of the park and a charming footbridge spans the water. Large shade trees line the banks. There are picnic tables with grills, and a modern playground that is shaded by giant oak trees. A huge grassy area is suitable for football, Frisbee, or kite flying. A popular feature is a 10,530 square-foot covered basketball court complex, providing shade during the peak of summer. A hike and bike trail loops around the park. Dittmar Park also has volleyball courts. There is plenty of parking. Wheelchair-accessible.

The Dittmar Recreation Center is 6,405 square-feet and has two gymnasiums. It also has a pottery room, multipurpose and meeting rooms, weights, showers, lockers, and a kitchen. Classes for children in tumbling and dance are offered, as well as aerobics and karate classes for older kids. Concessions such as soda and candy machines can be found inside the Recreation Center.

Dittmar Pool

DOTTIE JORDAN POOL

2803 Loyola Lane
Austin, Texas 78723
(512) 926-3491

STATISTICS

Open May through August
25 yards
Minimum Depth: 1 foot, 1 inch
Maximum Depth: 11 feet

Formerly known as University Hills, Dottie Jordan Park and Pool is a little off the beaten path but well worth the trip. The park is 11.8 acres, and was acquired by the city in 1973. It hugs Little Walnut Creek and is bordered by steep limestone cliffs, making it quiet and picturesque.

There is a rectangular swimming pool and a separate square wading pool. Two lap lanes are designated for swimming, and diving boards are popular. Swim lessons and team workouts are held here, so it's important to check the recreational swim hours each season. There is no bathhouse, but there are outdoor showers and rest rooms. The adjacent playground is nicely shaded, and picnic tables overlook the creek. A small hike and bike trail meanders through the park. There is a parking lot, and plenty of shady oak trees and grassy areas.

Dottie Jordan Pool

The Recreation Center has tennis and basketball courts, flag football, kickball, and concessions.

DOVE SPRINGS POOL

5701 Ainez Drive
Austin, Texas 78744
(512) 447-5875

STATISTICS

Open May through August
25 yards
Minimum Depth: 1 foot
Maximum Depth: 8 feet

Dove Springs Pool looks just like Dick Nichols Pool. In fact, Dove Springs is also a new pool and the recreation center has been totally renovated. For a neighborhood pool, Dove Springs is huge. The facilities are very clean and modern. Playful architectural features are painted in bright blue, purple, magenta and yellow. This is definitely a place to have fun!

There is a main pool with two to five lap lanes, and a separate wading pool. A large bathhouse provides indoor showers, rest rooms, and changing areas. A sprawling park surrounds the pool and has everything you can imagine. There is a group picnic area with a giant grill; individual picnic tables also have grills. A running track encircles the pool, and there are two soccer fields, basketball courts, tennis courts,

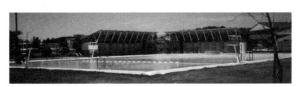

Dove Springs Pool

volleyball courts, and a modern playground. There is plenty of parking but minimal shade. The Recreation Center has concessions, aerobics, ceramics, fine arts, and much more. The facilities are completely wheelchair accessible.

Above: Entrance to Dove Springs Pool
Below: Dove Springs Wading Pool

GILLIS POOL

2501 South First Street
Austin, Texas 78704

STATISTICS

Open June through August
100 feet
Minimum Depth: 2 feet, 10 inches
Maximum Depth: 7 feet, 11 inches

This nice South Austin park and pool was named for Simon Gillis, a city councilman who served in 1934. Gillis objected to the construction of IH35, preferring the elm trees that used to line the highway, then known as East Avenue. He resigned over this issue when the highway finally went through. The elm trees were all cleared. Beverly Sheffield has one of these elm stumps in his recreation room. Judging from the massive size of the stump, I think I would have sided with Gillis, too.

The pool was built in 1947, and sits on the corner of a 7.7-acre park. There is no bathhouse, but an outdoor shower next to the pool and rest rooms in the park are available. There is medium shade from tall cottonwood and pecan trees, and grassy areas surround the pool. There isn't much to this pool and it often sits empty. Check ahead of time before heading out.

Gillis Pool

East Bouldin Creek winds through the park and alongside the pool. The park has picnic tables with grills, basketball courts, baseball diamonds with bleachers, and large, open grassy areas. A modern playground is popular with kids. There are no concessions but convenience stores are within walking distance. The park is wheel-chair-accessible and parking is allowed on the street or on the north side of the park in a small lot.

GIVENS POOL

3811 East 12th Street
Austin, Texas 78721
(512) 928-1982

STATISTICS

Open June through August
50 yards
Minimum Depth: 3 feet
Maximum Depth: 13 feet

Givens Pool is named for Dr. Givens, an African-American dentist. Givens Pool is a well-kept secret. Acquired in 1958, it's a fabulous swimming pool that is huge for a neighborhood pool. It never seems to be crowded and it's free. A grand hexagonal entrance welcomes you into a large shady area and the L-shaped pool stretches out before you. Givens is actually two pools, with a separate rectangular wading pool. One lane is designated for lap

Givens Wading Pool

swimming. A diving board is popular with the kids. The wading pool is adjacent to the main pool but on a lower level. It is surrounded on two sides by high concrete walls and faces the park. There are indoor showers and rest rooms. A large oak tree provides shade around the pool, and grassy areas are well kept.

Givens Park is a sprawling forty-six acres, and a wonderful place to spend the day. Tannehill Creek, named for an early Austin settler, winds through this extensive park. Mostly made up of low, rolling hills, the park has wide-open areas, groves of trees, and lots of amenities. A group picnic pavilion is available for parties. Individual tables with grills dot the park. A hike and bike trail and a nature trail will take you all around the park for a good overview. Baseball diamonds with spectator bleachers, basketball courts, lighted tennis courts, and a playground add to your fun. A covered outdoor amphitheater hosts plays and entertainment. Rest rooms and water fountains are located throughout the park. There is plenty of parking.

As if all that weren't enough, Givens Park also has a Recreation Center with a gymnasium, an activity center, arts and crafts classes, meeting rooms, and a weight room.

Givens Pool

GOVALLE POOL

5200 Bolm Road (just off of Airport Blvd.)
Austin, Texas 78721

S T A T I S T I C S

Open June through August
60 feet
Minimum Depth: 2 feet, 9 inches
Maximum Depth: 4 feet, 7 inches

Govalle was one of the first settlements in Austin. The log cabin that is currently located in Zilker Park was moved from Govalle.

This scenic twenty-six-acre park has a small pool near the entrance. The pool was built in 1946 and is surrounded by a high fence and thick hedges. It faces Boggy Creek where a footbridge crosses the water. Tall pecan trees provide plenty of shade. There is no bathhouse but an outdoor shower is provided. The park also has a playground, picnic tables with grills, open grassy areas, soccer fields, basketball courts, baseball, and lots of parking.

Govalle Pool

KEALING POOL

1500 Rosewood Avenue
Austin, Texas 78702
(Kealing Junior High School)

STATISTICS

Open June through August
60 feet
Minimum Depth: 2 feet, 8 inches
Maximum Depth: 4 feet, 8 inches

This little pool sits smack in the middle of Kealing Junior High School, but the public may use the pool and surrounding twenty acres of park land. Built in the 1960s, Kealing Pool is fairly minimal. There are rest rooms, and some grassy areas. Shade is provided by pecan trees. Parking may be found at the school or the museum/library. The pool is surrounded by open grassy areas, and a Moontower shines forth. On campus you may also enjoy basketball courts, a playground, and a picnic area.

Kealing Pool

George Washington Carver Museum

1165 Angelina Street
Austin, Texas 78702
(512) 472-4809

Tuesday through Thursday 10:00 A.M.–6:00 P.M.
Friday and Saturday noon–5:00 P.M.
Free admission

Before or after your swim at Kealing Pool, visit the first neighborhood African-American history museum in Texas. The George Washington Carver Museum opened in 1980. The building, which was originally located at Guadalupe and Ninth streets, was moved in 1933 to its current location. It originally housed the Austin Public Library and was built in 1926. The exterior was resurfaced in brick and it reopened as the Carver Museum. A current branch of the library is next door to the museum today. Exhibits change regularly.

KENNEMER POOL

1032 Peyton Gin Road
Austin, Texas 78758
(Lanier High School)

```
┌─────────────────────────────────────┐
│           S T A T I S T I C S        │
│                                       │
│       Open June through August        │
│              25 yards                 │
│         Minimum Depth: 3 feet         │
│        Maximum Depth: 11 feet         │
└─────────────────────────────────────┘
```

T his pool at the Lanier High School campus is a memorial to David Kennemer, a former Assistant Superintendent of Parks, who was killed in a head-on collision.

Although it has shared the Lanier High School facilities since 1974, Kennemer Pool is open to the public. There is one designated lap lane, and swim teams practice here. An outdoor shower is located next to the pool, and rest rooms may be found on campus. Kennemer Pool is on a busy stretch of Peyton Gin Road, but is screened from the street with trees. The pool is nicely landscaped with lush grassy areas, pink crepe myrtles, and young oak trees. A gazebo provides shade. Parking is available next door at the high school.

Kennemer Pool

MARTIN POOL

1607 Haskell Street
Austin, Texas 78702
(512) 478-8716

STATISTICS

Open June through August
25 meters
Minimum Depth: 2 feet
Maximum Depth: 11 feet

This neighborhood pool and the school are named for Sam Martin. Just a stone's throw from Town Lake, Martin Pool is a welcome sight when you reach the east end of the hike and bike trail. From the pool, you can take in a beautiful view of Town Lake and Fiesta Gardens. The pool is a good size and has a separate wading area. There is no bathhouse but outdoor showers are available.

The wide-open park has a playground, covered picnic tables and grills, and lots of huisache, pecan and cottonwood trees. A moontower casts luminescent rays on the water, and cultural murals face the pool.

Martin Junior High School has a Satellite Center which serves the neighborhood youths with foosball, a pool table, a piano, and a big-screen TV. Adolfo Mendez, the program specialist, is justly proud of his center. They work in connection with Ballet Austin and Ballet Folklorio to teach dance to children. Ceramics classes, tennis, sandlot baseball, basketball, and cooking classes are also offered.

Martin Pool

83

METZ POOLS

2407 Canterbury Street
Austin, Texas 78702

STATISTICS

Open June through August
100 feet
Minimum Depth: 3 feet, 4 inches
Maximum: 10 feet

The Metz Pools are named for Dr. Metz, an educator at the University of Texas; there is also a building on the UT Austin campus that bears his name.

The neighborhood pool was the very first in Austin to be built at a public school. Completed in 1932, it is rectangular and has murals, rest rooms, and an outdoor shower. There is good shade and grassy areas surround the pool. A small parking lot is adjacent to the pool.

Metz Pool

If you have always wanted to jump into a downtown water fountain in the middle of July for relief from the heat, head over to Metz Wading Pool to live out your fantasy legally. This thirty-foot circular pool is located in front of the Recreation Center as you approach the entrance. It is somewhat level with the sidewalk and has a low wall. When the fountain is flowing, it sprays water over swimmers. An outdoor shower is available at the main pool.

Metz Park is located in the shadow of the Holly Power Plant, and a constant hum is audible. The park is a nice one though, and has colorful murals, an amphitheater and stage, a playground, picnic areas, a recreation center with a ceramics kiln, and shaded basketball courts. There is off-street parking, eight acres of grassy space, and pecan and elm trees for shade. Concessions are available inside the recreation center.

Metz Wading Pool

MONTOPOLIS POOL

1200 Montopolis Drive
Austin, Texas 78741
(512) 385-5931

STATISTICS

Open June through August
25 meters
Minimum Depth: 2 feet
Maximum Depth: 11 feet

Montopolis was an early settlement of Austin. This neighborhood pool was built in 1977 by Hans-Stringer Architects. There are up to six designated lap lanes, and the pool has its own swim team. There is no bathhouse, but an outdoor shower and rest rooms are available. Murals face the pool. There is minimal shade around the pool, but you can take cover in the park.

The newly improved park is 7.5 acres and has a new baseball field, basketball courts, picnic tables, a playground, and open grassy areas. The Recreation Center has a gymnasium with weights. There is plenty of parking, and the park is a designated 'Drug-Free Zone'.

Montopolis Pool

MURCHISON POOL

3700 North Hills Drive
Austin, Texas 78731

STATISTICS

Open June through August
25 yards
Minimum Depth: 3 feet
Maximum Depth: 11 feet

Murchison was the superintendent of the Austin Independent School Disrict. This nice little neighborhood pool is the only one in the Far West neighborhood. Built in 1973, there is one designated lap lane; swim lessons are available and teams practice here. There is very little shade or grass, but an arbor gives some relief. Pretty crepe myrtles surround the pool. There is no bathhouse but an outdoor shower and rest rooms are provided.

The pool is located at Murchison Middle School, and a playground on the school grounds is open to the public. The school's soccer fields are very popular, as is the baseball field. There is plenty of parking and a soda machine provides cold

Murchison Pool

PALM POOL

201 IH35 Frontage Road
Austin, Texas 78701

STATISTICS

Open June through August
60 feet
Minimum Depth: 2 feet, 6 inches
Maximum Depth: 6 feet, 10 inches

Most people think that this pool is named for the beautiful palm trees in front of Palm School at East Cesar Chavez Street and IH35, but it goes back further than that to Sir Swante Palm. Sir Swante Palm was a leader of Swedish immigration to Texas. A native of Smaland, Sweden, Palm came to Austin in 1850. Palm served as Vice Consul to Texas for Sweden and Norway, and helped thousands of Swedish immigrants in Texas. Swedish King Oscar II knighted him in 1883 for his work. A highly educated man, Palm was one of Texas's first bibliographers. He amassed a huge library which he donated to the University of Texas, more than doubling its holdings. Palm served as Justice of the Peace, Alderman, and Postmaster. He was a founder of Gethsemane Lutheran Church. Palm School is named for him.

This endearing little pool is like an oasis in the heart of downtown Austin. It sits between the Convention Center and IH35, so it's not the most peaceful park in the system, but for people who work downtown, this is the perfect place for a lunch-time dip in the pool. Built in 1935 before IH35 and most downtown office buildings existed, it was probably once a popular place to get away from it all. The pool is practically in the center of a five-acre park, and is surrounded by some grass and a fence. There are rest rooms in the park, but they are a short walk from the pool. An outdoor shower is close to the pool. The park also has a playground, access to the Waller Creek hike and bike trail, tennis courts, a baseball diamond, and basketball courts.

Palm Pool was closed for a long time due to budget cuts and low attendance, but has recently re-opened. Palm Pool, along with thirteen other pools in the city system, are draw and fill pools. Palm Pool requires 94,000 gallons of fresh water to be pumped in every morning, which is then emptied into Waller Creek. The water becomes valuable during times of drought. A recent bond election earmarked funds to improve and develop Waller Creek, so perhaps Palm Pool will once again thrive.

Palm Pool

PARQUE ZARAGOSA POOL

800 Pedernales Street
Austin, Texas 78702
(512) 472-7142

STATISTICS

Open May through August
100 feet
Minimum Depth: 3 feet
Maximum Depth: 8 feet

Named for General Zaragosa, this park has been a gathering spot for Hispanic celebrations and festivals since the 1930s. The park has nine acres of beautiful, gnarly oak trees which provide great shade. Boggy Creek runs through the park and a footbridge spans the water taking you to the pool. There are sand volleyball courts, a baseball field with covered bleachers, basketball courts, a stage and performance area, a playground, and picnic tables and grills.

The pool is a simple rectangle with few amenities. Swim teams practice here, and rest rooms and an outdoor shower are available.

A 17,500 square-foot recreation center was built in 1992. Constructed of limestone, the building has interesting curves and metalwork. The recreation center has everything you can imagine, from pool tables, Ping Pong, shuffle board, wrestling, a weight room and gymnasium, to classes in tumbling, arts and crafts, mechanics and sewing.

A 2.6-mile trail is being proposed which would run through Parque Zaragosa and link the Downs-Mabson Ballfield just north of 12th Street with the Town Lake Trail. The existing trail along Boggy Creek would be improved and bike lanes would be added to connect with Pedernales Street. Call the Austin Metropolitan Trails Council at (512) 478-4644 for more information.

PATTERSON POOL

1400 Wilshire Boulevard
Austin, Texas 78722

STATISTICS

Open May through August
60 feet
Minimum Depth: 2 feet, 9 inches
Maximum Depth: 4 feet, 11 inches

Y ou'd never guess there was a pool here when you're whizzing down Airport Boulevard trying to make your flight on time. The pool is named for the Patterson Family who donated the land for Robert Mueller Airport. If you are the type of person who likes to watch the bellies of airplanes zoom overhead as they descend to the runway, Patterson Park will please you. Located right across the street from the air-port, planes buzz overhead so close you can practically touch them. When the airport relocates to Bergstrom in 1999, this feature will change. Until then, if you've got time to kill while waiting for Aunt Sally's flight to arrive, why not go for a swim?

Patterson Pool

The pool is identical to Brentwood Pool (see page 66) in design. Acquired in 1952, it sits on ten acres of park land which extends south to Schieffer Street. The main pool is rectangular, and the wading area is a separate octagon with a fountain in the center. The wading pool has a nice wooden deck and gazebo. There is no bathhouse, but there is an outdoor shower and rest rooms. Patterson has a swim team. The park has a playground, picnic areas and grills, and plenty of parking. There is minimal shade from oak and cottonwood trees, but there are plenty of grassy areas. Enjoy baseball fields and basketball and volleyball courts. The Burnett 'Blondie' Pharr Tennis Center is also popular. The park is well-lit and well-maintained.

RAMSEY POOL

1400 West 42nd Street
Austin, Texas 78756

STATISTICS

Open May through August
100 feet
Minimum Depth: 3 feet
Maximum Depth: 9 feet

This popular neighborhood pool was built in 1941. Amenities were donated by the Ramsey Estate. The pool is at the south end of a five-acre park near Austin's medical community. There is one designated lap lane. Ramsey Pool has a swim team. There is no bathhouse, but an outdoor shower and rest rooms are provided.

The park covers two city blocks and has a playground, picnic tables with grills, tennis courts, and baseball. Parking is only available on the street. Pecan trees provide shade, and a soda machine has concessions.

Ramsey Pool

93

REED POOL

2600 Pecos Street
Austin, Texas 78703

STATISTICS

Open May through August
60 feet
Minimum Depth: 2 feet, 9 inches
Maximum Depth: 4 feet, 6 inches

This tucked-away neighborhood pool is named for Roberta Reed, an Austin citizen, and her daughters. It is located deep in the old Enfield neighborhood on the shores of Lake Austin. Set back from the street, you'll have a nice stroll through the grassy park past Taylor's Lime Kiln as you approach the pool.

The pool, built in 1954, has an irregularly-shaped main swimming area and a separate wading pool. There is one designated lap lane. There is no bathhouse but an outdoor shower and rest rooms are provided. Shade can be found under some oak trees which hang over the fence, and willow and elm trees surround the park. Reed Pool is a quiet, neighborhood swimming spot, but very popular with local residents. It is completely wheelchair-accessible. Reed Pool also has a swim team.

The six-acre park has a playground, picnic tables and grills, and large grassy areas. Lake Austin is a very short walk down a trail in the back of the park. There is parking on Pecos Street, and in a small lot next to the pool. Soda machines provide concessions.

A vestige from Austin's history, Taylor's Lime Kiln still stands in Reed Park. The lime manufactured in this kiln was used in the building of the original Austin capitol building. Peter Calder Taylor (1829-1895) moved to San Antonio from the Orkney Islands in Scotland in 1851 with fifty cents in his pocket. He built a kiln in San Antonio in 1860, then when the railroad came to town in 1871 he moved to Austin.

Construction projects were sprouting up everywhere, and land in Austin was selling for fifty cents an acre! The construction of Taylor's kiln cost $5,000. This original kiln was built in 1871. Taylor later built a second kiln about one mile south of Reed Park. Taylor was so successful because he devised a way of keeping the fire inside the kiln going while the lime burned continuously. This allowed more control over the process. The quarry where he extracted limestone is now submerged under Lake Austin at Taylor's Slough. However, the wagon trail he used to haul materials back to the workshop still exists between Reed Park and the submerged quarry. The wooden braces on the present day kiln have deteriorated, and some modern repairs have been made. Taylor patented his braces because they contained the walls while expanding with heat. The original firebox entrance has been closed with cement since children began playing inside. It originally had a burning well thirty feet deep and ten feet in diameter. At its peak, the kiln produced up to one hundred barrels of lime per day that was sold as far south as Galveston. Horse stables, carpenter and blacksmith shops, and wheelwright and paint shops surrounded the original kiln. If you look hard at the present-day Reed Park, you can easily imagine what a bustling scene it was. Taylor's Lime Kiln was designated a historical landmark in 1974, affirming Taylor's integral role in the development of Austin's economy and architecture.

Taylor's Lime Kiln

Reed Pool

ROSEWOOD POOL

2300 Rosewood Avenue
Austin, Texas 78702
(512) 476-4118 Doris Miller Auditorium
(512) 472-6838 Recreation Center

STATISTICS

Open May through August
130 feet
Minimum Depth: 1 foot, 1 inch
Maximum Depth: 8 feet

Built in 1929, Rosewood Pool was originally designated for African-Americans. The area residents held beauty pageants and picnics there, and it became a center of community spirit. Rosewood reminds me a lot of Givens; in fact, they bracket the Boggy Creek Greenbelt like bookends, and are similar in design. The main pool is a whopping 130 feet. When I visited on a hot day in July, there wasn't a soul in the pool! If you're looking for a lot of elbowroom, try Rosewood. It's a lovely, simple pool with plenty of amenities. There is a separate, rectangular wading pool below the main pool. Rosewood hosts a swim team. An outdoor shower and rest rooms can be found at the pool.

Rosewood Park is twelve acres of gentle hills. The park has a playground, picnic tables with grills, tennis courts, volleyball, and baseball diamonds with bleachers. Elm, pecan and huisache trees provide shade, and concessions can be found in the Recreation Center. A famous moontower glows over the park.

While you're there, check out the Madison Cabin which is now an African-American heritage exhibit. Henry G. and Louisa Madison were farm laborers and pioneers. They built this log cabin in 1863 near the present location of 807 East 11th Street. In 1886 they built another structure around the original log cabin and lived there until

1912. When a wrecking crew was razing the outer house in 1968, they discovered the log cabin inside. Historical relics and documents were found regarding black pioneers. In 1973 the city carefully deconstructed the cabin and rebuilt it at Rosewood Park where it can be seen today. The interior is not open to the public, but tours are available by calling the Rosewood Recreation Center. It is open Monday-Friday, 9:00 A.M.-5:00 P.M. Admission is free.

The Boggy Creek Greenbelt has a 1.2-mile trail of gravel and concrete. The trail begins just north of Parque Zaragosa along Boggy Creek at the Conley-Guerrero Senior Center on Nile Street, travels north along the creek through Rosewood Park, and ends just north of 12th Street. There are rest rooms at the 12th Street trailhead, and in Rosewood Park. Parking is available at Parque Zaragosa, the Boggy Creek trailhead, Rosewood Park and 12th Street.

The Rosewood Recreation Center has a theater and gymnasium, and tons of activities such as arts and crafts, after -school tutoring, cheerleading, flag football, basketball, ceramics, dance, bridge, sign language, self-defense for women, karate, etc. Doris Miller Auditorium also has a stage. Doris Miller was the first African-American to be killed during WWII. He was a cook, but fought valiantly at Pearl Harbor by shooting at enemy planes when his comrades fell.

Rosewood Pool

ST. JOHN'S POOL

910 East St. John's Avenue
Austin, Texas 78752

STATISTICS

Open May through August
60 feet
Minimum Depth: 2 feet, 9 inches
Maximum Depth: 4 feet, 9 inches

S t. John's Pool is the most minimal pool in the City of Austin system and looks like a giant kitchen sink. Acquired in 1961, the pool was popular for thirty years or so. The Home Depot and other retail stores have encroached on what was once a large meadow, and the pool is now wedged between stores and residential back yards. There are absolutely no amenities, including rest rooms; however, an outdoor shower is provided. There is minimal shade and grass, and the pool is rectangular.

SHIPE POOL

4400 Avenue G
Austin, Texas 78751

STATISTICS

Open May through August
100 feet
Minimum Depth: 3 feet, 3 inches
Maximum Depth: 10 feet

Shipe was the developer of Hyde Park. You can learn more about him by visiting his residence, a designated historical landmark.

Shipe Park used to overlook Gem Lake where the Baker School is located today. Gem Lake covered the entire block. Bridges spanned the water for pedestrians, while ducks swam underneath. There were boat rides and summer stock plays. The park also had a zoo.

In August of 1935, residents of Hyde Park marched before the city council and demanded that bathers at Shipe Pool wear robes while coming and going from their swim. Apparently, nothing came of this push for modesty, and bathers of all sorts frequent Shipe Pool today.

Shipe is a very popular neighborhood pool with some loyal fans. Many city pools close when school begins in August because the lifeguards are mostly young students. Recently, area residents took up a collection to pay for the maintenance costs of keeping Shipe Pool open for another month beyond the usual close date. They held a benefit with live music and activities, and were successful in their efforts. What a wonderful display of community spirit and pool loyalty!

Shipe Pool is part of a two-acre park that takes up an entire city block in the heart of Hyde Park. The main neighborhood pool is rectangular and was built in 1929.

Shipe is one of the oldest pools in the city system. One designated lap lane is always occupied, and the Shipe swim team practices here. An outdoor shower is provided, and grassy areas surround the pool. Maple trees provide good shade. Rest rooms are located in the log building next to the pool. There is a separate wading pool that is separately fenced and located next to the main pool.

The park has a fabulous playscape which was voted 'Austin's Superior Playground' in 1957. Cottonwood and oak trees give the park a natural look. Waller Creek flows through the north end of the park where you can wade up to your ankles. The park also has basketball and volleyball courts, and lots of wide-open grassy space. Soda machines have concessions. Parking is available on the street.

Shipe Pool

Elizabet Ney Museum

304 East 44th Street
Austin, Texas 78751
(512) 458-2255

Before or after your swim, visit the Elizabet Ney Museum. The castle-like building houses statues and sculptures by Texas's first popular sculptor. Ney emigrated from Germany with her husband in 1870, and was famous for sculpting notable Texans such as Sam Houston and Stephen Austin. The museum, built in 1892, used to be Ney's studio, and was modeled after a studio she kept on the island of Madeira, called Formosa. Today, classes in sculpture are offered to the public. Open Wednesday-Saturday 10:00 A.M.-5:00 P.M. and Sunday noon-5:00 P.M.

WESTENFIELD

2000 Enfield Road
Austin, Texas 78703

STATISTICS

Open May through August
100 feet
Minimum Depth: 2 feet, 1 inch
Maximum Depth: 6 feet, 8 inches

N amed for the Westenfield neighborhood, this area was developed by the Graham Family, The Grahams were connected to the Pease Family, and Westenfield is one of the oldest neighborhoods in Austin.

This nice 5.5-acre park was acquired by the city in 1946. The pool has great shade and a wooden deck. There is one designated lap lane, but this is not an ideal pool for lap swimming. Nonetheless, it is ideal for swim lessons and swim team practice. There is an outdoor shower and rest rooms, but no bathhouse.

Westenfield Pool

In the park there are picnic tables, lots of pecan and oak trees, tennis and basketball courts, a baseball field and a playground. Soda machines provide concessions. Traffic noise from MoPac is constantly audible, but tolerable. The train can also be seen and heard when it goes by. Parking is on the street only.

The entrance to the 56-acre Johnson Creek Greenbelt is located kitty-corner to Westenfield Pool. The hike and bike trail is 1.11 miles of concrete and mostly follows MoPac to meet the mouth of the Town Lake Trail near the parking lot of Austin High School. From there it is a short walk west over to Deep Eddy Pool.

WADING POOLS

BAILEY POOL

1101 West 33rd Street (directly behind Bailey Medical Center)
Austin, Texas 78705

STATISTICS

Open June through August
30 feet
Minimum Depth: 2 feet, 4 inches
Maximum Depth: 3 feet

Bailey Pool is located on a two-acre section of land in the heart of Austin's medical community. The city acquired this property in 1935 and built a thirty-foot circular wading pool. The surrounding park has a playground with picnic areas, volleyball courts, baseball fields, and tennis courts. A picturesque garden has a picnic area under the shade of oak trees. Junipers and oaks populate the park, but there are grassy areas, too. Parking is on the street only.

Bailey Pool

CLARKSVILLE POOL

1811 West 11th Street
Austin, Texas 78703

STATISTICS

Open June through August
50 feet
Minimum Depth: 9 inches
Maximum Depth: 2 feet

The neighborhood known as Clarksville used to belong to Governor Pease. His African-American slaves made their homes there, and eventually Governor Pease deeded the land to them.

The fifty-foot wading pool is ample in size and has a wide wheelchair ramp leading into the water.

This 1.5-acre park is located within a residential neighborhood close to MoPac; it's fairly quiet but you can hear the highway noise. It has a wooden playground, picnic tables, a baseball field and basketball court. There is minimal shade and lots of flat, grassy space. Parking is allowed on the street.

EASTWOODS POOL

3001 Harris Park Avenue
Austin, Texas 78705

STATISTICS

Open June through August
50 feet
Minimum depth: 8 inches
Maximum depth: 2 feet

The City of Austin acquired nine acres for this park in 1929 in what was then Northeast Austin. The space was ideal as it was already wooded and Waller Creek ran through the back section. The pool is located right in the middle of the park with good shade.

Cactus Pryor recalls visiting J. Frank YDobie, who lived nearby, on the footbridge spanning Waller Creek. Dobie would smoke his pipe and stare contemplatively into the water.

Even before Dobie's time, Eastwoods Park was known as a popular picnic area called Christian's Grove. Today, the park is popular with University of Texas students who mostly populate the area. The park has lots of pecan and oaks trees which provide excellent shade and shelter to some very friendly squirrels. There are picnic tables, a playground, basketball courts, and a baseball field. A winding, walking trail encircles the park. The old footbridge over Waller Creek still stands. Parking is allowed on the street.

LITTLE STACY POOL

2000 Alameda Drive
Austin, Texas 78704

STATISTICS

Open June through August
50 feet
Minimum Depth: 9 inches
Maximum Depth: 2 feet

L ittle Stacy Park is linked to Big Stacy Park by a short but scenic trail along Blunn Creek. This is a four-acre park located in the heart of Travis Heights. There are picnic tables with grills, baseball fields, tennis courts, and a playground. The rectangular wading pool, built in 1937, has a wooden deck and is quite popular. Folks can also wander down to Blunn Creek and hike.

Little Stacy Pool

ODOM POOL

1010 Turtle Creek Boulevard
Austin, Texas 78745

STATISTICS

Open June through August
51 feet
Minimum Depth: 1 foot
Maximum Depth: 2 feet

This little pool, as well as the elementary school where it is located, is named after Lalla Odom. It is an exact replica of the Clarksville wading pool (see page 106) with a wheelchair ramp leading into the water. The pool is completely surrounded by concrete and there is minimal shade. There is also a wooden playground with grassy areas and baseball and basketball facilities. Parking is allowed on the street.

Odom Pool

PAN AMERICAN POOL

2100 East 3rd Street
Austin, Texas 78702
(512) 476-9193 (Recreation Center)

STATISTICS

Open June through August
50 feet
Minimum Depth: 6 inches
Maximum Depth: 1 foot, 8 inches

When the city acquired this nine-acre pool and park in 1954, a contest was held to determine a name, and Austinites chose Pan American.

This is another good pool where you can indulge your fountain-splashing fantasies. It is irregularly shaped and has a stair-step pyramid like a Mayan temple in the midst of climbing equipment. The water flows from the top over the steps into a shallow wading area.

The park has a brand new playground, picnic tables with grills, a baseball field with spectator bleachers, basketball courts, an amphitheater with a sloping hillside, and a football camp. Cottonwood and oak trees dot wide-open grassy areas. Concessions are available inside the Recreation Center. Parking is allowed on the street.

The Recreation Center also has volleyball courts, softball, and public information on illiteracy, immunizations, etc., plus encyclopedias, books, pool tables, a kitchen, and more.

PEASE PARK AND POOL

1600 Parkway at Kingsbury
Austin, Texas 78701

STATISTICS

Open June through August
48 feet
Minimum Depth: 6 inches
Maximum Depth: 1 foot, 5 inches

Pease Park was the first publicly owned park in Austin. Twenty-three acres of land were donated by Elisha Marshall Pease to the City of Austin in 1875. Pease had a long career as a politician. Born in Connecticut in 1812, he first came to Austin 1835 from New Orleans after reading a book by Mary Austin Holley, cousin of Stephen F. Austin, about the area. Pease fought in the Texas Revolution against Mexico as a soldier and civil servant. He was Comptroller of the Republic of Texas, a Representative in the first two sessions of the Texas Legislature, a Senator in the third session, then Governor from 1853-7. He became a Union leader during the Civil War, then an organizer of the Texas Republican Army. Pease also served as Provisional Governor from 1879-80. He founded the schools for the deaf and blind, which are still operating in Austin. The Pease Governor's Mansion, an example of classic Greek revival architecture, can still be seen at 6 Niles Road.

The Kiwanis Club constructed the wading pool, the main entrance to the park, and the bathhouse in June 1928. At the time, Pease Park was hardly ever used and the facilities quickly deteriorated. Jim Garrison then planted new grass, and opened the park to the public on July 23, 1928. It's been steadily used ever since.

Pease Park has some wide-open grassy areas, and also wooded areas thick with oaks. Shoal Creek meanders through the length of the park and almost always has some water in it.

The Shoal Creek Greenbelt and hike and bike trail, which begins at Town Lake and Cesar Chavez, and ends at 38th Street, will take you through this park. The three-mile trail is made of crushed granite, limestone and concrete. The only rest rooms along the trail are located in Pease Park. If you are interested in preserving the trail and greenbelt, join the Shoal Creek Greenbelt Coalition which represents the interests of hikers, bikers, runners, dog lovers, and disc-golf players. The group has 'adopted' a section of the trail between 24th and 29th streets, and volunteers hold periodic cleanups.

Pease Park is extremely popular because it is so extensive and has diverse activities. The pool is small and suitable for cooling off after enjoying the rest of the park. Pease Park is the only City of Austin park where dogs are not required to be on a leash, making it very popular with them. Frisbee Golf is also very popular here. A Frisbee Golf information center can be found near 24th Street, or call 477-7273. A new playscape recently replaced the older wooden one, and is now divided into sections for preschoolers and older children. The park has numerous picnic tables with grills, and a cluster of tables that may be reserved by calling 480-3036. There are baseball fields and basketball and volleyball courts. Parking is only available on the street.

RICKY GUERRERO POOL

500 Brodie Street (not Lane!) at South 6th Street
Austin, Texas 78704

STATISTICS

Open June through August
30 feet
Minimum Depth: 3 inches
Maximum Depth: 3 feet, 6 inches

Unless you already knew that there was a pool here, you'd miss it. This wading pool is a large cobblestone ring that slopes toward a drain at the bottom. In fact, I have not ever seen water in this pool, so don't get your hopes up if you visit.

The city acquired this two-acre park in 1972. Roy Guerrero was Director of the Pan American Club in 1947. His son died unexpectedly, and this pool was named for him.

The park leans up against Bouldin Creek and has a playground, picnic tables with grills, a small parking lot, and lots of grass and trees.

Ricky Guerrero Pool

113

WEST AUSTIN POOL

1317 West 10th Street
Austin, Texas 78703

STATISTICS

Open June through August
55 feet around
Minimum Depth: 3 feet, 4 inches
Maximum Depth: 4 feet, 6 inches

This lovely park was acquired by the city in 1930. It is a 3.27-acre square between city blocks, but is filled with nooks and crannies, shady hollows, and scenic vistas. It is grassy but hilly. Located in a residential Clarksville neighborhood, it is quiet, too. The circular pool is relatively deep for a wading pool. The park has an elaborate wooden playground, picnic tables, and fairly good shade provided by oak and mesquite trees.

West Austin Pool

THE HIGHLAND LAKES

THE HISTORY OF
THE LOWER COLORADO RIVER AUTHORITY

How High's the Water, Mama? Three Feet High and Rising!

Lower Colorado River Authority
Post Office Box 220
Austin, Texas 78767-0220
(800) 776-5272
(512) 473-3200
http://www.lcra.org
http://highlandlakes.com/

> *The best way to see the future was to look into the river, and the river that runs through the heart of all things Texan is called the Colorado.*
>
> Walter Cronkite

The Colorado River has been used by people for centuries. Historians agree that the Caddoan Indians called the Colorado River 'Kanahatino', and other tribes called it the 'Pashohono'. Spanish explorers called it both the San Clemente and La Sablonniere because of its numerous sandbanks. The name Colorado probably comes from the Spanish term for 'red'. It began appearing on maps as the Colorado in 1690, although perhaps by cartographers' error. Supposedly a mapmaker in Madrid transposed the names for the Colorado River and the Brazos River. The state capital was also planned for the Brazos, but the Colorado offered more opportunities to harness power. It was also more central and transportation and accessibility were key issues. Texas's Colorado River is not to be confused with the Colorado River that flows through the Grand Canyon to California. Our Colorado has its headwaters at the Texas-New Mexico border and travels 900 miles to the Gulf of Mexico. There are ten intrastate rivers in Texas, with the Red River and the Rio Grande bordering us to the north and south, respectively.

The Colorado River basin is in a primarily semi-arid region where rainfall increases as you move from west to east. The average annual rainfall over the Highland Lakes is about thirty inches, whereas in the upper basin near San Angelo, it's twenty inches, and at the Gulf it's forty-four inches. The basin is a 41,000 square-mile area, an area about the size of Ohio, that drains into the river. Its annual runoff is two million acre-feet.

The Colorado River is prone to flooding because warm, moist air from the Gulf often clashes with Pacific and Canadian air and causes heavy rainfall. Central Texas is also prone to drought.

FLOODING AND DAMS

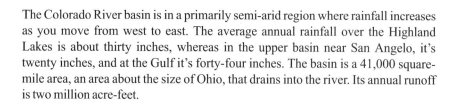

> *It rains about thirty-seven inches a year in Austin.*
> *You should have been here the day it all fell!*
>
> Anonymous

The history of flooding and flood control on the Colorado River is a fascinating one, filled with political intrigue and even murder. The Colorado has probably flooded since the beginning of its existence. In February 1843, water levels were recorded at thirty-six feet. There were numerous floods recorded between 1869-1870, and by then people were crying out for action, especially those downstream of Austin who bore the brunt of the flooding. At the time, the river was still used for navigation by boat, and wood and other debris would pile up and clog boating channels. A few companies tried to clear these channels out, but the costs were high and there were frequent setbacks. Initial attempts to dam the Colorado came from the private sector, not the federal government. In 1885, a farmer named General Adam Rankin Johnson tried to garner support for building a dam at Shirley Shoals (now Buchanan Dam), which had been plagued by flooding. In 1895, General Johnson died and transferred his land to C.H. Alexander, including the water rights. The City of Austin also became interested in harnessing the water and in 1893 built the Austin Dam and a generator at the site of the present Tom Miller Dam. The dam created Lake McDonald and a colorful regatta was held to celebrate. Unfortunately, it quickly eroded and then washed away during the flood of 1900 when the river again rose thirty-three feet. Eight people, including five children, were killed when the powerhouse was crushed by floodwaters. The limestone foundation had pre-vented a good, strong base and as silt built up it made construction efforts futile.

During this flood, an architect named Eugene T. Deats was working at his drawing board downtown when he heard a huge commotion and horses stampeding. He then heard Will Searight shouting from his horse "Run for your life! The dam is broke!" Water rushed up to the bank buildings at 6th Street and Congress Avenue and bridges were washed out. The Austin Dam was rebuilt in 1915, only to be destroyed by flooding again later that year. It was rebuilt a third time in 1937 and renamed Tom Miller Dam after the mayor who had worked for flood control. At the same time, Lake McDonald was renamed Lake Austin.

AUSTIN HISTORY CENTER, AUSTIN PUBLIC LIBRARY, PICB 04262

Guarding Lake Austin

C.H. Alexander tried to build a dam in 1912 at Marble Falls, but he was only able to complete a low-level structure about a third of the way across the river. He planned to build six dams in all but ran out of money.

Twenty floods between 1900 and 1923 caused the state to finally take notice. Hundreds of lives had been lost and the damages were running in the millions of dollars. Flooding was recorded on the first floor of the capitol and ruined millions of acres of farmland. Up to this point, efforts to dam the Colorado had been conducted by private enterprise, which at the time did not have the technical skills or resources to build a dam of large scope. In 1915, a group of landowners living in Travis, Bastrop, Fayette, Matagorda and Wharton Counties, who were interested in flood control, power development, irrigation, and growing rice, formed the Colorado River Improvement Association. An act passed by Congress in 1916, called the Rivers and Harbor Act, enabled surveys along the Colorado River bed to improve navigation, although there was little interest because the railroad and growing highway system

AUSTIN HISTORY CENTER, AUSTIN PUBLIC LIBRARY, PICA 04147

Congress Avenue from South Austin June 15, 1935

were now being used for transportation. In 1918, the Army Corps of Engineers released a report identifying three potential dam sites above Austin, but the state made little effort to realize the plans. No one yet fully realized the potential and resources of the Colorado, so the only thing that kept the interest going was public outcry about repeated flooding.

121

In 1919 the Army Corps of Engineers formally recommended that a dam be built above Austin to control the river. Although development of the river was slow going, it was prudent in the long run. Nowhere in the country had a project of such magnitude been considered.

With more floods in 1919, 1921 and 1922, funding was finally pushed through for surveys of several floodplains throughout the nation. A massive flood of the Mississippi in April 1927 covered 1,200 miles from St. Louis to New Orleans, and caused national outcry and attention. This prompted Congress to authorize $325 million to expand the duties of the Army Corps of Engineers to include flood control. The building of Hoover Dam in 1928 was a great influence because of its massiveness and the use of new technology, proving that such a feat of engineering was possible.

Alvin J. Wirtz, an attorney, and a lobbyist and state senator from Seguin, encouraged a development company called the Insull Utility Company of Chicago to take an interest in the Colorado. The firm was also working on a project on the Guadalupe River. A man named Holleman showed up one day to protest the building of the dam and fatally shot an employee. The development of the Colorado was an emotional one, and there is a long history of conflicting interests and people taking it all very seriously.

In 1931, construction began at a dam at the site that General Johnson had earlier recommended and created 2,000 jobs. The dam was to be two miles long and 137 feet high, but before it was completed, the Insull Utiltity Company went bankrupt. Wirtz organized the Colorado River Company and began looking for a new financier. Meanwhile, the population along the Colorado grew.

Wirtz got a break from James P. 'Buck' Buchanan, a friend and U.S. Representative whose district included Burnet County to Bastrop County, split by the Colorado. Buchanan had been a longtime advocate for control of the river and sat on the appropriations committee. Before the New Deal, most large development projects had been conducted by private sector entrepreneurs. But when Franklin Delano Roosevelt came into office, everything changed. The government had a new role supporting local efforts to change, fix, and build things. FDR announced the National Recovery Act and formed the Civilian Conservation Corps, the Works Progress Administration, and the Public Works Association. Wirtz applied for federal funds for his project, but was turned down. He then enlisted Buchanan to persuade FDR to fund four dams. Buchanan went directly to FDR and asked him to consider the dam as a birthday present to him. The funds were awarded on the condition that the Lower Colorado River Authority be created to manage them. Governor Ma Ferguson signed the bill in November 1934. In a mass meeting at

Hamilton Dam sponsored by the Austin Chamber of Commerce and the Colorado River Improvement Association, it was unanimously decided by the crowd to rename the dam for Buchanan. They had no authority, and federal law dictates that a dam cannot be named for a living person, but these little technicalities were of no concern to Central Texans, and they succeeded in changing the name. When Buchanan suddenly died of a heart attack in 1937, Lyndon Baines Johnson ran for his seat and won.

The LCRA set to work building six dams, two reservoirs and four pass-through lakes, to be known as the Highland Lakes, a 150-mile chain of water. Buchanan Dam was finished in 1937, Roy Inks Dam in 1938, Tom Miller Dam in 1940, J.J. Mansfield Dam (named for the Chairman of the Rivers, Harbors and Navigation Committee) on Lake Travis in 1941, Wirtz Dam on Lake LBJ in 1950, and Max Starcke Dam on Lake Marble Falls in 1951. The largest of these lakes are Buchanan and Travis, which contain 380 billion and 300 billion gallons respectively.

During the construction of Mansfield Dam, a workman from the Brown and Root Company purportedly fell into a deep concrete pour and became entombed inside. Supposedly, his body remains there. At 7,100 feet long, Mansfield Dam is one of the longest dams in the country. It is designed to withstand a flood peak of 748.9 feet. Normal levels are 681 feet. Lake Travis has about 260 billion gallons of flood storage control capacity, which means that Lake Travis and Lake Buchanan water levels will fluctuate dramatically as water is alternatively stored and released. Inks Lake, Lake LBJ, Lake Marble Falls, and Lake Austin were constructed primarily for hydroelectric power generation, so their water levels don't vary as much. The construction of the dams has largely eliminated flooding and has provided a dependable water supply and endless recreational opportunities. The water is used for municipal and industrial water supply and agricultural irrigation. The City of Austin is the biggest municipal user. Some of the water simply evaporates, but most just flows into Matagorda Bay in the Gulf of Mexico. The Colorado also maintains ecological systems. In 1995, the Texas Natural Resource Conservation Commission designated the stretch of the Colorado between Austin and La Grange as an "exceptional aquatic habitat." The state owns the water in the Highland Lakes, while the LCRA manages it.

TODAY

The LCRA receives no tax money or state assistance and operates on revenue generated from wholesale electric and water sales. The LCRA supplies electricity to over one million Texans. They have a base of forty-four wholesale customers, including thirty-three cities and eleven cooperative utilities. The LCRA also manages parks; recreational facilities; and several soil, energy and water conservation programs. The LCRA spans fifty-eight counties from San Saba to Matagorda.

The water levels of each lake fluctuate with rainfall and controlled flow. Weather conditions in Central Texas can change rapidly so always be careful when swimming. Each Highland Lake has multiple coves, creek mouths and inlets for exploring. You can swim at just about any place where you can publicly access the water, but please respect private property boundaries. Below Longhorn Dam the river is slow flowing. It is safe for swimming in terms of water quality. However, wherever signs are posted to not swim, obey. Water currents and boats can pose hazards. Releases at a rate of 1,500 cubic feet per second, or approximately two miles per hour, generally occur between March and October. The water levels and velocities will vary during this time. From October to March, releases are cut back to 300-350 cfs, less than one mile per hour.

Certain water and land use regulations apply to LCRA managed camping, boating and recreational facilities. For a full list, call (512) 473-4083.

Call the Lake Information Hotline at (800) 776-5272 x. 3333 or (512) 473-3333. The hotline provides lake levels, hydrogenation schedules, and emergency flood conditions.

AN OVERVIEW OF THE LCRA PARKS

There are many parks along the Colorado River and Highland Lakes that allow swimming. Swimming in the Highland Lakes is at your own risk as there are no lifeguards on duty. Always use common sense and obey posted rules. Above all, respect nature and clean up after yourself. Violation of park rules can result in confiscation of park permits and removal from the park for at least 48 hours. The parks are open year round and are free.

The LCRA has seven parks on Lake Travis alone totaling 20,000 acres. The smallest park on the Highland Lakes is 3.6-acre Dink Pearson Park on Lake Travis; Pace Bend is the largest park at 1,520 acres. Some parks are just minutes from downtown Austin, while others take a little more time to find.

LAKE BUCHANAN

Buchanan Dam/Inks Lake Chamber of Commerce
Post Office Box 282
Buchanan Dam, Texas 78609
(512) 793-2803

Lake Buchanan is 23,060 acres and thirty-two miles in length, with a maximum width of about eight miles. It is the highest and broadest of the Highland Lakes. Lake Buchanan is favored for boating because of the generous space. The reservoir provides Central Texas with hydroelectricity, flood control, water storage and recreation. Inflow comes from the central portion of the Colorado River and the water level fluctuates.

The boundaries of Burnet and Llano counties cross at the river channel. Black Rock Park is on the Llano County side. Cedar Point Recreation Area is the largest public park on the lake. It has three miles of shoreline but no amenities. On the Burnet County side is Burnet County Park, a small park with campsites and a boat ramp, and Burnet Park, close to the dam, also has a boat ramp. A new park, Canyon of the Eagles Park, just opened on the north end of the lake in 1999. The parks are operated by the LCRA.

The Buchanan Dam, completed in 1937, is 176 feet high and more than two miles long, the longest multiple arch dam in the country. Tours of the dam are available by advance arrangement by calling (800) 776-5272 ext. 3002. A small swimming beach at the base of the dam on TX 29 is quite an experi-

Buchanan Dam

ence. A pier leads out over the water. A visitors' center has a great view of the lake from an observation tower 145 feet up. They also have telescopes for viewing long distances. The dam has a small chamber of commerce and a museum dedicated to the construction of Buchanan Dam. Visitors can view photographs, get historical information and watch a videotape. You may also feed a school of fish that congregates below the observation deck daily. The museum is open 8:00 a.m. to 4:00 p.m. Monday through Friday, and 1:00 to 4:00 p.m. on weekends and holidays.

125

VANISHING TEXAS RIVER CRUISE
Post Office Box 901
Burnet, Texas 78611
(800) 728-8735

General Admission $15
Over sixty and students with ID $13 Ages
Six to twelve $10
Dinner Cruise $21.95

From TX 29, go NW 13.5 miles on RM 2341.

The Vanishing Texas River Cruise is a unique ecological tour of the Colorado River Canyon on Lake Buchanan. The Texas Eagle sports three decks and holds 200 people on its seventy-foot length. In June, cruisers can see wildflowers and birds. From November to March, people come to see the migration of bald eagles that nest there.

Cruises leave at 11:00 A.M. daily but do not run on Tuesdays. Sunset dinner cruises are available May through October on Saturdays at 6:00 P.M. Between September and December, cruises are on Wednesdays, Saturdays and Sundays at 11:00 A.M. The cruise lasts two-and-one-half hours and makes a thirty-six mile round trip tour of Lake Buchanan. The Vanishing Texas River Cruise will be relocating to Canyon of the Eagles Park soon.

The Texas Eagle

COURTESY OF TEXAS DEPARTMENT OF TRANSPORTATION

BLACK ROCK PARK

(512) 389-8900
(800) 776-5272 x. 4083
www.lcra.org

From Burnet, take TX 29 west and turn right on Hwy. 261. Drive about four miles to the park.

This ten-acre park is on a small peninsula on the western shore of Lake Buchanan. A sandy swimming beach has rest rooms and an outdoor shower. The water is shallow. Black Rock Park also has camping, a boat launch, hiking trails, and picnic areas.

CEDAR POINT RECREATION AREA

(512) 473-4083
(800) 776-5272 x. 4083
www.lcra.org

From Llano, take FM 2241 and turn right on FM 3014. Go .3 miles to the main site entrance. FM 3014 bisects the park in several points for additional access. From Buchanan Dam, take Hwy. 251 to Bluffton and follow the same directions.

This 350-acre park is one of the largest on Lake Buchanan. It is a long peninsula with four miles of lakeshore. There is also a boat ramp and paved parking. Otherwise, the park is quite primitive with diverse vegetation, including wildflowers in the spring. Birds such as heron, pelicans, and roadrunners are abundant. There is no running water or picnic tables.

INKS LAKE

Parks Superintendent
Inks Lake State Park
Route 2, Box 31
Burnet, Texas 78611
(512) 793-2233

Buchanan Dam/Inks Lake Chamber of Commerce
Post Office Box 282
Buchanan Dam, Texas 78609
(512) 793-2803

> Admission $5. Open year-round.

From U.S. 183, take TX 29 north at Seward Junction, then go west through Burnet about nine miles to Park Road 4, and another three miles to the park. About 1.5 hours from Austin.

Inks Lake, at 802 surface acres, is more like a reservoir than a lake, but it offers good swimming and recreation nonetheless. 1,200-acre Inks Lake State Park has lots of amenities, such as camping, picnicking, boat rentals, water skiing, Scuba diving, golf, and hiking. Devil's Hole on the north shore is an excellent swimming spot. Water cascades in stair-steps down to the lake, and deer often wander through. There are 7.5 miles of hiking trails with several loops of varying lengths. Since most people come to swim, the hiking trails are usually quiet and take you past large pink granite outcroppings, fields of wildflowers, and stands of cedars and oaks. A new trail is under construction which will link the park to Longhorn Caverns State Park and add 6-8 more miles of trail. The Pecan Flats Trail Camp in the southeast corner of the park offers primitive camping, and Rock-A-Way Park has a boat ramp and campground as well as showers. The park is wheelchair-accessible; concessions and groceries are readily available. Pets are allowed on leashes only. Visit Roy Inks Dam, formerly known as Alexander Dam, while you're there.

LAKE LBJ

Lake LBJ Chamber of Commerce
Post Office Box 465
Kingsland, Texas 78639
(915) 388-6211

Just south of Kingsland from FM 1431 on the east side, or from FM 2900 on the west side.

Formerly known as Granite Shoals Lake, this lake is named for Lyndon Baines Johnson (of course!). It is one of the more scenic lakes at 6,375 acres, and is surrounded by steep hills and granite outcroppings. The water in Lake LBJ comes from both the Colorado River and the Llano River. Lookout Mountain on FM 1431 offers an incredible view. Lake LBJ is twenty-two miles long.

The Cottonwood Resource Area near Alvin Wirtz Dam on the lower end of the lake is mainly a boat dock and observation area, but swimming is allowed below the dam. It is currently being developed into a marina and recreation area and will have a nice public beach.

The Flying K Recreation Area is across the lake from the Cottonwood Resource Area; it's a 13-acre, day use only park with picnic facilities and a shoreline.

LAKE MARBLE FALLS

Marble Falls Chamber of Commerce
801 U.S. 281
Marble Falls, Texas 78654
(800) 759-8178

Lake Marble Falls is the smallest of the Highland Lakes at 780 acres. It winds its way along six miles of steep limestone cliffs and hills in the City of Marble Falls. It is named for a series of waterfalls which have since been inundated by the lake waters. The marble part of the name comes from a great granite dome used for quarrying in the area. The view from the dome, off of U.S. 281, gives a great overview of Lake Marble Falls. It is popular for boating, sailing, water-skiing and swimming. Boat ramps give access to the water, which is otherwise surrounded by steep cliffs and not easily accessible. However, just below Max Starcke Dam there are wide, flat rocks and a decent swimming hole. Max Starcke was once the Mayor of Seguin, and was an expert on water law.

Falls Creek Park, Johnson Park and Lakeside Park are municipal parks located adjacent to each other on either side of an inlet of Lake Marble Falls. A public boat ramp can be found where the lake travels under a bridge at U.S. 281.

Lakeside Park has grassy slopes leading down to the lake. There is a man-made swimming pool in the park shaped like a cross. The pool has a diving board, and the bathhouse has rest rooms and showers. There is minimal shade except for three covered spectator benches. Lakeside Park also has tennis courts.

Falls Creek Park is a very simple park with concrete picnic tables and minimal landscaping. Here you can swim in the creek, a small tributary of the lake, next to the boat ramp.

Johnson Park has two playgrounds, one older and one modern. A covered amphitheater looks out over the lake for a spectacular view and a delightful setting for entertainment. There are picnic areas, plenty of parking and volleyball courts. Swimming is permitted near the boat ramp, and the waters are particularly serene and calm here. Ducks tend to gather here on the grassy banks, or seek shade under oak trees.

COURTESY OF TEXAS DEPARTMENT OF TRANSPORTATION

Lake Marble Falls

Lakeside Park Pool

$1.50 for adults
Open 11:00 A.M.-7:00 P.M. Tuesday through Saturday
2:00-7:00 P.M. on Sundays
Closed Mondays

LAKE TRAVIS

Lake Travis Chamber of Commerce
Post Office Box 340034
Austin, Texas 78734
(512) 263-3188

At sixty-five miles long, 18,930 acres, and with 270 miles of shoreline, Lake Travis is definitely the most popular of the Highland Lakes with Austinites. In fact, it's often referred to as 'The Lake', as if there were only one. With seventeen public parks totaling six thousand acres, and numerous private facilities, you're bound to find fun at Lake Travis, whether it be boating, water-skiing, sailing or swimming. Mineral outcroppings and fossils are abundant around Lake Travis, which is the primary flood control for the Colorado River. Many creeks and rivers flow from Lake Travis, really too many to mention, but the Pedernales River and Hamilton Creek are some of the larger ones.

The parks on Lake Travis are alternately owned and/or operated by Travis County and the LCRA. The Travis County parks are generally more developed, while the LCRA parks are more primitive. Travis County operates nine parks, with Pace Bend being the largest. Travis County parks are generally located on the lower half of the lake and have paved access roads. User fees are charged.

COURTESY OF TEXAS DEPARTMENT OF TRANSPORTATION

Lake Travis

LCRA PARKS ON LAKE TRAVIS
(512) 473-4083
(800) 776-5272 x. 4083

Camp Creek Recreation Area

Take FM 1431 to County Road 343 and continue one mile to the entrance.

This 350-acre park on the north side of Lake Travis completely surrounds tiny Burnet County Park. There are a few good swimming spots on the lake that have a short and steep shore, and Camp Creek runs through the park which is good for wading. A hiking trail loops around the park. There is a boat ramp, picnic tables with grills, and overnight camping. Pecan groves provide shade. Pets are allowed.

Gloster Bend Recreation Area

Take FM 1431 to Singleton Road and continue 3.3 miles to the entrance.

This 580-acre park on the north side of Lake Travis has a boat ramp. Camping and picnicking are allowed but the facilities are primitive. There are some nice swimming spots along the shore but it is a long trek from the entrance to the water.

Grelle Recreation Area

From TX 71, turn north on Spur 191 and go one mile to Spicewood. Take a right on County Road 404 (Paleface Ranch Park) and go one mile to the intersection with County Road 412 (a gravel road). Turn left and go 6.10 miles to the entrance.

This 400-acre park on the south side of Lake Travis is used primarily for launching boats and has the only public ramp on the south side of Lake Travis. There is paved parking for cars and trailers, and a few campsites are centered around fire rings. There is no running water at Grelle and it is very primitive.

Muleshoe Recreation Area

Take TX 71 and turn right on County Road 404 (Paleface Ranch Road) and go 4.5 miles to County Road 414. Turn right and go 1.5 miles, then take another right just before the entrance to Ridge Harbor. After about one mile the road will turn to gravel. Continue for .3 miles to the entrance.

At 900 acres, Muleshoe Recreation Area is the largest park in the primitive recreation system on the south side of Lake Travis. There are several miles of varied shoreline, from quiet coves to steep outcroppings. A two-mile looped hiking and equestrian trail is scenic. Overnight camping and picnicking are permitted but facilities are not provided. Pets are okay.

The Narrows Recreation Area

From TX 71 turn north on Spur 191 and go one mile to Spicewood. Continue 1.1 miles north on County Road 410 to the intersection with County Road 411 (a gravel road). Travel 1.5 miles north to the entrance.

This 29-acre park on the south side of Lake Travis is near Max Starcke Dam and is very primitive. There is a boat ramp where you can also swim. Camping and picnics are permitted but facilities are not provided. Pets are allowed.

Shaffer Bend Recreation Area

Take FM 1431 to County Road 343A and continue one mile to the entrance.

This 535-acre park is on the north side of Lake Travis. There is extensive low and gentle shoreline, spectacular views, and abundant native vegetation and wildlife, such as guayacans, which are not normally found east of Del Rio. The park has an upper section which is hilly with cliffs overhanging the lake and covered in cedar, and a lower section which is more open and sloped toward the shore. Overnight camping and picnicking are permitted but amenities are not provided. Pets are allowed.

Turkey Bend Recreation Area

Take FM 1431 to Shaw Drive and continue 1.8 miles to the entrance.

This 400-acre park on the north side of Lake Travis is a picturesque cove on a long and narrow bend, with two miles of shoreline and steep shores, and flat open areas that are full of wildflowers in the spring. Turkey Bend is one of the most tucked away places on Lake Travis and feels very natural. Overnight camping and picnicking are permitted but facilities are not provided. Pets are permitted. A circular equestrian and hiking trail winds through the park. Hunting is prohibited in the park but allowed on private lands surrounding the property. Caution is advised during hunting season, and visitors should respect property lines.

TRAVIS COUNTY PARKS ON LAKE TRAVIS
(512) 473-9437

Arkansas Bend

This 195-acre park made up of four peninsulas is quiet and out of the way on the north shore of Lake Travis. Two miles of shoreline have some great swimming spots. Shaded picnic tables with grills front the water where you can swim. Camping is permitted.

Cypress Creek

This is a small fifteen-acre park on Bullick Hollow Road with a large and open area sloping down toward the water combined with a steeper shore in the day use area. A boat ramp and small cove offer easy access to the basin area of the lake.

Dink Pearson Park

At the end of Lohmann's Crossing Road and FM 1431.

This small 3.6-acre park on the north shore of Lake Travis can get crowded quickly. It is adjacent to Point Venture which has rest rooms, food, gas, and a golf course. Dink Pearson Park has picnic tables with grills, camping, and a boat ramp. Swimming in Lake Travis is allowed, and juniper and oak trees provide some shade.

German immigrant John Henry Lohmann came to Texas in 1842 with his wife and four children. They landed in Galveston and made their way to Austin via ox cart, stopping briefly at Hornsby Bend. They settled on a hill overlooking Austin and called the place Ridgetop. We know it today as the University of Texas.

Lohmann was a dairy farmer and established the first dairy in Travis County with eleven cows. At the time, his supply was enough to feed the entire Austin community. Lohmann moved in 1861 to a site along the Colorado 17 miles north of Austin, where he built a house and five cabins. He also built a road to a shallow water crossing, or ford, of the Colorado River. According to Lohmann, normal river levels were "up to a horse's belly" but during drought conditions a man could jump across the water. The crossing became known as Lohmann's Ford, and appears on today's maps as Lohman's Crossing Road, someone having dropped the extra 'n' along the way. Lohmann's Ford was one of several accesses across the river used by pioneers to socialize with their neighbors. Lohmann resisted serving for the Confederates, and he was captured by a band of zealots who tried to hang him. Friends held the gang at gunpoint and Lohmann got away with his life. Travis County eventually took over the ford and built a bridge across it. The original bridge and Lohmann's homestead are now 150 feet below Lake Travis. If you stand on the deck of the Lakeway Inn and look halfway across the lake, between the boat ramp and Point Venture, you can find the spot.

Hippie Hollow/McGregor Park
On Comanche Trail

Hippie Hollow is the only public park in Texas where clothing is optional. It is extremely popular with sunbathers and swimmers. Regular ranger patrols make it safer. Hippie Hollow, at 109 acres, has great views of Lake Travis along the hiking trail which hugs the cliffs. There is paved parking and wheelchair access, but the shore itself is rocky. Junipers jut out from the hillside. You must be 18 or over to use Hippie Hollow Park.

Mansfield Dam Park

Sixty-five-acre Mansfield Dam Park, located just below the dam, is the main access point for boaters on Lake Travis and is very popular. There is an adjacent primitive area for hiking, camping, picnicking with grills and swimming. Plans for major renovations are underway.

Pace Bend Park

Pace Bend Park is very popular and heavily used. It is the largest park in the LCRA/Travis County system at 1,368 acres. It's only forty-five minutes from downtown Austin, which makes it especially popular. Pace Bend Park was originally called Paleface Park after a cattle ranch which was there. In 1983, the county began charging admission and changed the name.

You can choose from camping, horseback riding, hiking, picnicking and swimming. From over nine miles of shoreline for swimming and boating, and over twenty coves and inlets, people pick their favorites. Some have designated swimming beaches (Kate's Cove, Mudd Cove, Levi Cove and Gracy Cove). The coves tucked around the bend are named after the former owners of the land. A new swimming platform was added at Mudd Cove, and Jet Skis can be rented on the weekend. There is a Jet Ski course on the east side of the park. There is new terracing on Kidd's Cove to control erosion. The sheer cliffs are popular with cliff divers, and toward the northern part of the park the land evens out for more relaxing activities.

There are also large open areas perfect for hiking. There is a main road that winds through the park and gives access to each camp. A 3.5-mile hike and bike trail cuts through the center of the park, and a wildlife preserve makes up the middle. The trail leads up to a peak with spectacular views. The very tip of the peninsula is privately owned and closed to the public. You can still drive to the water's edge and dogs can run free if they are kept close.

Pace Bend Park was recently revamped between 1993-1997, and during the drought of 1996 when the lake levels were low, the County Parks Department filled eroded areas with sediment, and put boulders in the park to prevent people from driving off the roads. The northeastern portion of the park is closed temporarily so that it can recover from the heavy use while the county raises money to restore it. Eventually, the county hopes to build another campground and extend the hiking trails.

Tom Hughes Park

Off of RR 620 just north of Mansfield Dam.

Tom Hughes Park is famous for its sunset views. It's not as heavily used as some other parks because parking is limited and the trail leading to the lake access is steep and primitive. Still, swimming, Scuba diving and sunbathing are popular. It is only five acres, but has hiking trails and picnic areas.

Sandy Creek

Lime Creek Road

This little twenty-five-acre park is a quiet peninsula that is ideal for swimming, watching endangered birds, or primitive hiking up to a peak with a view. Overnight camping facilities and picnic tables with grills are provided. A boat ramp gives access to the water. Pets are permitted.

Bob Wentz Park
Comanche Trail
(512) 266-3857 Visitors' Center

Bob Wentz Park is one of the busiest parks on Lake Travis, and Windy Point is a privately owned park with lake access. The two parks are divided by a fence.

With a brand-new $2.5 million renovation, Bob Wentz Park is more popular than ever. Picnicking, swimming, windsurfing, sailing and Scuba diving are all popular. The shoreline is 211 acres, and another 150 acres of undeveloped park is located toward the back. There are two sand volleyball courts, a hike and bike trail, and a pavilion for party rental. The boat ramp is for sail craft only. You can rent Jet Skis and sail boards. The swimming beach is rocky and gravelly and has minimal shade.

Windy Point
(512) 266-3337

Monday through Friday, $5 for adults
Saturday and Sunday, $10 for adults
or $5 after 3:00 P.M.
Kids under 11 are always free.

Windy Point is a privately owned and requires an entrance fee. It is quiet and grassy with shade trees and a picnic area. The shoreline has large boulders that you can climb down to access the water. Swimming areas are marked by buoys.

MORE FACILITIES AND PLACES

Lakeway

The Lakeway area was once populated by Tonkawa, Comanche, Apache, and Mesolero Indian tribes. Ancient camp sites of mounds, cliffs and caves, and even a 'flint factory' can still be found in the area. When Anglos settled the area, it became ranch land with cattle, goats and sheep. In the 1960s, the land became too expensive to ranch and was subdivided for residences. The Lakeway Inn was built in 1962 and the community, mostly retirees, grew up around the resort. At first there were no phone lines or electricity lines to the area. Lakeway Park is on Hurst Creek Road along the waterfront, and charges $5 per vehicle for nonresidents.

At the Lakeway Marina you can take two-hour sunset cruises aboard a sixty-foot yacht, or rent a boat by calling 261-7511. You can also take the Flagship Texas from the Lakeway Boat ramp at 261-6484.

The Hudson Family, for which Hudson Bend is named, settled in Lakeway in 1854. They acquired four of the original twenty-five land surveys on the four thousand-acre tract. One of their descendents, 'Cotton' Hudson, worked on the Mansfield Dam. Their property is now covered by water, but a historical marker honors them.

Camp Chautauqua

Open year-round: April 1 through September 30, 9:00 A.M.-5:00 P.M.; October 1 through March 31 10:00 A.M.-2:00 P.M.

Operated by the Chautauqua Foundation, Inc.
Route 1, Box 30
Spicewood, Texas 78669
(512) 264-1752

From Austin, take TX 71 west to FM 2322. Go north 4.6 miles to Pace Bend Park. The gate ranger will direct you to Camp Chautauqua.

Camp Chautauqua is much more than just a place to swim. It is 115 acres within

Pace Bend Park which is owned by the LCRA and operated by the Chautauqua Foundation, Inc. The camp is designed for individuals, families, classrooms, public agencies and private businesses to use for family reunions, seminars, and educational events. The camp has volleyball, camping, canoeing, picnicking, swimming, and sunbathing. They offer informal environmental studies, such as taking water quality samples. Patrons sit around the campfire at night. The term Chautauqua refers to a tent, popular at the turn of this century, wherein plays, lectures, concerts, etc. took place. The atmosphere is peaceful and unhurried. There is a pier, a boat ramp, and two coves for swimming. A playscape and ball field round out the amenities.

The Oasis

6550 Comanche Trail
Austin, Texas 78732
(512) 266-2442 (restaurant)
(512) 266-2441 (guest suites)

There are many places to eat on Lake Travis, but the Oasis is a landmark in itself. Sitting 450 feet above the water, the Oasis has spectacular views of the lake and sunsets. There are twenty-eight outdoor decks to view from, or choose from several dining rooms inside with panoramic views. The Oasis is available for weddings, private parties, and meetings for 10-1,000 people. The grounds are beautiful with sculpture, art, antiques, and lush gardens. The restaurant serves fajitas, steaks, seafood, pasta and Mexican food for up to $20 a plate, and has a full bar. Lunch is served on weekdays and brunch on Sundays. Live music often wafts over the decks. A gift shop has souvenirs. The Oasis also has guest suites in multilevel cottages featuring fireplaces, lofts, private decks, baths and great views. Rates range from $195-240. The Oasis has a tradition where patrons applaud and rate the sunsets when the hostess chimes a bell. A man-made swimming pool is available for overnight guests.

Volente Beach Club

16107 Wharf Cove
Leander, Texas 78641
(512) 258-5109 (business office)
(512) 258-9993 (Sundowner grill)
(512) 258-8400 (boat rentals)

> Open daily Memorial Day through Labor Day
> Flexible hours September through May.

From RR 620, take Anderson Mill (turns into FM 2769) seven miles. FM 2769 dead-ends at Volente Beach Club.

You bring the swimsuit and sunscreen, Volente Beach Club will do the rest. This private facility has three acres of beach front on Lake Travis, a restaurant, a beachside bar, three lighted volleyball courts, boat rentals, swimming, and sunsets. You can also rent Waverunners, windsurfers, sailboats, pontoons, water-skiing boats, cruises, party barges, and take sailing and water-ski lessons. The entire facility is available for parties of 20-500 people. The restaurant features fried catfish, barbecued ribs, salads and desserts.

LAKE AUSTIN

Riverboats were very popular at the turn of the century and made regular excursions to what was then known as Lake McDonald. A paddleboat called the Ben Hur used to take people up to Camp Chautauqua for parties before the Colorado River was dammed. The water level is fairly constant. At 1,830 acres and twenty-two miles long, Lake Austin is ideal for water skiing, boating and swimming.

What is now Lake Austin was once a thriving area of early settlements. The water has since covered up several springs. Power House Springs was discovered during the construction of one of the dams in 1893. Bee Springs, just above Tom Miller Dam, is under the convergence of Bee Creek and Lake Austin. Mormon Springs was the site of a Mormon settlement in 1846 and was also used for a gristmill. Mount Bonnell Springs is a cluster of water sources near the mountain. Santa Monica Springs was also a popular watering hole and many artifacts were found there. The waters of Lake Austin, being rich in minerals, were once bottled by early settlers in the 1890s.

Lake Austin as seen from Mount Bonnell

Courtesy of Texas Department of Transportation

Walsh Boat Landing

This is a great place to stop and rest on Lake Austin Boulevard just north of Oyster Landing—a very popular little strip of trendy restaurants and shops. The boat launch has a dock where you can swim up to fifty feet out from the shore. An open water swim is held here each September. There are a couple of picnic tables and bathrooms for public use. The LCRA headquarters is located across the street and has a information about Lake Austin and other facilities

Fritz Hughes Park

This park is off of RR 620 on Low Water Crossing Road (turn left on Fritz Hughes Road). It's a five-acre day use park with rest rooms, picnic tables and grills, a playscape and sports courts. The park is faced by residential housing on one side and the lake on the other. The access road winds around to the lake front. It's not a great swimming spot because the water can be swift, but it is allowed.

Fritz Hughes Park

Mary Quinlan Park

Mary Quinlan Park

This park at the very end of Quinlan Park Road, has the only boat ramp within several miles. It is 5.8 acres and for day use only. The park has rest rooms, a few picnic tables and grills, sports courts, and easy access to the lake.

Selma Hughes Park

This park off of Quinlan Park Road on Selma Hughes Park Road is a quiet five acres for day use only, with rest rooms, picnic tables and grills. It is a small shaded park with a sandy beach.

Selma Hughes Park

The Hwy. 360 Boat Ramp

Located just under the Percy Pennybacker Bridge, there is a three-acre grassy area where picnicking is allowed. The boat ramp and park are for day use only, and rest rooms are available. This park has gained a reputation for moonlight skinny-dipping. Swim at your own risk.

Access is limited to the narrow, northern portions of Lake Austin.

Pennybacker Bridge

Westlake Beach

2509 Westlake Drive
Austin, Texas 78746
(512) 327-9004

A privately owned park with picnic areas, a marina, concessions, diving, a playground, showers and volleyball. The Ben Hur is long gone, but the Commodore Riverboat ((512) 345-5220) will still cruise you up and down Lake Austin.

Ski Shores Waterfront Cafe

3103 Pearce Road
Austin, Texas 78730
(512) 346-5915

Since 1954, Ski Shores Café has been feeding hungry visitors to Lake Austin in droves. It's a typically Austin burger joint serving burgers, fries, fried okra and cold drinks. Try a 'Border Burger' with guacamole, sautéed onions and jalapeños, or a classic cheeseburger with coleslaw and fries. A sign over the order window reads "Life is too short to live in Dallas," which pretty much sums it up. You can enjoy your meal at a series of picnic tables overlooking the lake. The tables are outdoors but covered. Ski Shores Café has a very low-key and casual atmosphere, and is a family-style eatery.

144

Ski Shores not only has great food and atmosphere, it also has three miles of shoreline on Lake Austin where you can swim or water-ski. It can get pretty crowded during the summer, but it's worth the trip.

TOWN LAKE

Town Lake is the most stable portion of the Highland Lakes chain, and in my opinion, Austin just wouldn't be Austin without it. To me, Town Lake is the heart of Austin. The little camp called Waterloo that grew into Austin began right where the Congress Avenue Bridge is today. The Colorado River and all of its resources allowed Austin to grow into a thriving metropolis. The river has also divided north and south Austin for decades. When I have visitors from out of town, I tell them we're going to Town Lake, but when we get there they say, "Why, this is just a river!" Town Lake actually *is* a lake, created by the City of Austin in the 1960s as a cooling pond for the Holly Street Power Plant, with Tom Miller Dam and Longhorn Dam containing the water. Town Lake Metropolitan Park extends the entire length, five miles, on the north and south shores. The park includes seventeen ball parks, places to rent rowboats, canoes, kayaks and paddleboats, swimming pools, volleyball courts, picnic tables with grills, and lots of great scenery.

> *78704: Not just a zip code, a way of life.*
>
> A popular bumpersticker in South Austin

Cold Springs near Deep Eddy is a source of water for the lake. Today it is covered by Town Lake but it still flows and can only be seen by boat. It's on the south shore between Red Bud Isle and MoPac. A man-made pool has been built under a 100-foot waterfall.

> *The bridge company is having a gate put up at this end of the bridge which will be closed after a certain hour at night. Young bloods who live south of town have been in the habit of firing off their pistols at a late hour and running across the bridge at a terrible rate are informed that the latter part, at least of their performance, will be stopped. The gate will prevent their escape from town by way of the bridge.*
>
> From the April 16, 1881 Austin Democratic Statesman

Town Lake Hike and Bike Trail

Sailing and canoeing are permitted on Town Lake, but swimming and powerboats are not. However, you can swim in several swimming pools in the park within a stone's throw of the lake.

A popular feature of Metropolitan Park is a 10-mile hike and bike trail. The gravel and concrete trail begins at Riverside Drive and Congress Avenue, near the Hyatt. It goes west past Auditorium Shores, which has parking and rest rooms; Butler Shores, which also has parking; Zilker Park (includes a short skirt around Barton Creek); and crosses under MoPac, which also has a rest room. From there it is a short jog west to Deep Eddy where there is a shower; past Austin High School; across Lamar Boulevard; past Shoal Beach and the Buford Tower; past the trailhead to the Shoal Creek Greenbelt; and across South First and Congress Avenue Bridges. It intersects with Waller Creek Walkway, goes under IH35, past Festival Beach, Martin Pool and the U.S. 183 Bridge and follows Lakeshore Boulevard until it ends about one-half mile west. The trail crosses the river via footbridges at MoPac, South First Street, South Congress Street, and the frontage road of IH35.

On the north shore of Town Lake you'll find:

Holly Beach
A small 2.5-acre park between Longhorn Dam and Metz Park.

Fiesta Gardens

Popular for Hispanic celebrations, this sixty-acre park also has displays of exotic flora and a lagoon. Fiesta Gardens also has a boat launch and lots of open grassy space.

Waller Beach

Twenty-six acres of grassy park between IH35 and Congress Avenue. The park is filled with gazebos, boat launches and docks.

Congress Avenue Bridge

Built in 1910. A relief exhibit at the intersection of Congress Avenue and East Cesar Chavez (north of the river, in the southwest corner) shows Austin as it looked in 1889. It is displayed from the perspective as it would have appeared had you been standing in the same spot in 1889.

South First Street Bridge

Also known as the W.F. Drake, Jr. Bridge. Drake was mayor of Austin between 1951-1953.

Shoal Beach

An eighteen-acre stretch between Congress Avenue and Lamar Boulevard. This section includes Buford Tower, dedicated in 1978 to Fire Department Captain James T. Buford for giving his life in the line of duty to the citizens of Austin. Buford Tower was originally built in 1930 as a training place for Austin's firefighters.

Buford Tower

Lamar Beach

Extends from Lamar Boulevard to Johnson Creek. This forty-acre park includes several ballfields.

University Beach

Parallels the University of Texas property west to Red Bud Trail and has one acre of lake access.

Red Bud Isle

Thirteen acres of primitive wilderness just below Tom Miller Dam. It is literally an island; you can picnic and access the lake from a circular drive of very rough road.

Emmett Shelton Bridge

This bridge was the first low-water bridge over Town Lake. Originally built in 1849, it was the gateway to the foothills west of Lake Austin. Shelton is an attorney, author, land developer, marine captain, community benefactor, historian, and poet. There is a historical plaque just west of the bridge with an original block of Texas red granite that was part of the first dam built on Lake Austin in 1893 and destroyed by the flood of 1900. Portions of the bridge remain submerged by the water.

Tom Miller Dam

Finished in 1940, this was the third dam built in this spot, the previous dams having been destroyed by flooding of the Colorado River. The dam is accessible from Lake Austin Boulevard at Red Bud Trail. Tom Miller was mayor of Austin.

On the south shore:

Longhorn Dam

Has scenic overlooks and picnic areas.

Lake Shores

Thirty-five-acre undeveloped park east of the Kasuba property to Pleasant Valley Road.

Auditorium Shores

A popular gathering place for free concerts and other public festivals. It is a flat, grassy area from the South First Street Bridge to Lamar Boulevard. Twenty-five acres in all, it has a gazebo, a reflection pool, and numerous rest areas.

Butler Shores

Named for Roy Butler, mayor of Austin in the early 1970s. Butler Shores has parking and is adjacent to the Parks and Recreation Department headquarters. It extends from the Lamar Bridge to Barton Creek, and has seven acres of lake frontage.

For a spectacular view of Town Lake and Austin's skyline, check out Lou Neff Point located in Zilker Park. Isabella Neff was the namesake of the very first state park in Texas, and Lou Neff is a relative.

As of this writing, Austin is considering converting Town Lake Park into a performing arts center, parking garage, and park land.

Lone Star Riverboat
Post Office Box 160608
Austin, Texas 78716
(512) 327-1388

The Lone Star Riverboat is an old-fashioned paddleboat. Cruises are available to the public March through October, including moonlight and dinner cruises. Private parties by reservation are held year-round. The riverboat departs at the dock between the Hyatt Regency Hotel and the South First Street Bridge on the south side of Town Lake. Cruises last one-and-one-half hours, and no reservations are required. Boarding begins thirty minutes before the departure time. The riverboat travels leisurely under city bridges, past Barton Creek and Zilker Park, and offers excellent views of limestone cliffs and waterfowl. March through May, cruises depart on Saturday and Sunday at 3:00 P.M. June through August, cruises leave Tuesday through Sunday at 5:30 P.M., and Fridays at 10:30 P.M. for the moonlight cruise. There are half-price fares on Wednesdays. September through October, the boat departs at 3:00 P.M. on weekends. Adult fare is $9, children under 12 are $6 (under 2 is free), and senior citizens are $7. The trip is informative and scenic, and the captain 'married' me and my friend.

Capital Cruises
208 Barton Springs Road
Austin, Texas 78704
(512) 480-9264
http://www.io.com/~capcruis

Capital Cruises has tours available on Lake Austin as well as Town Lake for public and private parties. They also have sunset cruises and bat-watching excursions. Catering from the Hyatt is available on private cruises. Capital Cruises rents pontoons, pedal boats, electric boats, canoes and kayaks for $8-60. Call for group rates and cruise rates. Open June through August, weekdays from noon to dusk and weekends 9:00 A.M. to dusk. March through October, they are open Monday through Friday 10:00 A.M. to dusk, and Saturday and Sunday 9:00 A.M. to dusk. Rentals are available November through February, weather permitting and by reservation. All cruises depart from the Hyatt Regency dock on the south side of Town Lake.

BATS
http://www.batcon.org/

A discussion of Town Lake would not be complete without a word about the bats. Between April and October, North America's largest urban colony of Mexican free-tailed bats make Austin their home. More specifically, they live under the Congress Avenue Bridge and can be heard squealing as you walk under it. Hundreds of people gather on the bridge or shores to watch the colony, literally millions of bats, leave in a swarm at dusk to devour mosquitoes and other insects. The Austin America Statesman has set up a grassy beach and informational stand for viewing from the south side of the bridge. Another way to watch the bats is from your table at the Shoreline Grill. August is the prime month for viewing.

Lone Star Riverboat

COLORADO RIVER ACCESS POINTS

COLORADO RIVER ACCESS POINTS

A River Runs Through It

COLORADO BEND STATE PARK
Post Office Box 118
Bend, Texas 76824
(915) 628-3240

Admission is $3.00 per person for ages 13 and over.

Tours to Gorman Falls are at 10:00 A.M. and 2:00 P.M. on weekends only. Ages 6 to 12 are $1.00, all ages over 13 are $2.00. There are also 'crawling cave tours' for $15 at 1:30 P.M. each Saturday. The walking cave tour is $8 at 9:15 A.M. every Saturday and Sunday. Reservations are not necessary for the Gorman Falls hike, but are for group tours. No pets on the tour.

From U.S. 183 North, take FM 580 west at Lampasas. About two hours from Austin.

Just ten miles above Lake Buchanan and one of the newest state parks, Colorado Bend State Park is spacious and uncrowded. No more than 300 vehicles are allowed into the 5,328-acre park. There are over twelve miles of hiking and interpretive trails that take you past swimming holes, wildlife, and hill country vegetation. The 2.7-mile Spicewood Springs Trail connects to another one-mile trail from the main camping area. It follows a creek down to the Colorado River with several holes for swimming along the way. The 5.7-mile Upper Gorman Creek Trail loops through woodlands and has several offshoot trails to customize distance. A 1.5-mile hike and tour of Gorman Falls is also worth doing. You should wear appropriate rubber-soled shoes for the hike, and drinking water and bathrooms are not available in the falls area. Colorado Bend State Park has six miles of lake frontage. Two spring-fed creeks form great swimming holes. There are picnic sites and great views of deep canyons. The park has primitive camping, chemical toilets, and a boat ramp.

There are a number of access points to the Colorado River east of Longhorn Dam. The river, of course, empties into the Gulf of Mexico and there are numerous parks the whole length. The segment of the river closer to Austin is developed with low water dams; in Webberville it becomes more rural with vegetation and wildlife. The river here is wide and has a slow current. The riverbed is mostly sand and gravel. The land along the Colorado River east of Longhorn Dam tends to be more flat and open prairie land than the rocky and hilly parks to the west. White egret populate the area.

U.S. 183 Bridge

This little access point is on the south side of the river and has a foot trail leading to the water. Swimming depends on rainfall and water levels.

Big Webberville Park
(512) 247-5360

Park hours: March 1-April 30, 9:00 A.M.-7:30 P.M.
May 1-Labor Day 8:00, A.M.-9:00 P.M.
Labor Day-October 31 9:00, A.M.-7:30 P.M.
November 1-February 28 9:00, A.M.-6:00 P.M.
Free, day use only

From FM 969, turn right on Webberwood Drive.

Big Webberville Park is an open-space project of Travis County that was built in 1990. The park offers access to the Colorado River with a small pier and boat ramp. Big Webberville is a large park (135 acres) with several sections and grand pecan trees. There are volleyball and basketball courts, softball and soccer fields, a 2-mile hike, bike and equestrian trail, concession stands, playscapes, and a large picnic area with grills. There is plenty of parking throughout the park. It tends to be uncrowded.

Little Webberville Park
(512) 247-5360

Little Webberville Park is located just five miles north of Big Webberville Park. This little six-acre park also has a boat ramp which accesses the Colorado River. Kayakers and canoeists often put in at Little Webberville and take out at Big Webberville. Little Webberville Park has a playscape and picnic tables with grills. There is plenty of parking.

Windmill Ranch
(800) 776-5272

In the future, Windmill Ranch at McKinney Roughs may open as a regulated canoe launch and nature park. This park is still in the development stage.

CITY OF BASTROP FISHERMAN'S PARK
(512) 321-3941

Near downtown at the end of Farm Street. Day use only.

Fisherman's Park in downtown Bastrop is a nice, new park built in 1994. Located on the banks of the Colorado River, this small park has picnic facilities and access to the river for boats and canoes. You can wade into the river via this paved access, but the water can be swift.

Fisherman's Park has a nature trail and modern playground. Shade is provided by pecans and oaks. The park is both pretty and historical, and within walking distance of antique shops and the heart of Bastrop. The park also has basketball courts, baseball fields, and tennis courts. The LCRA Conference Center and Bastrop's water well are on the site. There is plenty of parking.

Fisherman's Park

The Iron Bridge spanning the river is historic and has been integrated into the park with picnic tables, benches and a walkway across the water. The Riverwalk connects with Terry Park. No alcohol is allowed. Open dawn to dusk.

FM 969 Crossing

On Water Lane just north of the FM 969 and FM 1209 crossing in Utley. It has a tiny playground and is absolutely minimal with one picnic table. A paved boat ramp and parking lot are available, and concrete steps lead down to the river.

La Grange

Take TX 71 to Business 71 into town, cross the bridge over the Colorado and turn right immediately. This access point on the Colorado has no amenities except for an unpaved public boat ramp. A few picnic tables with grills are shaded by the bridge. Swimming is at your own risk near a jetty, and the current is swift here.

White Rock Park
La Grange City Hall
(409) 968-5806

From TX 77 just north of the Colorado River take East Elbin Street to South Mode Street.

White Rock Park is a sprawling open space in La Grange. The park has camping by permit only, baseball fields and modern play equipment. A zig-zag path leads down to some concrete steps into the Colorado River. The water here has a muddy bottom, but it is calm and wide, perfect for swimming laps. Someone has built wooden planks on a tree which leans out over the water for diving. This is a peaceful, quiet stretch of the river. Swimming is at your risk.

White Rock Park

ARMY CORPS OF ENGINEERS and LCRA LAKES

LAKE BASTROP

Lower Colorado River Authority
Post Office Box 220
Austin, Texas 78767
(512) 303-7666
http://www.lcra.org/lands/northshr.html

L ake Bastrop, nestled among the Lost Pines, was built by the LCRA in 1965 as a cooling pond for the Sam Gideon Power Plant. There are parks on the north and south shores of the 906-acre lake. The water is a mixture of warm and cold, and swimming beaches are gravelly. The endangered Houston Toad is often spotted near the water.

The park is located not far from the heart of Bastrop, but has an 'away-from-it-all' feeling. The landscape is so unlike anything else in Texas that you feel transported to a far-away place. And with Bastrop so close by, if you get an urge for a meal in a restaurant or other amenities, everything is readily available. Both parks take reservations and are open year-round.

NORTH SHORE PARK

From Bastrop, take Hwy. 95 north and go right on FM 1441. Go 2.5 miles to the park entrance on the right.

Lake Bastrop

North Shore Park is a twenty-three-acre park offering swimming, camping, picnicking, canoeing, windsurfing, sailing and water-skiing. There is a public boat ramp for motor and sailboats. Swimming areas are designated around the shore, but no lifeguards are on duty.

The park has 66 campsites, 44 of which have electricity and potable water, and 14 of which have water only. Eight sites have screened shelters. Hot showers are available, and each campsite has a picnic table and grill.

SOUTH SHORE PARK
(512) 321-5048

From Austin, take TX 71 to TX 21 north. About forty miles east of Austin.

Recently renovated, South Shore Park has modern camping facilities such as paved camp sites, RV hookups, electricity, and a sanitary dump station. If you prefer primitive camping, South Shore Park can accommodate you. There are picnic sites with grills, hot showers, rest rooms, a boat ramp, and water-skiing, sailing and canoeing. The swimming area is protected from boats but no lifeguards are on duty. This park has a group picnic pavilion, a playground, and volleyball and horseshoe pits. Firewood can be bought at the park or brought in, but not gathered in the park.

LAKE BELTON

Reservoir Manager
99 FM 2271
Belton, Texas 76513
(254) 939-1829
http://bellnetweb.brc.tamus.edu/res_grid/mspubs/lakbeltn.htm

Four miles northwest of Belton via Texas 317 north, then FM 2271 west.
About eighty miles from Austin.

Lake Belton is a 12,300-acre impoundment of the Leon River. Numerous creeks, coves and long peninsulas make the lake scenic and account for over one hundred miles of shoreline. Built by the Army Corps of Engineers between 1949 and 1954, Belton Dam is 3,800 feet long and 172 feet high. Lake Belton extends to the boundaries of Mother Neff State Park, the first park in the state system. The lake provides water for nearby Fort Hood and spans Bell and Coryell counties. A mural on the east side of Belton Dam tells the story of this area's history. Lake Belton is calm and has lots of swimming docks and picnic areas. Of the thirteen public parks, three have swimming beaches: Cedar Ridge, Westcliff and Temple's Lake.

Temple's Lake Park

Of interest is Miller's Spring Park created when Lake Belton overflowed in 1992, carving out a huge canyon and wetland. This area is now a nature preserve referred to as the 'Miracle Mile', and includes a boardwalk trail that is fully accessible to people with disabilities. Hiking is allowed but swimming is not. Open dawn to dusk.

Temple's Lake Park

Day use fee of $1.00

From IH35, take TX 36 north to FM 2305, then to the north side of the dam on FM 2271.

Claiming 172 acres on Lake Belton, this park is the best for swimming. A sandy beach is roped off, and there are open, grassy areas with shade. Several peninsulas create protected swimming areas. A bathhouse with showers is nearby. Boat rentals are available, as well as skin diving and Scuba equipment. Camping facilities dot the park. Private and group picnic areas have a great view of the lake. Pets are okay on leashes. There is plenty of parking.

Lake Belton as seen from the dam

CANYON LAKE

Canyon Lake Chamber of Commerce
(830) 964-2223 or (800) 528-2104
3934 FM 2673
Post Office Box 1435
Canyon Lake, Texas 78130

Reservoir Manager
Canyon Project
HC 4, Box 400
Canyon Lake, Texas 78133-4112
http://www.wildtexas.com/parks/canyon.htm

Sixteen miles northwest of New Braunfels via SR 306.

C anyon Lake is an impoundment of the Guadalupe River built by the Army Corps of Engi-neers, and offers eighty miles of scenic, protected shoreline for your enjoyment. Seven public parks surround the 8,240-acre lake, three of which have swimming beaches. Jointly operated by the Guadalupe and Blanco River authorities, the dam was built for flood control and water conservation in the surrounding communities. Construction began in 1958 and was completed in 1964. The dam is 224 feet high, 20 feet across, and is 4,410 feet long. Look for the black and brown rock squirrels that live around the dam. You can hike over the dam and around the lake ridge on a 5-kilometer trail with an excellent view called the Vereda Real. The scenic view at Overlook Park is spectacular, and it is still and quiet on top of the hill. A ranger station is located there and can provide brochures, maps and information.

Camping, picnic, and boating facilities are provided throughout the lake, including two yacht clubs, two marinas, and a ski club. Scuba diving is popular, as well. Resorts, bed and breakfast inns, motels, water sport rentals and restaurants can all be found close by.

Swimming beaches can be found at Comal Park, Canyon Park, and Potters Creek Park. Swimming is at your own risk as there are no lifeguards on duty.

The Canyon Lake area is in the heart of the Hill Country, and the hilly terrain is dotted with scrubby oaks.

There is absolutely no hunting at Canyon Lake, and wildlife is abundant. Pets are permitted on leashes, but not on the beaches.

North Park at the north end of the dam is for camping and has fair swimming; Jacob's Creek Park is for day use and has a large swimming beach, with   rest rooms, a boat ramp, and picnic areas. Canyon Park swimming beach is located near the entrance and has camping and a marina. Potters Creel has a small swimming beach and covered picnic areas on a little peninsula.

DECKER LAKE/WALTER E. LONG PARK

6614 Blue Bluff Road (off of Webberville Road)
Austin, Texas 78724
(512) 926-5230

> Entry fee is $3.00 Monday through Thursday
> $5 Fridays, Saturdays, Sundays and holidays

About 5 miles east of downtown Austin.

Decker Lake is a great alternative to Lake Travis when summer sizzles and everyone and their cousin is out on the lake. Although it is smaller, it never seems to get crowded, and it's conveniently close to Austin. Acquired by the City of Austin in 1968, the lake is 3,802 acres with 1,269 acres dedicated to sailing and skiing. Decker Lake boasts one-and-one-half miles of accessible shoreline and wide, open grassy banks. There are two boat ramps, plenty of parking, picnic areas and shade areas, an open playfield and volleyball courts. As for swimming, there is a dedicated sandy beach and the lake has a muddy bottom. Shorelines are reedy or grassy, and the lake is quiet and peaceful. Swimming is at your own risk, as there are no lifeguards on duty.

The park is laid out in two branches, and camping facilities front the lake on either side.

Before you head out to Decker Lake, make arrangements to visit the Indiangrass Wildlife Sanctuary next

Decker Lake

door. The Sanctuary is open by appointment only and tours are available. Two hundred acres of East Texas forestry meets the Blackland prairie at the park, and oak and elm trees integrate with the grasslands. The Blackland prairie is an endangered habitat made up of several types of grasses. The park is a unique geographic area offering great views from its hilltops. Five acres of the park are covered with gayfeather, a spiky purple flower which blooms in the fall. Birds nest in the wetlands along the shoreline of Decker Lake, and abundant wildlife, such as deer, armadillos, owls, hawks, osprey and snakes make their homes here.

LAKE FAYETTE

La Grange Chamber of Commerce
171 South Main Street
La Grange, Texas 78945
(409) 249-5208 or (800) LAGRANG

| Admission Fee $3.00 |

Take TX 71 to La Grange, then TX 159 about ten miles east toward Fayetteville.

L ake Fayette is an LCRA cooling lake for a power plant and a popular recreational site for locals. At 2,400 acres, there is plenty of fun to be had. There are two water access points and swimming beaches at Park Prairie and Oak Thicket Park, both off of TX 159 on the north side of the lake. The water is quite warm and good for swimming.

Park Prairie
(409) 249-3344

This fourteen-acre park has a designated swimming area on a small peninsula. There isn't really a sandy beach but just an abrupt and shallow shoreline. Expect to share the water with some friendly ducks. There is plenty of paved parking, potable water, rest rooms, a boat ramp and primitive camping. A sand volleyball court and a 3-mile multi-use trail add to the fun. There are picnic tables with grills and great views of the lake. Wheelchair-accessible.

Oak Thicket Park
(409) 249-3504

At eighty-five acres, Oak Thicket is bigger than Park Prairie and has more campsites with RV hookups, showers, a lighted pavilion and a playground. Oak Thicket has a sandy beach where the lake gently laps to shore. The Rice-Osborne Bird and Nature Trail connects the two parks.

Lake Fayette

LAKE GEORGETOWN

Route 5, Box 500
Georgetown, Texas 78726-9551
(512) 930-5253

Georgetown Convention and Visitors Bureau
Post Office Box 409
Georgetown, Texas 78627-0409
(512) 930-3545
http://swf67.swf-wc.usace.army.mil/georgetown/index.htm

*About thirty minutes from Austin. From Austin, take IH35 north to RM 2338 and
go west for four miles. Russell Park is at the north side of the dam and Cedar
Breaks is to the south.*

Georgetown was established in 1848 on the Chisholm Trail. The town was
founded when Mr. Washington Anderson and four other men were as
signed the task of locating a county seat. They decided to take a break
from their scouting under an oak tree when Anderson's cousin, a landowner named
George Glasscock, Sr., rode up on his mule. Anderson told Glasscock that if he'd
give him all the land from that point to the San Gabriel River, they'd name the
town after him. George agreed and donated 173 acres. The name stuck!

The North Fork of the San Gabriel River, part of the Brazos River system, flows east
across Williamson County to join with the middle and south forks at Georgetown.
Abundant fish and wildlife attracted numerous Indian tribes to the area along the
stream in historical times. Originally named Rio de San Javier by Spanish explorer
and priest Frey Isidro Felix Espinosa in 1716, it was known as the San Gabriel River
by the time Williamson County was created in 1848. Anglo settlements along the
river in the 1800s led to the establishment of four major crossings which took the
names of families living at the sites: Booty, Russell, Box and Hunt. Located along
the stream at the crossings were homes, mills, churches, schools, cemeteries, postal
stations and a gin. Booty, Russell and Box crossings were inundated by the waters
of Lake Georgetown but Hunt Crossing remains above the reservoir, planned as
part of the flood control for the Brazos River system. A dam creating Lake
Georgetown was completed by the Army Corps of Engineers in 1979. The lake and

171

Lake Georgetown

parks were opened in 1981. Lake Georgetown is an impoundment of the San Gabriel River, which flows through it. The lake is 1,200 acres and offers swimming, boating, water-skiing, camping, a wildlife preserve, and 16 miles of hiking trials. The Good Water Trail is a semi-loop built and operated by the Army Corps of Engineers. The trail mostly circles Lake Georgetown with a jog in between entrances. One entrance is at Cedar Breaks Park and the other at Russell Park. The trail begins as rocky, wooded terrain and then evens out into plains. Views of the lake can be found at many points. Bicycles are limited to Russell Park and Tejas Camp, a primitive campground with running water about half-way around the trail.

Fires are permitted in rings and grills only, no woodcutting is allowed, and no firearms, ammunition, or fireworks can be brought into the park. Pets on leash are permitted. Swimming is at your own risk and there are no lifeguards.

Russell Park
At the end of CO 262
Open April 1-September 30

There is no camping allowed here, but there are seventy picnic sites, a swimming beach, a boat ramp, and a group picnic pavilion. The trailhead for the Good Water Trail begins here and connects to Cedar Breaks Park.

Cedar Breaks Park
South of the dam

This park has a swimming beach, sixty-four campsites with water, electricity, showers and rest rooms, and forty-one picnic sites.

Jim Hogg Park
at the end of FM 2338
Sites 1-78 open year-round
Sites 79-148 open April 1-September 30

Jim Hogg Park has camping with water, electrical hookups and showers, and a boat ramp where you can also swim.

LAKE GRANGER

Project Office
Route 1, Box 172
Granger, Texas 76530
(512) 859-2668
http://swf67.swf-wc.usace.army.mil/granger/index.htm

Seven miles east of Granger on FM 971, or eight miles northeast of Taylor via SR 95 and FM 971. FM 971 connects via the dam to FM 1331 and makes a nice scenic loop around the lake.

There is a dispute over whom Granger was named for, John R. Granger, an early settler, or the Grange organization. Whichever it was, Granger was built up around the railroad in 1882. The area is beautiful in the spring when bluebonnets abound. Lake Granger is an excellent alternative to the Highland Lakes which can have one to two-hour waits for boat launches in the summer. Lake Granger has no virtually no waiting.

The staff in the project office is exceedingly friendly. They feature exhibits with photographs of the early flooding in the area, the building of the dam and lake, and information on indigenous animals, plants, and people. Many artifacts excavated during the dam construction are on display, including a woolly mammoth's pelvic bone.

Lake Granger

Opened in 1981 and built by the Army Corps of Engineers, Lake Granger is 4,400 acres. The dam is 2.54 miles long. A 5-mile nature and hiking trail loops around the shoreline in Taylor Park.

There are swimming beaches at Wilson H. Fox Park on the southeast end and at Friendship Park on the northeast end. Swimming beaches are grassy, not sandy, and lead right to the water's edge. Gentle waves lap at the shore. The lake has a pebbly bottom. Sheltered, individual picnic areas on the grass look out over the swimming area. Swimming is unsupervised. The water temperature is comfortable for swimming.

Lake Granger also has camping, water-skiing and boating.

Wilson H. Fox Park is open year-round, while Friendship Park is open April 2–September 31.

Pets on leash are permitted.

LAKE SOMERVILLE

Reservoir Manager
Post Office Box 549
Somerville, Texas 77879
(409) 596-1622

Somerville State Park
Route 1, Box 192A
Somerville, Texas 77879
(512) 389-8950
(800) 792-1112
http://swf67.swf-wc.usace.army.mil/somerville

Birch Creek Unit
(409) 535-7763

About 108 miles from Austin. Take U.S. 290 and turn onto FM 180 to get to the western side of the lake. Or take FM 1948 in Burton to get to the Corps of Engineer parks. Continue on FM 1948 to TX 36 in Somerville and then take FM 60 west to the other parks.

Somerville, like so many other Texas towns, grew up around the railroad. Lake Somerville is a little off the beaten path, south of Bryan, and is not crowded.

Lake Somerville has eighty-five miles of shoreline and covers parts of Washington, Burleson and Lee counties. The lake is an impoundment of Yegua Creek, the main tributary of the Brazos River. Built by the Army Corps of Engineers, Fort Worth District, between 1962-1967, the dam is over 26,000 feet long and the lake is 11,640 acres.

At Big Creek Marina on the north side of the lake there is a convenience store and camping area. The marina has leased a part of the park on a peninsula and provides excellent swimming and scenic overlooks. The other swimming beach is at Birch Creek Unit, which has a 150-foot long rock jetty.

Lake Somerville's trail system is one of the longest in the state park system at 37 miles and is open to horses, cyclists and hikers. The trail loops around the park linking campsites. Some of the trails are wheelchair-accessible.

Courtesy of Texas Department of Transportation

Lake Somerville

STILLHOUSE HOLLOW LAKE

Project Manager
Stillhouse Hollow
Route 3, Box 3407
Belton, Texas 76513
(254) 939-2461
http://swf67.swf-wc.usace.army.mil/stillhouse/index.htm

Admission to the day park is $1.00

About 80 miles from Austin. In Salado take Exit 286 and follow the signs.

The first thing people want to know about Stillhouse Hollow Lake is how it got its name. There are several legends surrounding the name. Some say that moonshiners stored their whiskey stills during Prohibition in a hollow created by the river at Dog Ridge. However, the name has appeared on deed records since the 1850s, so its source remains a mystery.

Stillhouse Hollow Lake is an impoundment of the Lampasas River about 5 miles southwest of Belton. It was built by the Army Corps of Engineers between 1962-1968 to provide flood control for the Brazos River Valley. The dam is 15,624 feet long and the lake is 6,430 acres. The lake level will fluctuate, though they strive to maintain it at 622 feet.

Dana Peak, on Comanche Gap Road off of FM 2410, and Stillhouse Park, on Simmons Road off of TX 190, are the best bets for swimming. The lake has an irregular shape and rocky, chalky shores.

Other parks around the 58 miles of shoreline have facilities for water-skiing, sailboarding, boating and Jet Skis. Camping sites and numerous picnic areas can be found throughout the parks. Chalk Ridge Falls has an environmental nature trail that winds behind the dam; a small waterfall provides lovely scenery from a suspension bridge, and swimming below the dam is permitted. Cedar Gap has a boat ramp. Overlook Park has a picnic area with a breathtaking view. River's Bend Park also has picnic facilities. Union Grove Park has picnicking, camping and boating. Group picnic pavilions are available by reservation. A day-use park at the marina on the northeast shore has a playground and picnic facilities, as well as swimming off a small peninsula. Stillhouse Hollow Lake is rarely crowded.

Stillhouse Hollow Lake

UNIVERSITY FACILITIES

ST. EDWARD'S UNIVERSITY

3001 South Congress (at St. Edward's Drive)
Austin, Texas 78704
(512) 448-8400
http://www.stedwards.edu

STATISTICS

25 meters long
6 lap lanes
Minimum Depth: 3 feet, 6 inches
Maximum Depth: 12 feet

Enter from South Congress and take the first driveway on the right; follow the street as it curves around. The pool is in the first building on the right.

If you are looking for a free place to swim during the winter months, or just a nice indoor pool, St. Edward's University is a splendid alternative. The Old Main Building is a historical landmark built of limestone, and Gothic towers and turrets decorate the campus. Large windows in the pool room look out onto a grove of oaks. The pool tends to be less crowded than Stacy Pool in the winter, but it is still quite popular.

There is limited public access on weekday mornings. Generally, the public may swim on the weekends before noon. Check for current hours posted on the front door.

NOTE: The City of Austin did not renew their contract with St. Edward's University as of this writing, so the public may not be able to access the pool. I have included this chapter in hopes that St. Edward's University pool will become accessible to the public again in the future, and for the information of the students, faculty and staff of St. Edward's University.

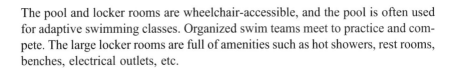

The pool and locker rooms are wheelchair-accessible, and the pool is often used for adaptive swimming classes. Organized swim teams meet to practice and compete. The large locker rooms are full of amenities such as hot showers, rest rooms, benches, electrical outlets, etc.

The track is also open to the public. Parking is adequate for visitors.

After your swim, enjoy the Blunn Creek Nature Preserve: forty acres of stream, upland woods and meadows located between Oltorf Street and St. Edward's Drive, just west of Travis High School. The trailhead is at St. Edward's Drive just west of Eastside Drive. Spring-fed Blunn Creek meanders through the preserve. Persimmon and oak trees dot the area. An ancient coral reef can be seen with compacted volcanic ash deposits which are one hundred million years old. The cone of the volcanic eruption can be see beneath the main building at the University.

SOUTHWESTERN UNIVERSITY

1001 East University Avenue
Georgetown, Texas 78626
(512) 863-1381
http://www.southwestern.edu/

The Robertson Swim Center is available to the public through the purchase of a swim pass. There is currently a waiting list for swim passes. Call for more information.

SOUTHWEST TEXAS UNIVERSITY

601 University Drive
San Marcos, Texas 78666
(512) 245-3941
http://www.swt.edu/

The Recreational Sports Aqua Sports Center is open to students, faculty and staff of Southwest Texas University. The pool is open for lap swimming every day but hours vary from semester to semester. There is generally an early morning session, a lunch session, and late afternoon and evening session. For more specific information, call the Aqua Sports Center.

UNIVERSITY OF TEXAS AT AUSTIN RECREATIONAL SPORTS

Division of Recreational Sports
The University of Texas at Austin
GRE 2.200
D-7500
Austin, Texas 78712-2078

Administration	(512) 471-1155
Memberships	(512) 471-6370
24 hour Facility Hotline	(512) 471-4373
Swimming Office	(512) 471-7433
Swim Lessons	(512) 471-1272
Longhorn Swim Camp	(512) 475-8652
Jamail Texas Swim Center	(512) 471-7771

http://www.utexas.edu/main/content/banner/helpful-information

You don't have to be a student at the University of Texas at Austin to access its facilities, including the pools at Gregory Gym and the Jamail Swim Center. Anna Hiss Gymnasium used to be a favorite swimming spot, but was demolished to make room for the new microbiology building. To access the pools along with all other recreational facilities at UT, choose one of the following options:

If you are already a faculty member, staff member or student at UT, prices will vary. Call for specific rates. The general public must be sponsored by one of the above. Options include a one-semester membership, two-semester membereship, and annual membership (including summer). Lockers are given first to UT people, then sold to the public for an additional fee. You may pay in cash in the administrative office, or mail a check to UT, or charge your credit card. For annual and two-semester memberships, a monthly payment plan is available.

Hours vary semester to semester, so it is best to call ahead. Pools close briefly between semesters and at end of summer. Gregory Gym and the Jamail Texas Swim Center are both open for circle swimming at lunch time. A separate children's schedule is available.

The water is maintained at a temperature conducive to the activities of each pool. Target temperatures are as follows:

Gregory Gym 82-84°F
Gregory Gym Shallow Pool 88-90°F
Swim Center 79-81°F

UT's facilities are for the use of students, faculty, staff, and affiliate members of recreational sports. You must show a valid UT identification, a recreational sports facility card with a photo ID, or a guest pass.

Parking is a nightmare around the University. The lots are all permit-only and the campus is surrounded by State lots. Friday afternoons, weekends and holidays are the best bets for parking in permitted areas when they become unrestricted. You might consider taking the UT shuttle, the Dillo, or Capital Metro.

JAMAIL TEXAS SWIM CENTER

Martin Luther King, Jr. Blvd. at Trinity Street

You'd never know it by looking at the monolithic, windowless building, but inside there is a 50-meter by 25 yard, world-class competition pool with a separate diving well. If you are a serious swimmer preparing for a competition, the Jamail Texas Swim Center is the best place in Austin to train.

Lee and Joe Jamail Swim Center

Inside the Jamail Texas Swim Center is a massive spectator stand done completely in burnt orange (what else?). Toward the back of the building is the Skippy Browning Diving Facility, named for a champion diver who attended UT. The diving well has five diving boards and five diving platforms. The pool is eight lanes but the bulkhead can convert it into split sections for practice and competition areas. This pool is totally-state-of-the-art with 'waveless' shock absorbers, and is fully regulated for competition. There are two announcement boxes, award stands, and scoreboards. Banners, flags and trophies decorate the walls. With all that water indoors, the environment is humid and chlorinated. There are benches and grassy areas outside.

Concession stands are open during events, but soda machines and water fountains are available all the time. There is a small store that sells souvenirs and equipment such as caps, water bottles, swimsuits, training suits, goggles, fins, kickboards, Powerbars, and Gatorade. Kickboards and pull buoys are available at both pools.

The Jamail Texas Swim Center is open for lap swimming. Coordinate through the facilities operations office located in Gregory Gym at 2.200.

GREGORY GYM

Located at the corner of Speedway and 21st Street.

From the outside, Gregory Gym looks and feels like an old gymnasium; in fact, it is a historical building. In the 1930s, Tommy Dorsey's Orchestra with Frank Sinatra played in Gregory Gym to hundreds of enthralled students. With its arched, cavernous shape resembling an airplane hanger, the building recently underwent a major

Gregory Gym

renovation, and the new facility is spectacular. The renovations include remodeling of the swimming pool and a new shallow, warmer pool. The main pool is 100 feet long, has seven lanes, and the shallow pool is four-and-one-half feet deep. There are two retractable diving boards. There is a family swim time, an outdoor program, and handicapped lifts. Lifeguards are on duty. Gregory Gym pool hours vary from semester to semester, so it is best to call ahead.

Beyond swimming there is a three-tier suspended indoor track, an indoor climbing wall, twice the weight training space as the old gym, an exercise room with step climbers, stationary bikes, treadmills and rowers, new lockers and showers, saunas

187

and steam rooms, international-sized squash courts, two aerobics rooms, new floors for basketball, badminton and volleyball, an outdoor resource center, a wellness center, a sports café, and much, much more. Whew! You could spend all day working out. By far the best improvement is the addition of AIR CONDITIONING!

Gregory Gym Pool

GENERAL RULES AT UT

You must show valid ID (ID cards are only for the program indicated).

Enter and exit during 7:00 A.M.-10:00 P.M.

Spectators and visitors are not allowed to participate in practice sessions, and are required to sign in at the front desk and proceed directly to the grand stands.

Minors are not allowed without direct supervision.

UT is not responsible for lost items.

Report any problems to the front desk.

No smoking, bicycles, skateboards, balls, rolling objects, glass, food, or alcohol.

Only proper swimming attire is allowed. No cut-offs, shorts or jeans.

No rowdy behavior, no gum, hairpins or foreign objects.

No children on the deck during recreational sports hours.

Enter the water by sitting down and sliding into the water feet first.

No street shoes on the pool deck.

People with infectious diseases are prohibited from swimming.

Must take a soap shower before you get in.

Must demonstrate advanced swimming skills.

Lifeguard must be on deck.

MUNICIPAL UTILITY DISTRICTS

A WORD ABOUT MUDS

A MUD is a municipal utility district, a residential area with its own utility infrastructure, usually water and wastewater. These subdivisions fall outside of Austin's city limits and are newer neighborhoods dating from the 1970s. Austin has grown so fast that the city cannot always finance construction of utilities before building is complete, so residents pay taxes and water bills to their MUD. The City of Austin may buy back the MUD over several years. Many MUDs have their own swimming pools. If you look in the phone book under 'private swimming pools' you'll see a whole slew of them. Some are truly private and cater to neighborhood residents or members of a club. Others are funded and maintained by the residents of the MUD, but allow public access for a fee. There are dozens of MUDs around Austin, but I have included only a sampling here to get you started.

ANDERSON MILL MUD

Anderson Mill was originally a water-powered mill in Austin's early days. Anderson's Mill diverted water from the Colorado to a natural fall where the mill stood on top of a bluff. Water was diverted from the Colorado River to fuel the mill and produce flour, among other things. During the Civil War, Confederate

Anderson Mill Pool

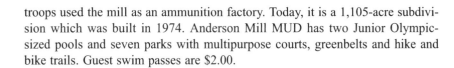
troops used the mill as an ammunition factory. Today, it is a 1,105-acre subdivision which was built in 1974. Anderson Mill MUD has two Junior Olympic-sized pools and seven parks with multipurpose courts, greenbelts and hike and bike trails. Guest swim passes are $2.00.

Anderson Mill Pool
10701 School House Lane
Austin, Texas 78750
(512) 258-3687

> Monday through Friday 6:00-11:00 A.M.
> and 1:00-7:30 P.M. open swim.
> Hours change when school starts.
> Call for the most current schedule.

Right off of Lake Creek Parkway.

Both Anderson Mill Pool and El Salido Pool have an L-shaped design, with diving boards and a deep end and lap lanes. Both also have a separate wading pool. Arbors provide shade at Anderson Mill and there are grassy areas surrounding the pool. A large bathhouse has showers and changing rooms.

El Salido Pool
11500 El Salido Parkway
Austin, Texas 78750
(512) 250-8427

> Monday through Friday open swim 1:00-8:00 P.M., Saturday and Sunday 10:00 A.M.-8:00 P.M. Monday and Wednesday 6:30 A.M.-8:00 A.M. adult swim.
> Hours change when school starts. Call for the most current schedule.

From U.S. 183 take Anderson Mill Road to RR 620. Turn right onto RR 620 and go right again on El Salido. The pool is on the corner.

El Salido Pool has some shade provided by arbors, and lounge chairs surround the pool. The bathhouse also has a weight room, a recreation center, a playground, and covered picnic pavilions with grills. The pool is wheelchair-accessible on one sloped shallow end. The adjacent park has tennis courts, and baseball, football, and soccer fields.

CAT HOLLOW POOL

8600 O'Connor Drive
Austin, Texas 78717
(512) 244-2934

$4.00 admission.

Monday, Wednesday, and Thursday 10:30 A.M.-6:00 P.M.
Closed Tuesdays.
Friday and Saturday 10:30 A.M.-10:00 P.M.
Sundays 12:00-8:00 P.M.

---

*From IH35 take the RR 620 exit and go west to the stoplight at O'Connor Drive.
Turn into the Cat Hollow Subdivision.*

Cat Hollow has a very nice, new swimming pool. The bathhouse is accented by magenta and teal-colored tiles and is surrounded by lots of grass for spreading out. Depths in the main pool range from two to six feet, and there is one dedicated lap lane. A separate wading pool has a fountain for frolicking. There is plenty of parking out front, but virtually no shade near the pool. The adjacent park has volleyball courts, playgrounds, tennis courts, and a hike and bike trail. Concessions are available.

Cat Hollow Pool

195

WELLS BRANCH MUD

KATHERINE FLEISCHER POOL
2106 Klattenhoff Drive
Austin, Texas 78728
(512) 251-9932

Monday-Saturday 10:30 A.M.-9:00 P.M., Sunday 12:00-9:00
$2.50 admission

From IH35 take Wells Branch Parkway west under the interstate. Go right at Wells Port, then left at Klattenhoff Drive.

Katherine Fleischer Pool is located on a historical site. The original build-ings which were part of the Wells Branch and Gault homestead, a 320-acre land grant, are still standing next to the pool. Although the property has been sold through several families over the years, a log cabin, a farm, and a home remain as a reminder of the area's early rural heritage.

The L-shaped pool is popular and well-maintained. Depths range from three to nine feet, and a separate wading pool is provided for kids under age 5. Katherine Fleischer Pool has one dedicated lap lane and a diving board. Wooden arbors provide shade, and picnic tables and benches let patrons relax.

The adjacent community center has a modern playground, more picnic tables with grills, a hike and bike trail, soccer and football fields, a baseball diamond, basketball and tennis courts, and a dock and mill pond. The park is very nicely landscaped with wildflowers and native grasses.

WILLOW BEND POOL

2801 Sauls Drive
Austin, Texas 78728
(512) 310-1833

Willow Bend is also a newer, regulation-size pool. There is a separate wading pool with a mushroom fountain for the tots. Willow Bend has dedicated lap swim daily from 11:00 A.M.-1:00 P.M. and 3:00-4:00 P.M.

Both pools have large, clean bathhouses with full amenities.

Willow Bend Pool

MUNICIPAL POOLS OUTSIDE OF AUSTIN

CEDAR PARK MUNICIPAL POOLS

Cedar Park Parks and Recreation
(512) 331-0645
http://www.ci.cedar-park.tx.us/services/parks/
community_parks.html

BUTTERCUP CREEK POOL
Off of Buttercup Creek Boulevard and Twin Oaks
(512) 250-9578

$2.00 for guests for over 17
$1.00 for seniors and under 17

Buttercup Creek Pool serves the Buttercup Creek subdivision, but everyone is welcome. It is a new pool with a modern playground, tennis courts, a senior center, rest rooms, concessions, and plenty of parking.

The pool has two diving boards. The shallow end is 2 feet deep and the deep end is 13 feet. Buttercup Creek Pool is totally wheelchair-accessible with ramps. There is some shade over a group of picnic tables inside the pool area. Chaise lounges surround the pool. There is a separate wading pool.

Buttercup Creek Pool

While you're in the Cedar Park area, consider that Pond Springs Road was named for a spring about 1.6 kilometers north of Jollyville that once formed a pond. Early settlers in the area used it as a gathering area, and from 1854 to 1880 a post office was stationed there.

ELIZABETH M. MILBURN POOL

Admission $2.00 for adults
$1.00 for 17 and under
Seniors and kids under 7 are free

Take U.S. 183 toward Leander. Turn left on Cypress Creek Road and you'll see the pool on your right.

Milburn Pool looks a lot like Micki Krebsbach Pool in Round Rock (see page 214). It's ultra-modern with a water slide and fantasy fountains. There are eight lap lanes. A large bathhouse provides plenty of comfort with hot showers, restrooms, etc.

Dedicated in 1995, the park is new and very nicely outfitted with tennis courts, picnic areas, gardens, a football field, open spaces with lots of trees, and sand volleyball and basketball courts. Concessions are available and there is plenty of parking.

A historical marker indicates a cemetery of the original homesteaders, the McRae family. Murdock McRae, wife Isabella, and son Daniel are all buried there. The McRaes were early Williamson County pioneers and farmed this tract of land. The original farmhouse stood 300 yards east of the cemetery, and the original limestone walls still exist. Milburn Pool is near an Austin Community College campus and the new Cedar Park High School.

Milburn Pool

GEORGETOWN MUNICIPAL POOLS

Georgetown Parks and Recreation
1003 North Austin Avenue
Georgetown, Texas 78626
(512) 930-3595
http://www.georgetown.org/tourism/html/parks.html

Georgetown is a fast-growing community with some fine parks and pools. The municipal pools were built in the 1970s. Williams Drive Pool is by far the largest, and San Gabriel Park Pool and River Ridge Pool are about the same size.

Pools are open Memorial Day to Labor Day. Between the start of school and the week after Labor Day, pool hours will be reduced and posted at each pool.

Admission to all pools is $1.00 for children under 18, and $2.00 for adults. Punch cards for ages under 17 for fifteen swims are $13.50; Adult punch cards are $27. Unlimited season passes are $65 for children and individuals, $150 for families. Passes are prorated as the summer progresses, and discounts apply if purchased before the season opens. Fees for non-residents are slightly higher. For more information, call the Georgetown Parks and Recreation Department.

RIVER RIDGE POOL
(512) 930-3533

Tuesday through Saturday 1:00-7:00 P.M.
Sunday 2:00-6:00 P.M.
Closed Mondays

At the corner of River Ridge and South Ridge in the River Ridge subdivision. River Ridge is off of Leander Road (RR 2243).

This pool has a lengthy shallow area and a deep diving area. There is also a one-foot deep, square wading pool separate from the main pool. The pool is surrounded by grass and concrete, and picnic tables and lounge chairs are provided. There is some shade from oak trees, and rest rooms and changing areas are well- maintained.

Georgetown has 'Dive-In Theater' at the Williams Drive Pool, just like Austin's (see page 333), where movies are shown outside at the pool. Refreshments are available for purchase. A $3.00 entry fee includes raft rental so you can kick your feet up and float. Movies start at 9:30 P.M. and the pool closes at midnight.

Pools can be rented between Memorial Day and Labor Day for reasonable rates. Call Georgetown Parks and Recreation for more information. Parks and Recreation also offers classes in lifeguarding, water safety, and water aerobics. Swim lessons are given for ages six months and up, and are $25 per session, a session lasting about a week to ten days.

River Ridge Pool

SAN GABRIEL PARK POOL
(512) 930-3530

> Monday and Wednesday through Saturday 1:00-7:00 P.M.
> Sunday 2:00-6:00 P.M.
> Closed Tuesdays

Inside San Gabriel Park off of Business IH35.

This pool is operated by Georgetown Parks and Recreation but is idyllically set in San Gabriel Park. There is a large pool laid out like a cathedral with a square deep end under the diving board and a rounded apse at the opposite end. A separate, rectangular wading pool is adjacent to the pool. The drawback to this pool is that there is absolutely no shade. Tents have been erected which provide some relief. There are some grassy areas inside the fence, and the pool looks out over the park's flower gardens, fountains, and playscapes. Rest rooms and changing rooms are next door in the recreation center.

San Gabriel Park Pool

WILLIAMS DRIVE POOL
(512) 930-3529

At the corner of Lakewood and Williams Drive (RR 2238).

Tuesday through Saturday 1:00-7:00 P.M.
Wednesday 8:00-10:00 P.M. for Family Swim Night
Sunday 2:00-6:00 P.M.
Closed Mondays

This large pool is L-shaped with a huge shallow area and a diving board in the deep end. There aren't many amenities, but the pool accommodates a large number of people. There isn't much natural shade either, but there are grassy areas surrounding the pool. The pool is on a busy corner, so it's not very idyllic. It is a popular pool with kids, and they don't seem to mind. There is plenty of parking on the street and in an unpaved lot next door. A large bathhouse has rest rooms and showers. Concessions can be purchased from vending machines. A basketball court sits next to the pool.

Williams Drive Pool

LA GRANGE MUNICIPAL POOL

La Grange Chamber of Commerce
171 South Main Street
La Grange, Texas 78945
(409) 249-5208 or (800) LAGRANG

> Tuesday through Sunday 2:00-7:30 p.m.
> Closed Monday
>
> 50¢ admission for all ages

Take TX 71 to Business 71 into town, cross the bridge over the Colorado, take the first left, go one block, turn right and you'll see the pool.

There is a nice little pool inside Kruschell Memorial Park which was built in 1996. The pool is rectangular and has a diving board. Depths range from three to twelve feet. Concrete and some grass surrounds the pool, and there is very little shade. A small bathhouse has rest rooms. The pool has a handicap lift. Kruschell Memorial Park has a small, modern playground and picnic tables.

LEANDER MUNICIPAL POOL

601 South Bagdad Road
Leander, Texas
(512) 259-8115

> $2.00 admission
>
> Tuesday through Saturday 12:00-8:00 P.M.
> Sunday 1:00-6:00 P.M.
> Closed Mondays

From FM 1431 in Cedar Park head north on Bagdad Road at the Diamond Shamrock and go past Leander High School.

L eander was a railroad town, named for the settlers of Bagdad, a tiny town near Leander about a mile away on RR 2243. Leander Brown was the director of the company that built the railroad.

Leander Pool is located in an undeveloped area in a small park. This is your basic rectangular pool with very few amenities except for two diving boards. There is a changing room and bathroom, but no shade. Concrete and grass surround the pool. The park has basketball courts, a small playground, a baseball diamond, and some covered picnic tables with grills. Antique barns next door are an interesting conversation starter.

LLANO'S ROBINSON POOL

Llano County Chamber of Commerce
700 Bessemer
Llano, Texas 78643
(915) 247-5354
http://www.llanochamber.org/recreation.htm

Open daily in the summer 2:00-7:00 P.M.
Closed Mondays

$1.00 admission

On RR 152 about two miles east of the courthouse.

T his nice pool is idyllically set on the banks of the Llano River. The pool, built in 1953, is Junior Olympic-size and has a separate, square wading pool. Depths in the main pool range from 2 to 9 feet, and there are high and low diving boards. There is also a bathhouse with rest rooms and showers. An arbor provides shade.

The surrounding park has picnic tables, basketball courts, a sports stadium, camping, a 9-hole golf course, and a community center. You can walk along grassy banks on the Llano River and feed geese and ducks. This portion of the river is dammed and is calm, wide, clear and blue.

LULING MUNICIPAL POOL

Luling Parks and Recreation
Post Office Box 630
Luling, Texas 78648
(830) 875-2713
http://www.bcsnet.net/lulingcc/index.htm

Open daily 1:00-7:00 P.M.
Closed Mondays
Adults 13 or older $1.50
Children 5-12 $1.00
5 and under free

Off of TX 80 at the edge of the city limits.

Luling Municipal Pool is located in a lovely park on the banks of the San Marcos River. The main pool, built in 1954, is large and has a diving board. The pool is painted in bright blue and red. A bathhouse has rest rooms and dressing areas, and a square wading pool is separate from the main pool. Concrete and some grass surrounds the pool. The pool and park are populated by towering pecan trees and wide-open grassy space. The park has a golf course, a town meeting hall, and picnic tables with grills on the riverbank. There is plenty of parking throughout the park. There is also a dam on the San Marcos River which forms a picturesque waterfall.

The San Marcos River as seen from Luling

GILLELAND CREEK POOL

700 Railroad Avenue
Pflugerville, Texas 78660
(512) 251-5082
http://www.io.com/~flagship/parks.html

$1.00 for kids 6-18
$2.00 for adults 18 and over
Kids under 5 are 50¢

Tuesday through Sunday 12:15-8:00 P.M.
Closed Mondays

From IH35, take the FM 1825 exit and continue on FM 1825 about four miles to downtown Pflugerville. At the stoplight at Railroad Avenue, turn left. The pool is about one-quarter mile down on the left.

The town is named for the Pfluger family. Henry Pfluger (1802-1867) migrated from Germany to Texas in 1849 with his large family. George Pfluger gave the right of way to the land where the train depot was built, and the town grew up around it. He also built some of the brick buildings downtown.

Gilleland Creek is named for James Gilleland who settled in the area in 1832. He organized a Methodist church for Travis and Bastrop counties.

This large, L-shaped pool was built in 1991 and has lots of amenities. Depths range from shallow to deep, and there are eight dedicated lap lanes. There is minimal shade around the pool, but there are expansive grassy areas close by, and lots of chaise lounges for relaxing. A large bathhouse has showers, rest rooms and changing areas. There is lots of elbowroom at Gilleland Creek Pool, and a variety of activities, such as lessons, to choose from.

Outside there is plenty of parking and concessions. A large picnic pavilion hosts parties, and a wooden playscape entertains the kids. A hike and bike trail connects to Pfluger Park on City Park Road, and follows Gilleland Creek. The park has picnic tables with grills. There are magnificent shade trees throughout the park, and pretty crepe myrtles near the pool.

Gilleland Creek Pool

ROUND ROCK

Parks and Recreation Department
605 Palm Valley Blvd.
Round Rock, Texas 78664
(512) 867-6442 Recorded Information
http://www.ci.round-rock.tx.us/parks-rec/pard.html

Round Rock Chamber of Commerce
212 East Main Street
Round Rock, Texas 78664
(800) 747-3479

Round Rock is named for an old round rock (actually it's more anvil-shaped) that sits in the middle of Brushy Creek. The rock was a landmark for early settlers indicating when the water was low enough to cross. Round Rock was originally called Brushy after the creek, but the postmaster suggested changing the name in honor of the big rock. Today, Williamson County is the fastest-growing county in the country.

Sam Bass, an infamous outlaw, has become a small claim to fame for Round Rock. His tale is a classic story from the Old West. Bass was from Indiana but came to Denton as a teenager. He robbed trains and planned to rob the Round Rock Bank in July 1878 with help from his gang of outlaws. Jim Murphy, a Texas Ranger, got word of Bass's plan and alerted Texas Rangers who were camped on Brushy Creek. When Bass went into town to survey the bank, a Ranger stopped him for wearing his guns. A shooting spree broke out. Bass was shot by the local deputy but managed to escape. He was eventually tracked down by Rangers and died the next day, his twenty seventh birthday, July 21, 1878. He is buried in the Old Round Rock Cemetery on the fence line between the Anglo burial sites and the old slave cemetery, near the St. Charles Hotel. Over the years tourists have chipped off pieces of the tombstone as souvenirs and it has been replaced many times. Buried next to Bass is Sebe Barnes, 'right bower' to Bass.

Brushy Creek flows through Old Settlers' Park, where you can see the round rock. Memorial Park has a softball field, a hike and bike trail, picnic tables, a playground, and lots of grassy areas and shade. A footbridge extends over the creek, which flows south under the highway to the Chisholm Trail.

Lake Creek Pool
Park Lane
(512) 218-7030

Friday through Sunday 1:00-8:00 P.M.
Tuesday through Thursday 1:00-6:00 P.M.
Closed Mondays

Children 75¢ and adults $1.25

Take IH35 to the RR 620 exit, go east on Main Street through downtown. Turn right on Burnet Street and then go left immediately after the railroad tracks on Park Lane. You'll see a small sign for the pool. Park Lane dead-ends into the pool.

Lake Creek Pool was built in the 1970s. It's a little out of the way, but well worth the peace and quiet once you get there. There are two diving boards, a low and a high. The main pool is mostly deep for this reason. A separate wading pool accommodates shallow water swimmers and is well-shaded. A nice, meandering park runs next to the pool with covered and shady picnic tables, grassy areas, ballfields, and lovely places to wade through Lake Creek.

Lake Creek Pool

Micki Krebsbach Pool
Deepwood Drive
(512) 218-7090

Resident Admission: Adults $1.25, Under 17 75¢
Resident swim passes good for 10 swims: $11.50 for adults, $6.50 for children
Non residents: $1.50 adult, $1.00 for children
Non resident swim passes: $14 for adults and $9 for children

Daily 1:00-8:00 P.M.
Tuesdays 5:00-9:00 P.M.
Lap swim for adults 11:00 A.M.-1:00 P.M.
Monday, Wednesday, Thursday and Friday

From IH35, take the RR 620 exit and go west. Take Deepwood Drive to the left and you will see the pool on the left.

Micki Krebsbach was a young Round Rock student who accidentally fell off of her bike and died. Her mother later married a coach at Round Rock High School and the pool became a memorial to Micki. Micki's mother became an advocate for bicycle safety headgear.

Micki Krebsbach Pool is the larger of Round Rock's municipal pools. It is spectacular and looks like a water theme park. After parking in a huge lot, you are welcomed through a pavilion-style entrance. The pool has amusements and regulation swimming, and is the best of both worlds. For fun, an aqua-colored water slide plunges into the deep end. To use the slide you must be at least 48 inches tall. A mushroom-shaped fountain sprays water over swimmers like a shower, while sprinkler-style fountains wave water back and forth. Moveable bulkheads create superb swimming spaces for lap swimmers and can be adjusted to twenty-five-meter lanes for competition and meets. The pool has full amenities including a spacious bathhouse, and lounge chairs surround the pool for sunbathing. Lynn Allen is the manager and a swimming coach with ambitions for building his own pool. His staff is very friendly and helpful. The pool is quite new and clean, and just opened in May 1996.

Micki Krebsbach Pool

214

CITY OF TAYLOR MUNICIPAL POOLS

Taylor Chamber of Commerce
Post Office Box 231
Taylor, Texas 76574
(512) 352-6364
http://www.lone-star.net/mall/txtrails/taylor.htm

Thirty-six miles from Austin, eight miles from Lake Granger.

Between Round Rock and Taylor lies Kenney Springs. About four kilometers east of Round Rock on TX 79, look for the historical marker for Kenney Fort. The Tonkawas had a racetrack there. In 1839 Thomas Kenny built a fort at the springs on the south side of Brushy Creek. Santa Fe organized his expedition there in 1841. The springs were described by a member of the group as "cool and most delicious water" (Kendall 1844). In 1842, the state archives were moved from Austin to this fort when a Mexican threat was imminent, but they were only kept overnight. The foundations of the fort remain, and the springs are in the bed of Brushy Creek.

Taylor is another railroad town which grew up around 1876. It was originally named Taylorsville for Edward M. Taylor, a railroad worker.

Taylor Independence Festival Days are held in Murphy Park on the Fourth of July every year. The festival includes diving and swimming competitions and exhibitions plus a carnival, magic shows, parades, and a whole lot more.

Murphy Park Pool

Take Main Street (TX 95) to Westlake Drive and turn left. Cross the water over a small bridge and take an immediate left into the park. Murphy Park is located behind the Chamber of Commerce.

Murphy Pool is located in splendid Murphy Park. The mint green pool has depths ranging from three to six feet and the shallow and deep ends are separated by a low wall. A large bathhouse has showers and rest rooms. Concrete sidewalks surround the pool, and benches and grass let spectators watch the swimmers in

215

Murphy Park

comfort. There is no shade around the pool. A man-made lake is visible from the pool and offers a nice view. Funds from a bond election held in 1997 will be used to build a brand new pool in Murphy Park. Construction begins in the fall of 1998, and the existing pool will be filled in.

Murphy Park also has tennis courts, baseball diamonds, a bandstand, picnic areas, a playground, miniature golf, assembly halls, a hike and bike trail, bird watching, and football and soccer fields. A man-made lake supports ducks and geese, and a small creek, crossed by footbridges, meanders through the park.

Robinson Park Pool

To get to Robinson Park Pool from Business 79 (4th Street), turn right on Dolan Avenue after you go under the railroad trestle. You can also take Business 95 under the railroad tracks to Walnut Street, go left through the entrance of the park, then take a left on Dolan Avenue.

Robinson Park Pool is a small pool with minimal amenities. Depths range from two to six feet, and the pool is painted mint green. There is a small bathhouse, and vending machines provide cold drinks. Concrete and some grass surrounds the pool, and benches are provided for spectators. There is very little shade. Robinson Park consists mostly of open space. A small creek winds through the park, and patrons can enjoy baseball diamonds and picnic tables. This is not the most idyllic park, being situated amongst a grain mill, railroad tracks, and a power plant that generates an audible hum.

NATURAL SPRINGS AND RIVERS

ABOUT SPRINGS

Texas abounds with thousands of springs due to its unique geography. Unfortunately, many springs have run dry due to well drilling, clearing and plowing of the land, and the pumping of ground water. Springs that still flow are often polluted with runoff of insecticides, herbicides, sewage and oil fields. Many of these springs were the sites of Indian, Spanish and early American camps, as evidenced by bedrock mortars, middens, and rock and cave paintings. Springs were a refreshing 'rest stop' on trails for stagecoaches, explorers, and riverboats. Early Indian trails formed a sort of connect-the-dots between springs. These trails later developed into major transportation routes followed by De Vaca, Coronado, and Moscoso. Springs also powered mills and provided health-restoring properties to spas. Hundreds of towns grew up around these springs and many are named for them. The springs were often referred to as fountains because they were so powerful as to gush high into the air, sometimes as high as 26 feet! When early Texans built forts, they were almost always nearby springs to provide water, and this sometimes meant the difference between life and death.

Some springs are fed by surface runoff and will periodically dry up; others are fed by underwater springs and will be more constant. The springs in our area along the Balcones fault line are the largest and oldest in Texas. During the Miocene age, about 15 million years ago, the present springs 'sprang' and have been present ever since. They have changed slowly in geological time with erosion and slippage. Central Texas contains some of the world's largest springs, including Comal Springs with 9,000 liters flowing per second, San Marcos with 4,300 liters per second, and Barton at 1,400 liters per second.

Ebb and flow springs may have periods of heavy flow alternating with a dormant period. These types of springs usually issue from limestone. Perhaps the 'miracle waters' described in the Bible (John 5:2-9) were ebb and flow. These springs are rare, and 27 can be found in the United States, 8 of which are in Missouri. Seiders Springs in Austin (in Pease Park, see page 317) is the only one in Texas.

Other springs are thermal. Hot springs are classified as 37 Celsius or higher, and warm springs range from 1-2 degrees warmer than the local average atmosphere up to 37 degrees Celsius.

Why have springs declined? It began with the Spanish missionaries when they began to dig ground water reservoirs, but it took several centuries to really make a difference. As Texas developed and urbanized, forests were cleared, wells were dug, and livestock grazed on the grassland. Buffalo had done this for years in a migratory fashion, and the grass always grew back, but when cattle were placed on a permanent pasture, the grass could not renew itself quickly enough. The soil became compacted and could no longer absorb the recharge waters effectively. Brushy plants such as mesquite took over with their long roots and sapped water. Anglos began settling here with their huge cattle herds and compounded the problem. In the mid-1800s, deep wells were drilled which drastically reduced the spring flow as they diverted water above. The springs had no pressure to keep pumping on their own, so humans began doing that for them, and in the 1930s irrigation waters were withdrawn in huge quantities. The paving of urban areas has also reduced some of the recharge run-off.

Texas's springs should be enjoyed and protected as much as possible.

BLANCO RIVER

Blanco Chamber of Commerce
Post Office Box 626
Blanco, Texas 78606
(830) 833-5101

Blanco State Park

Post Office Box 49
Blanco, Texas 78606
(830) 833-4333
http://www.tpwd.state.tx.us/park/blanco/blanco.htm

Just off U.S. 281 in town.

Dinosaurs were probably the first to enjoy this park as evidenced by tracks in the river bottom. Later, Tonkawa and Comanche tribes had sites here. The 110-acre state park was built by the Civilian Conservation Corps in 1934. The Blanco River cascades over small dams with grassy slopes on one side, while the other bank is rockier and wooded. The river bottom is limestone, hence the name Blanco (white), and makes the water very clear and pretty, like a man-made swimming pool. You can access the river via ladders on either side of the dam. Swimming and tubing are popular, and camping, picnicking, a children's play area, hiking and concessions are available. The river is swift and shallow, but perfect for distance swimmers with more than 1,000 feet of uninterrupted length. This is sort of a plain park with sloping banks lined with willow and oak trees, but is quite scenic. You can rent tubes, canoes and boats. The Town Creek Nature Trail connects the state park to a square downtown.

Blanco State Park

223

Five Mile Dam

Take IH35 to Yarrington Road just south of Kyle. Follow the frontage road to the 'Y', then take the right on FM 2779.

This Hays County park is on the banks of the Blanco River. The river is deep enough for swimming above the dam, and there is good wading below the dam. Further east are some flat rocks good for sunning. A small concrete bridge spans the river and a railroad trestle crosses it above. There are no beaches to speak of, just brushy banks. There are picnic tables, a pier and a playground. Development nearby is encroaching on this swimming hole.

Five Mile Dam

Little Arkansas

(512) 847-2767

$5 a day per car.

Go east on RR 3237 and at the Corral (an outdoor movie theatre), turn right on CR 173 (Flite Access Road). Turn right again on CR 174. Follow the signs for several miles of unpaved road. You will cross the river several times. About 7.5 miles from Wimberley.

Little Arkansas is a privately owned recreation spot run by Liza Howell, an old matriarch. Howell has been likened to a stern schoolteacher. There are 'No' signs all over the place telling you what you can't do during your visit. Don't let the signs scare you, though. Little Arkansas is a family-oriented place with camping and great swimming. Surrounded by wooded and rough country with abundant springs, tributaries of the Blanco River come together in a 15-foot waterfall. A small concrete dam makes a nice shallow swimming area with two docks. The springs are also known as Fern Bank Springs and Krueger Springs.

Courtesy of Texas Department of Transportation

Little Arkansas

BULL CREEK PARK

6701 Lakewood Drive
Austin, Texas 78731

This forty-eight-acre park and swimming hole is an underused gem. It was acquired by the City of Austin in 1971 with some federal assistance, and is a very natural park.

Bull Creek cuts through a steep granite ridge where it flows over a small man-made dam. The dam forms two pools. Behind the dam the water is deep enough to have a rope swing and is framed by large boulders. The water cascades over the dam into a shallow area with fish and a gravelly bottom. Water levels will vary with rainfall. There is no lifeguard on duty. Bull Creek Park is very popular with dogs, so you just might have to share the pool with them. Often you must drive through a low water crossing, so be careful. This is a spot in Austin that always floods first when it rains.

The park also has plenty of parking, a volleyball court, picnic tables, and a large, permanent grill. Rock climbers use the face of the granite ridge to practice. The park is close to Loop 360 so you may hear the traffic in the distance. Oak, pecan and juniper trees provide plenty of shade.

Bull Creek

Bull Creek Greenbelt

The Bull Creek Greenbelt begins at Loop 360 and Spicewood Springs Road and then travels south along Bull Creek through the park. The 3-mile trail is under construction by volunteers of the Bull Creek Foundation with no public funding.

Barrow Preserve

The Barrow Preserve is ten acres full of Bull Creek tributaries in northeast Austin, dedicated by David Barrow's family in 1974. There is a small, permanent spring with lovely columbine blooming in the springtime. The trailhead is at Stepdown Cove.

226

CAMP BEN McCULLOCH

FM 1826
Austin, Texas 78737

Located off U.S. 290 about twenty miles from Austin, right across the street from the Salt Lick; About two kilometers east of Driftwood.

Ben McCulloch was one of Austin's first 300 settlers. He arrived in 1835 and was the first cotton farmer in Guadalupe County. Beginning in 1896, the park was the reunion spot of the Confederate Veterans, and in 1904 was opened as United Confederate Veterans Park.

In the southwest corner of the park is a nice swimming hole. A shallow, spring-fed creek with a pebbly bottom feeds the pool. It is entirely dependent on rainfall. Sometimes it is deep enough to dive into, while other times the creek slows to a trickle that you can hop across. The swimming hole has a rope swing and is adjacent to the dance hall.

Camp Ben McCulloch is a good place for a reunion or large event. There aren't many amenities, but it is quiet and picturesque. The park is privately owned and allows camping for $5 for tents and $10 for recreational vehicles. There is a covered and open-air dance pavilion and café. A small playground will entertain the kids.

Camp Ben McCulloch

COMAL RIVER

The World's Shortest River

Greater New Braunfels Chamber of Commerce
Post Office Box 311417
New Braunfels, Texas 78131-1417
(830) 625-2385 or (800) 572-2626
http://www.nbcham.org

The Comal River became famous when Ripley's Believe It or Not featured it as the shortest river in the world. The 2.5-mile river rises from Comal Springs in Landa Park where it fuels a swimming pool, past Schlitterbahn, and meets the Guadalupe River in the heart of downtown New Braunfels. The Comal is more popular with tubers and swimmers, while the Guadalupe is more choppy and rapid and is favored by canoeists. The Comal is one of the largest springs in Texas with 8 million gallons of water flowing through every hour. The water is pure, clear and cold, about 23-29 Celsius.

Spanish explorers 'discovered' Comal Springs in 1691 and found many Indian tribes living there, who referred to it as Conaqueyadesta meaning 'where the river has its source'. In an excerpt from his diary, Espinosa, who accompanied Domingo Ramon's expedition in 1716, described it this way: "Groves of inexpressible beauty are found in this vicinity. The waters of the Guadalupe are clear, crystal and so abundant that it seemed almost incredible to us that its source arose so near. It makes a delightful grove for recreation." Comal is the Spanish word for basin, which somewhat describes the local geography. The springs were later visited in 1764 by French explorer St. Denis, and eventually became a stop on the El Camino Real.

When German immigrants arrived, they called Comal Springs Las Fontanas and purchased the 1,300 acres around it for $1,111. By 1860, they had installed several mills, wool and cotton factories, a paper mill, an ice plant and a brewery along the springs. They also harnessed the water for their public water supply and electrical power.

Comal Springs

From 1896 until the Depression, the park was a private recreational area owned by Harry Landa. The City of New Braunfels then bought the springs in 1946 and turned it into a municipal park.

Landa Park
(830) 608-2164

In New Braunfels is das Leben Shöen
Landa Park has both a man-made Olympic pool and a gorgeous swimming hole that rivals Barton Springs. Both are spring-fed. There is a large bathhouse, built in 1937 by the Works Progress Administration, with showers, dressing rooms and full

> 11:00 A.M.-7:00 P.M. daily
> Ages 3-17 are $2.00
> Adults 16-64 are $3.00
> The admission price lets you into both pools.

amenities. The Olympic pool is surrounded by concrete and grass. Shade is provided by giant umbrellas over picnic tables. There are dedicated lap lanes and a large shallow area. A separate wading pool is quite large and has fantasy mushrooms and other fun things for kids to play with. The swimming hole is L-shaped and has grassy banks on either side which are well-shaded. There are rope swings, wooden platforms in the middle for sunning and diving, a water volleyball court, and a slide that plunges you into the cold water. Lifeguards are on duty at all three pools.

In addition, the Comal River has been dammed in several areas throughout the park, creating small wading pools where you can splash with the geese. Landa Park's amenities have been extremely well-incorporated into the natural landscape. The grounds are beautiful and seem to go on forever.

Landa Park Swimming Hole

229

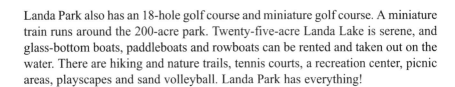

Landa Park also has an 18-hole golf course and miniature golf course. A miniature train runs around the 200-acre park. Twenty-five-acre Landa Lake is serene, and glass-bottom boats, paddleboats and rowboats can be rented and taken out on the water. There are hiking and nature trails, tennis courts, a recreation center, picnic areas, playscapes and sand volleyball. Landa Park has everything!

Hinman Island Park

If you want to swim and not tube, this is the place to do it. Hinman Island Park is a small, quiet stretch between Landa Park and Prince Solms Park. The river is 30 feet wide and 10 feet deep, just right for swimming laps. However, this stretch can get crowded on the weekends. It is free and there is a nice bathhouse.

Prince Solms Park

Tube Chute
(830) 625-4251

Prince Carl of Solms-Braunfels established a German colony on the Comal River in 1845 and named it after Braunfels, Germany, the site of his castle on the Lahn

Hinman Island Park

River. Prince Solms Park was once the site of an early mill and factory founded in 1850 by John F. Torrey (1821-93), a pioneer promoter of Texas industry. He operated a flour, grist and saw mill, a sash door and cotton factory, and the first woolen factory in Texas. With indomitable spirit, he rebuilt the plant after it was destroyed by both tornado and flood.

Admission is $4.00 to the park
$2.50 for the tube, plus a refundable deposit of $2.50

Parking fees are collected on weekends
and holidays from Easter to Labor Day:
$2.00 for cars and motorcycles
$5 for buses and campers

Prince Solms Park is a lot like Barton Springs with a concrete embankment and sidewalks containing the Comal River, and tall shade trees like cottonwoods, oaks and pecans, Spanish moss, and well-manicured grounds. Tropical vegetation lines the shores, and charming footbridges span the river. Prince Solms Park has lots of amenities but still has a very natural feel. The river is clear, blue-green and calm. It can be quite deep in some areas. During the peak of summer it can be very crowded, with everyone tubing the river including families with children, students, and teen-agers with dogs, coolers, and radios in tow. The water is not too cold and is perfect for a leisurely float. You can rent tubes across the street from the park from several vendors. Private property lies on one side of the river. There is plenty of parking. No glass is allowed in the park, and pets must be on a leash. The park also has picnic tables with grills, bicycling, golf, hiking, tennis, and a playscape.

The Tube Chute

The most popular attraction is the Tube Chute, an S-shaped slide down Stinky Falls. The ride is swift, and you should wear tennis shoes or Aquasox to protect your feet from the concrete and because the rocks are covered in algae and can be slippery. You can go through the Tube Chute as many times as you want. The Tube Chute is not recommended for children under 6.

Camp Warnecke
(830) 620-3500

Admission is $2.25

Camp Warnecke is an old-fashioned family resort. A screened pavilion is cooled by water, which trickles down the metal roof. A small dam on the river creates a nice swimming space with rapids for tubing, and the current is strong enough to bring you almost full circle at the dam. There is a bathhouse and cabins. No lifeguard is on duty.

Cypress Bend Park

Cypress Bend is a nice little park on the Guadalupe River at the end of Peace Avenue, across from the fairgrounds. It's a shady park with picnic areas, a playground and swimming in the Guadalupe River.

GUADALUPE RIVER

Greater New Braunfels Chamber of Commerce
Post Office Box 311417
New Braunfels, Texas 78131-1417
(830) 625-2385 or (800) 572-2626

The Guadalupe River was one of the earliest-explored rivers in Texas, and was named for Our Lady of Guadalupe by Spanish explorer Alonzo de Leon in 1689. During 1691-93, Domingo Teran de los Rios, the Spanish Governor of Texas, maintained a colony on the river, and an early Anglo-American settlement, with thirty to forty families living along the banks, formed the boundary of the Power-Hewitson Irish Colony. Near the mouth of the river, historic Victoria was founded. Sixty miles above the headwaters is Gonzales, where the first shot for Texas freedom was fired on October 2, 1835. The Guadalupe River is 250 miles long and supports some of the finest recreation spots in Central Texas.

RIVER ROAD

Take IH35 to Loop 337 (TX 46) and go west from New Braunfels. Take a right at the first stoplight after crossing the river and follow the blue signs.

River Road is a 10.6-mile scenic drive between Loop 337 in New Braunfels and Canyon Lake Dam which crosses the Guadalupe River four times. There is no stopping or parking allowed on the road, so the best way to see this area is from an innertube on the river. Millions of people float this 20-mile stretch of the river between Sattler and New Braunfels every summer. The river flows from Canyon Dam toward the coast, and is *extremely* popular. There are over two dozen outfitters along the shore where you can rent tubes and canoes and buy concessions. Most outfitters offer a shuttle service to bring you back to your point of entry. Styrofoam and glass are prohibited on the river, and officers patrol the waters for safety. Whitewater rafting, canoeing, and kayaking are also

River Road

popular, but tubing seems to be the mode of choice. The river cuts through tall limestone bluffs and towering cypress trees. There are occasional rapids, but for the most part the river flows along lazily. The riverfront property is all privately owned, and there are many places to camp and spend the night, as well as restaurants.

KERRVILLE-SCHREINER STATE PARK

2385 Bandera Highway (TX 173)
Kerrville, Texas 78022
(830) 257-5392
http://www.tpwd.state.tx.us/park/kerrvill/kerrvill.htm

Kerrville Convention and Visitors Bureau
1700 Sidney Baker, Suite 200
Kerrville, Texas 78028
(830) 792-3535

Open year-round 8:00 A.M.-10:00 P.M.
Entrance fee $3.00 daily

Three miles southeast of Kerrville on TX 173.

Kerrville-Schreiner State Park has 517 acres fronting the Guadalupe River on the north side and enjoys the Hill Country as its back yard to the south. Swimming is allowed in the Guadalupe River and is at your own risk. The park also has 7.7 miles of hiking and interpretive trails, picnic sites, a boat ramp and rentals, and camping sites. The park is wheelchair-accessible. A gift shop has souvenirs and concessions for sale. An amphitheater is also available for entertainment. Pets are allowed on leashes.

GUADALUPE RIVER STATE PARK

3350 Park Road 31
Bulverde, Texas 78163-3608
(830) 438-2656
http://www.tpwd.state.tx.us/park/guadalup/guadalup.htm

Admission: $4.00 per person
Seniors $2.00
Children under 12 free

Take IH35 south to TX 46 in New Braunfels and go west about 40 miles.

Thanks to a handful of canoeists who lobbied the Texas Legislature in the mid-1970s, this 20-mile stretch of the upper Guadalupe River is now preserved as a state park. As you approach the park you drive through the scrubby Hill Country terrain dotted with live oak and juniper trees. The closer you get to the river, the lusher the vegetation becomes. Once you enter the park you drive through three different camping areas to get to the river itself, a jewel in the heart of the Hill Country. A large parking lot leads to a sloping, grassy bank overlooking the water. The hill is dotted with picnic tables and ends at a sandy beach at the waterfront. The river makes a wide bend through limestone cliffs and shady cypress trees to form an ideal swimming spot. The cliffs have numerous tiny caves which are home to a variety of wildlife. A small series of rapids empties into a calm, glassy pool which is deep enough to swim in over your head. Other water sports are popular on other sections of the river, such as water-skiing and canoeing. Concessions and rest rooms are available. Pets are allowed on leashes.

Guadalupe State Park

COURTESY OF TEXAS DEPARTMENT OF TRANSPORTATION

CASCADE CAVERNS

100 Villita Street
San Antonio, Texas 78205
(210) 226-2970

> Memorial Day through Labor Day 9:00 A.M.-6:00 P.M.
> Winter 10:00 A.M.-4:00 P.M.

Fourteen miles northwest of San Antonio, Exit 543 off IH 10.

Since 1932, tours of this unique cave structure on the Guadalupe River have been given to the public. The cave is well-lit and easily navigated, and has large caverns and natural pools, including a 90-foot underground waterfall. The pool levels fluctuate with rainfall and may be dry during periods of drought. One-hour guided tours are offered every thirty minutes. Although you cannot swim in the underground pools, the resort has a man-made swimming pool. It also has a dance pavilion and camping facilities.

LOUISE HAYS PARK

Greater Boerne Chamber of Commerce
1 Main Plaza
Boerne, Texas 78006
(830) 249-8000
http://www.stic.net/users/texian/boerne/recreat.htm

> Free
> 7:30 A.M.-11:00 P.M.

Thompson Drive west of Sidney Baker South in Boerne.

Louise Hays Park is a lovely little spot in the heart of downtown Boerne. The Guadalupe River flows through the park and has been dammed to form a natural swimming pool. The river bottom is rocky. Sloping, grassy banks are dotted with picnic tables, gazebos, and swans. A footbridge offers access to Tranquility Island where you can swim and picnic under tall cypress trees.

236

MAX STARCKE PARK
Business 183
Seguin, Texas

This glorious municipal park, operated by the City of Seguin, is beautiful and rich with the area's history. Built by the National Youth Administration in 1937 on the banks of the Guadalupe River, this large park has small rolling hills which are grassy and densely shaded by the most pecan trees you have ever seen. Other attractions include standard and miniature golf courses, playgrounds, picnic areas, volleyball, and basketball. The vegetation is lush with vines and caladiums along the riverbanks. Numerous picnic tables can be found right on the banks and throughout the park. Small motorized boats operate upstream.

The best swimming can be found behind Saffold Dam. A series of steps lead down to a concrete dock. It is recessed enough to offer privacy from the rest of the park. The river here is glassy, green and calm. Lap swimmers can journey back and forth in the rectangular space between the shores, which is quite deep. You may also dive from the dock.

Saffold Dam is named for William Saffold who owned the park land in the mid-1800s. Saffold Dam was originally a natural rock outcropping, which was typical of dams built in the late nineteenth century. The dam was first improved by Henry Troell in the late 1800s when he added more rock to it to raise the water level and power a cotton gin. Troell was a native of Germany who immigrated to Seguin sometime prior to 1860. He served in the Confederate Army and married Johanna Wohler in 1872. A successful freighting business enabled him to invest in several local properties and enterprises, including the Saffold Dam and gristmill. He expanded the hydroelectrical capabilities of the dam and in 1890 provided the City of Seguin with its first water and electrical utility system. The City of Seguin bought Troell's property in 1907 to further develop hydroelectricity, and subsequent improvements have led to the establishment of a hydroelectric plant on the south side of the river.

Max Starcke Park

HAMILTON POOL

(512) 264-2740

Take TX 71 west and go south on Hamilton Pool Road (FM 3238) for about 13 miles. About thirty minutes from Austin. $5.00 admission per vehicle.

W hen I think of the typical, old-fashioned swimming hole, Hamilton Pool immediately comes to mind.

Hamilton Pool formed when a cave over an underground river collapsed thousands of years ago, creating a waterfall and swimming grotto. Hamilton Pool is an excellent example of the typical geology of the Balcones Canyonlands and the Edwards Plateau. The pool is on the convergence point of the Pedernales River and Hamilton Creek in southwest Travis County.

There is evidence of Tonkawa Indians around the area, and it is a very old swimming hole. Land grants from the state and the H. Reimer family preserved the area. Hamilton Pool is named for Andrew Jackson Hamilton, a Texas State Representative, Attorney General, U.S Representative, tenth Governor of Texas and a noted anti-secessionist.

One hundred paved parking spaces are available at the ranger's station. From there it is a short hike down to the swimming hole. The trail travels under shady juniper and mesquite trees. Watch out for prickly pears! You may see armadillos, wren, squirrels and swallows along the way. A limestone outcropping frames the circular swimming hole. Hamilton Creek flows over the cliff and falls 60 feet into the pool. There is a large rock under the falls where the water splashes in a shower. The shoreline is made up of rocky limestone and extends across one side of the pool.

COURTESY OF TEXAS DEPARTMENT OF TRANSPORTATION

Hamilton Pool

There is minimal shade around the pool. The pool closes to swimmers occasionally when naturally occurring bacteria levels are too high. There is no drinking water; pets, glass, fires and cooking are prohibited, but the park does have rest rooms and picnic areas. Guided tours are available by reservation.

The Westcave Preserve
(830) 825-3442

Open weekends with tours every two hours
beginning at 10:00 A.M. and ending at 4:00 P.M.

At FM 3238 and FM 962l, 15 miles west of TX 71 near the intersection with U.S. 281.

The Westcave Preserve is a thirty-one-acre park with cypress, moss, ferns, orchids, travertine pools, a waterfall and a cave. There is no swimming allowed.

KRAUSE SPRINGS

Post Office Box 114
Spicewood, Texas 78669
(830) 693-4181

Monday through Thursday, children 4-11: $2.00, 12 and up $2.50
Friday, Saturday and Sunday, children 4-11: $2.50, 12 and up $3.00
Overnight camping for children 4-13: $3.00
14 and up: $6
RV spaces $3.00 extra
No pets
Open year-round
Available by reservation for weddings, receptions, company parties,
reunions, etc.

Take TX 71 west about seven miles past the Pedernales River. Turn right on Spur 191 at the Exxon station (it really sneaks up on you) and go about one mile. The road curves sharply to the left and you'll see a sign and driveway on your right just after you complete the curve. Turn right at the red arrow and sign for Krause Springs, then stay left at the fork in the road. It's 34 miles west of Austin.

Krause Springs is one of my favorite places on the entire planet. It is so wonderful, I was tempted to exclude it from this book and keep it all to myself. But that would not have been fair, so...

As you approach Krause Springs, you travel down a dirt road through a meadow full of pecan trees, wildflowers, and peaceful cows. A volleyball net and grassy areas wait for someone to use them. Then you see foreboding signs about signing liability releases and surveillance cameras. Don't be put off by these warnings.

Elton and Jane Krause own and operate Krause Springs, which is on the National Historical Register as an undisturbed midden, or Indian burial ground. Elton Krause used to live in Austin until he retired from the Austin American States-man. The Krauses bought the land, which had been in the family for two generations, from an aunt in the 1950s. The aunt kept a hog farm there on 115 acres. The first thing Elton did was to remove the hog pens. Then he built the swimming pool, doing 90% of it himself. One thing led to another, and the grounds today are filled with his handiwork. He has made all the tables and gazebos by hand and says you can pick out his first table and see the progression of his abilities. Eventually the Krauses opened their land to the public and built up the campgrounds. A Texas Monthly article in the 1980s listed it as one of the best swimming holes in Texas. Elton and his sons continually improve and build on the grounds. The landscaping is all done by them, as well as the rock picnic benches. They went with concrete because people would move the wooden tables together in clumps and he'd have to rearrange them each time. Elton officially retired in 1994 but says he's busier now than when he was working for the newspaper.

Krause Springs Swimming Pool

The 70 x 20-foot swimming pool is just below the well, which is the source of the springs. It pumps at a rate of 70 gallons per minute. It is beautifully made with stonework, a diving board, and a concrete patio. Depths range from deep enough for diving to shallow enough to wade in. The water is blue-green, very clean and natural, and it reflects the sky and trees beautifully. The spring trickles out from the well on the shallow end, goes through the pool into canals, flows over a cliff and cascades 25 feet into a waterfall into the lower pool, a natural swimming hole. The waterfall has changed since a portion of the overhang broke off in 1985. The fallen rock is still in the middle of the water. The lower pool is deepest, about eight feet, beneath the falls. There are numerous boulders in the water, so no diving is allowed. Flat limestone rocks have water rushing over them which pools into a great swimming hole with a rope swing, caves, and beautiful, mossy cliffs. To get down to the swimming hole, there is a new set of wide limestone flagstones, a great improvement over the old, rickety, steep stairs.

Krause Springs Swimming Hole

Krause Springs is so quiet and still, you can hear the birds, crickets and cicadas chirping. When I visited on a Friday, there were only five other people there. It is easy to get spoiled by having it all to yourself, and it is so intimate that it feels full when just a handful of people are around. The giant wind chimes, built in Austin, are some of the largest in the country. They sound like cathedral bells and resonate all over the grounds. Lush, green, tropical plants like taro and elephant ears are growing all over the park. Magnificent trees such as cottonwoods, pecans, cypress, and oaks preside over the park. Some of the cypress trees are estimated to be over 1,000 years old, and the live oaks are 100-200 years old. Dozens of butterflies fly through in the spring and fall migrations. I think Krause Springs has done an admirable job of incorporating man-made elements into the natural world. The result is a beautiful park that is obviously well-loved and cared for.

Krause Springs also has camping for those who want to spend a few days. There are three tiers of campsites with the bottom level backing up against Lake Travis. Boaters can travel up to the boat ramp at the end of Spur 191 and ride to the campground. There are many picnic areas, rest rooms, and grills. Proper swimwear is required. Loud music is prohibited. Elton's policy regarding trash? The sign says it all: My hired hand just quit!

LADYBIRD JOHNSON METROPOLITAN PARK

Fredericksburg Chamber of Commerce
106 North Adams Street
Fredericksburg, Texas 78624
(830) 997-6523
http://www.fredericksburgtexas.net/fun.htm

> Open dawn to dusk

South of Fredericksburg on Hwy. 16 about 3.5 miles.

This gem of a park is operated by the City of Fredericksburg and is located just south of downtown. It has typical Hill Country terrain with scrubby oaks, grassy hills, and, of course, wildflowers. At 190 acres, Ladybird Johnson Park has a little bit of everything. A small lake allows boating, canoeing, and pedal boats. A creek has been dammed and forms a nice swimming hole with friendly turtles. The water is shallow and has a gently sloping grassy bank on one side, and scrubby wilderness on the other side. Ladybird Johnson Park also has a ballpark, camping facilities, a modern playscape, covered group and individual picnic areas with grills, an 18-hole golf course, and tennis, volleyball, and badminton courts.

LAMPASAS

Lampasas Chamber of Commerce
501 East Second Street
Lampasas, Texas 76550
(512) 556-5172

L ampasas is like a giant sieve with springs just oozing out of the ground everywhere. These springs brought the first settlers to the area and put Lampasas on the map for its famous mineral spas. Several legends surround the springs, including one about members of a 1735 Spanish expedition who were travelling through the Lampasas area and were parched. They were on their way back to San Antonio after establishing a mission in San Saba. The area had been under a severe drought, and the party moved hopefully toward the Colorado and Lampasas rivers, which they'd heard about from earlier expeditions. Unfortunately, they found them dry as a bone. The party was without hope and their animals were dying. The resident priest, Saint Juan, threw his crucifix to the ground and cursed "This horrible country!" The legend goes that a spring erupted right there and other springs popped up where the other party members had spread out in search of water. The party was saved. However, the curse the priest incurred made the waters sulphurous and stinky.

Spaniard Bustillo y Ceballos probably did stop in Lampasas for a rest in 1732. The name Lampasas was earlier given to the river by the Spanish Aquayo Expedition in 1721. Supposedly, it was named for a town in Mexico that also had beautiful springs.

In 1853, Moses Hughes, who lived in Williamson County, heard about the curative powers of the medicinal springs in Lampasas and took his wife, who was suffering from a mysterious illness, to try them out. They stayed in a tent near the springs, and Mrs. Hughes's recovery was miraculous. In three weeks she had completely recovered. Word spread and Lampasas became known as a healing place to live, even called 'The Saratoga of the South'.

As word spread about the famous Lampasas springs, it became a stage stop and major tourist attraction. John Hanna, a member of a locally prominent family, formed the Central Texas Town Company to promote the springs. In the 1880s, he built a bathhouse around Hanna Springs (which now bears his name). A huge resort was constructed that held operas, conventions, dances, and entertainment. Hanna spent $200,000, which was a lot of money in those days, and expanded the bathing pools and dressing rooms that were separated by gender. There were offices, reception areas, concessions, and an orchestra pit all on the first floor! Above these rooms was a large convention hall built without central support. It was a significant architectural accomplishment for the day. The 1892 Democratic Convention met there and nominated Grover Cleveland for president and James Hogg for governor. Both won. Hanna Springs later closed in the early 1900s.

Hancock Springs

Off U.S. 281

> 11:00 A.M.-6:00 P.M. Tuesday through Saturday
> 2:00-6:00 P.M. Sunday
> Closed Monday

The Park Hotel became Hanna Springs' chief competition when it was built in 1883. The Park Hotel had 200 rooms on 200 acres in the 700 block of South Spring Street. Hancock Springs, named for the landowner, was the chief attraction. It was quite fashionable to take the mineral baths at the Park Hotel. A car pulled by a mule would shuttle folks between the train depot and the hotel. Hydraulic rams supplied water to the hotel, which was built on a hill, and pipes pumped the mineral water to the hotel rooms for hot steam baths, which was quite a luxury. The hotel later housed a college but it burned in 1895. A historical marker commemorating the hotel is located in the park.

Hancock Springs

Today, Hancock Springs is dammed to form a swimming pool and a separate, circular wading pool. The water is very sulfurous and stinks like rotten eggs, but you really do get used to it and it's so good for you. The pool has a natural rock bottom but is surrounded by concrete like a man-made pool. It is the best of both worlds. Hancock Springs is also the city's water supply.

Adjacent to Hancock Springs is the Hostess House and Green Frog Tea Room. The Tea Room used to be the social center of Lampasas, and has been lovingly restored to its former elegance. It is a fine place to get married, hold a prom, or have a family reunion.

W.M. Brook Park

W.M. Brook Park is 109 acres on Sulphur Creek. Located across the street from Hancock Springs, Brook Park has picnic tables with grills along the creek, playgrounds, and an 18-hole golf course. Cottonwood trees provide shade and the grounds are well-manicured. The Ruth F. Eakin amphitheater is a lovely place to watch a play. A tributary of the creek runs between the audience and stage, and a grassy hillside faces the stage. There is a kiosk located in the park with brochures and maps about local attractions. The pedestrian suspension bridge was inspired by a similar one near this location at the turn of the century, dedicated to citizens of Lampasas and commemorating the bicentennial.

W.M. Brook Park

Old Hancock Springs

2nd Street deadends at the railroad tracks. Go left on Hackberry Street and about half a block later you'll see a field on your left. The springs are set back from the road.

The Old Hancock Springs is a magical place. I could gaze into the water all day. It is somehow enchanting. With amazingly blue-green water, tiny bubbles rise to the surface while aquatic plants sway to and fro. Blue dragonflies dart around. You half expect to see a mermaid swimming by in the iridescent water! A circular rock wall surrounds the springs. The old springs used to be a bustling place. At the Visitors Center on 2nd Street you can view historical pictures of the springs. Lampasas hopes to eventually restore the springs and surrounding grounds. It currently sits in the middle of a vacant field.

Old Hancock Springs

As this book goes to press, Lampasas is building a new municipal pool in the Hanna Springs area on North Street. Texas Parks and Wildlife has issued a grant which will be matched by the LCRA and the City of Lampasas. The unique environmental and archeological factors of Lampasas will be considered in the construction of the pool. The initial design is for a sloped pool with a wading area gradually deepening to nine feet. Underwater lights and a heating element will be included for year-round use. The pool will have a modern water slide and a raindrop fountain. The entire facility will be 7,000 square-feet, including a deck area, a large bathhouse and staff office, sand volleyball courts, hiking trails, a large parking lot, professional landscaping, and an open-air pavilion housing basketball and volleyball courts.

LLANO RIVER
Land of Legend and Lure

Llano County Chamber of Commerce
700 Bessemer
Llano, Texas 78643
(915) 247-5354

L lano is the deer capital of Texas because they are so profuse in the Llano Basin. It's no wonder when they have the spring-fed Llano River to help sustain them. 'Llano' means plain. The Llano River was originally named 'Rio do los Chanas' (Chanas being a tribe of the Tonkawas) which is phonetically similar to Llano and eventually changed through misuse. Llano is home to Llanite, a brown granite with blue crystals and pink feldspar which is very rare and found only in this area. Rock hunting for quartz, granite, gneiss, flint, schist, feldspar, limestone and llanite is a popular pastime.

The Slab

On FM 3404, 1.5 miles west of FM 1431 in Kingsland.

The Slab is a spot in the Llano River where the water runs over large granite outcroppings and sandy beaches have formed. It is a popular swimming, tubing and picnicking site. The water is perfect for both wading and deeper swimming. The Slab is open to the public, but not maintained as a city park. Therefore, there is no drinking water or rest rooms.

The Slab

MCKINNEY FALLS STATE PARK

5808 McKinney Falls Parkway
Austin, Texas 78744
(512) 243-1643 Smith Visitors' Center
http://www.tpwd.state.tx.us/park/mckinney/mckinney.htm

$2.00 entry fee for everyone over age 12

From Austin, take U.S. 183 south 13 miles to McKinney Falls Parkway. Just ten short minutes from downtown Austin.

Often overlooked since it is so close to Austin, McKinney Falls is perfect for an afternoon picnic or a quick trip to get away for the day. McKinney Falls State Park is in the center of an early Texas land grant that originally fell within the impresario contract of a Texan hero, Ben Milan. Ten acres of the land were transferred to Santiago Del Valle who at that time was Secretary of the Mexican government, and who had previously served in the Mexican Congress. In 1835, Del Valle sold a portion of his land to Michael Menard who helped found the town of Galveston. Thomas F. McKinney was one of his business associates and bought the Del Valle grant in 1839. His family occupied the land but sold almost all of it off by the time of his death in 1873. Some of the land remained agricultural and became the City of Del Valle, the north tract became urbanized, and the remainder is preserved in the park.

McKinney was also one of Austin's first 300 colonists. He settled on Onion Creek and became a breeder of racehorses. You can still see the remains of the trainer's cabin in the park. The cabin was built in the early 1850s and served as quarters for John Van Hagen, McKinney's thoroughbred horse trainer, until Hagen moved to New York in 1873. There were nearby exercise and training areas. McKinney also owned a steamboat that he used to take to Mexico to trade horses.

249

McKinney Falls

McKinney Falls is at the confluence of Onion and Williamson creeks. The water changes from calm and quiet to rapids and falls depending on rainfall. The swimming hole is similar to Hamilton Pool with a large circular pool underneath a rock overhang. The swimming hole is also closed occasionally due to pollution.

In addition to swimming, 640-acre McKinney Falls State Park has several trails for hiking and bicycling. The 3.7-mile Onion Creek Trail is paved for hikers and bicyclists. Swimming is allowed in Onion Creek but is at your own risk. The three-mile Homestead Trail is unpaved and is designed for mountain biking and rough hiking. There are shorter interpretive trails, such as the Smith Rockshelter Trail that leads to an Indian rock shelter. A 3.5-mile paved trail runs along Onion Creek and passes the upper falls. Another 3.75-mile interpretive trail begins near the visitors' center and runs under huge limestone bluffs. Yet another trail is unmarked and crosses the main falls. It also passes the historical McKinney homestead and flour mill from the 1820s and then goes on about a mile through cedar and mesquite.

McKinney Falls State Park has camping, picnicking, and a variety of terrain and wildlife, including half-brown, half-black rock squirrels. Pets on leash are permitted. Wheelchair-accessible.

PEDERNALES FALLS STATE PARK

RR 1, Box 450
Johnson City, Texas 78636
(210) 868-7304
http://www.tpwd.state.tx.us/park/pedernal/pedernal.htm

From Austin, take U.S. 290 west for about 30 miles, then turn north on RM 3232 for about seven miles. Or go east via FM 2766 about eight miles. About forty-five minutes from Austin.

Pronounced 'Pur-da-nal-es' by locals, this 4,800-acre park is a wonderful place to explore. Massive, chalky white limestone outcroppings characterize Pedernales Falls, with the Pedernales River flowing over the wide bluffs and cascading down through the park. This is a scenic park with great views of the Pedernales River, numerous streams, and dramatic canyons and bluffs.

Until the early 1970s you could swim in the falls. Today, you can swim in other parts of the Pedernales River which are accessible from many points along the hiking trails. There is a great variety of pools, from shallow wading areas to holes deep enough to dive in. There are multiple miniature waterfalls and tide pools throughout the park. Swimming is generally allowed one mile above and two miles below the falls. The falls are best viewed from a scenic overlook at the north end of the park.

The 7.5-mile Wolf Mountain trail is popular with hikers and mountain-bikers. Another 6.5-mile, less-defined trail is across the river via a trammel crossing, just below the main camping area. There are other small trails throughout the park that focus on equestrian riding, bicycling, and nature.

Pedernales Falls

In addition to great swimming, Pedernales Falls has camping, picnicking, showers, and concessions. Pets on leash are okay. Oak and juniper trees populate the park, and it is a consistently good place to see monarch butterflies during their spring and fall migrations.

COURTESY OF TEXAS DEPARTMENT OF TRANSPORTATION

251

SALADO

Salado Chamber of Commerce
Post Office Box 849
Salado, Texas 76571
(254) 947-5040
http://www.lone-star.net/mall/txtrails/salado.htm

Salado, which means 'salty', is an old Tawakoni Indian settlement, although Paleo-Indian tribes were there even earlier. Bustillo y Ceballos probably stopped here, too. Originally called Salado Springs, it was settled in 1851 by Archibald Willingham and became a well-known stage stop on the Chisholm Trail. A stone wall was erected around the springs to keep the cattle out, since the springs supplied water for the town. Today it is a large, wide swimming hole behind a dam located downtown. One hundred years ago, the springs gushed so strongly that they produced a five-foot fountain. Between 1851 and 1868, eleven mills were built in Salado around the springs.

W.A. Pace Park

Take exit 284 from IH35, go right at the first stop sign, cross Main Street, and continue on into the park.

This park was given to the people of Salado by John W. and Elizabeth Pace Hodges in honor of their parents, William Alexander Pace and Sarah Jane Hankons Pace, on August 16, 1936. The land was once at the northwest corner of a 100-acre tract set aside by Colonel E.C. Robertson in 1859 to be sold to benefit Salado College. The property was purchased by a man named Stinnett who resold it to Pace in 1888. Pace was a Virginian who came to Texas to farm and had 17 children with his wife. During the Civil War, Pace Park was a safe haven to Company G.

Pace Park is a very simple park with few amenities. The main attractions are Salado Creek and lots of open, grassy space. The creek is shallow and suitable for wading. There are picnic tables and gazebos on the gently sloped shores, and private property is on the opposite side. The picnic tables are built of natural, uncut rocks from the creekbed. Cottonwoods provide shade. A covered pavilion has ceiling fans, a fireplace, and electricity.

252

A succession of fine boiling springs which from year's end to year's end send up great volumes of pure, clean water and which in their course to the Leon River cross many rapids and form many pools of rare beauty and utility. The certain supply of water and swiftness of the stream makes the Salado one of the best streams in the state for water power, and it is only a matter of time until it will be utilized..

Anonymous

COURTESY OF TEXAS DEPARTMENT OF TRANSPORTATION

Salado Springs

SAN GABRIEL RIVER

Take IH35 Business (Austin Avenue) north into Georgetown. After crossing the bridge over the South San Gabriel River, turn right. There is another access road a few hundred yards down the road.

Georgetown Springs is located within San Gabriel Park. Williamson County abounds with springs and has a very old history of occupation. Turkeys, chickens, mountain lions, fish, alligators, otters and beavers all called this place home at one time. This park has been used for large meetings and gatherings since at least 1879, and Santa Fe's expedition spent the night there in 1841.

The South San Gabriel River flows through beautiful San Gabriel Park and creates a wonderful swimming hole, and one of my favorites. The river has been dammed and creates a serene area for swimming. It is wide and perfect for swimming laps. The water is green and the banks are lush with vegetation; tall cottonwood and pecan trees provide wonderful shade. Ducks and fish willingly share the water with swimmers. There are no lifeguards on duty. The rush of the water spilling over the dam is a nice sound.

San Gabriel River Dam

The park is situated in downtown Georgetown within walking distance of the historical district. It is quiet, peaceful, and well-manicured. Lush flower gardens with fountains and benches for courting can be found throughout the park. There are covered picnic tables with grills, Frisbee golf, a playground, horseshoe pits, and volleyball courts, as well as numerous ballfields and open spaces. A footbridge connects the park to the opposite bank. The park also has a recreation center with lots of amenities, as well as a municipal swimming pool (see Georgetown Municipal Pools, page 203). The three-mile, concrete Pickett hike and bike trail begins at the south end of Blue Hole and leads to Chautauqua Park. There are many scenic overlooks of the river along the trail.

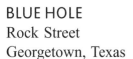

BLUE HOLE
Rock Street
Georgetown, Texas

North of downtown Georgetown off TX 81 and Austin Avenue at the end of Rock Street. Turn onto 2nd Street just below the South San Gabriel River Bridge.

Blue Hole reminds me of Barton Springs before the concrete retaining wall and amenities were installed. It has picturesque blue-green water which cuts through the San Gabriel River valley. The park is primitive, but the city has tried to keep it in its natural state and still accommodate the heavy traffic. There are two short dams that divide the water into sections. Behind the first dam is a deep and wide pool where people dive from the surrounding cliffs and float on rafts and tubes. Just beneath the first dam the water flows over rock outcroppings forming two gushing waterfalls and small rapids for playing in. There is a smaller dam below that with a shallow, but still wide, area to swim and float in. One side of the shore is rocky and pebbled, and the other is covered in vegetation. There is minimal parking and no stopping on the one-way road that parallels the river. A small dirt lot up the road holds some cars, but otherwise you just have to park and walk from neighboring streets. A few picnic tables dot the sloping hillside facing the pool.

Blue Hole

SAN MARCOS RIVER
Los Fontanas

San Marcos Convention and Visitors Bureau
Post Office Box 2310
San Marcos, Texas 78667
(512) 393-5900 or (888) 200-5620
(512) 396-6080 Parks and Recreation
http://ci.san-marcos.tx.us/

San Marcos is about 26 miles south of Austin and 45 miles north of San Antonio on IH35.

Hays County abounds with springs, and for that reason attracted many early settlers to the area. San Marcos is believed to be the oldest continuously inhabited site in North America, and Clovis Indian artifacts have been found there dating back 12,000 years. Spearheads have been found which evidence Paleo-Indian presence at least 8,000 years ago. The first Europeans to see San Marcos Springs were likely members of the expedition of Espinosa-Olivares-Aguirre in 1709. They estimated that there were 200 springs in the area. They found grapes, nuts, hemp and fish here, plus deer, bears, wolves, foxes, mountain lions and turkeys. Naturally, the robust spring supported abundant wildlife, even alligators! The river was 'discovered' on St. Mark's Day, hence the name. San Marcos Springs was called Canocanayesatetlo, meaning warm water, by

San Marcos River

Spaniards. The springs were anything but warm, with a constant temperature of 72°F. In 1755, the San Xavier missions were moved to San Marcos from Milam County because of a drought there. At that time, the water pressure was so great that McClintock described it as "so strong is the ebullition of the spring that the water is thrown two or three feet above the surface of the stream." Settlers harnessed the power of the spring for power plants, mills and ice factories. Pioneers William Moon and Mike Sessom made a permanent settlement at the springs, and in 1851 General Ed Burleson, William Lindsey and Eli Merriman bought the adjacent land and laid out the town of San Marcos. In 1867, San Marcos became a stop on the El Camino Real which stretched from Nacogdoches to Mexico.

Pouring forth millions of gallons of clear, icy water daily, San Marcos Springs feeds the San Marcos River and the 1,380 square-mile area into which it drains. The immense springs rise at the Balcones escarpment, a geologic fault line that slices across the state, separating upland from lowland.

Aquarena Springs

One Aquarena Springs Drive
San Marcos, Texas
(512) 245-7575 or (800) 999-9767
http://www.sanmarcostexas.com/tourism/default.htm

> Open year-round, daily 9:30 A.M.-6:00 P.M.

Aquamaid

Aquarena Springs is primarily the source of the San Marcos River, rising from hundreds of fissures under Spring Lake. A Spanish mission was established on the site, and later became the homestead of General Burleson and Eli Merriman. For many years, Aquarena Springs was a resort and entertainment park with boat rides and features such as mermaids. The 'Aquamaids' would wear oxygen tanks to eat pickles and drink Dr. Pepper underwater. Attracted by the scenic beauty of the area, A.B. Rogers started the park in 1926 and developed it into a popular tourist attraction. The park had a large hotel, a Swiss sky ride, glass- bottom boat rides, and a submarine theater with mermaid performers. By far the most popular attraction was Ralph, the Swimming Pig. Ralph swam around Aquarena Springs performing tricks and dives until the early 1990s when he retired.

Today Aquarena Springs is being converted into a wetlands project developed by the Southwest Texas University life sciences department. The park has a natural aquarium with endangered species that can be found only in the San Marcos River and archeology exhibits with artifacts dating back 12,000 years. Some of the original buildings still stand, such as Dr. Merriman's log cabin, General Burleson's home, and a 100 year-old gristmill that still operates. Ralph the Swimming

Ralph the Swimming Pig

Pig no longer performs, but you can still take glassbottom boat rides and view the bubbling springhead of the San Marcos River. Aquarena Springs has a restaurant and other concessions, a gift shop and picnic sites. The grounds are tropically landscaped. Picturesque swans sail over Spring Lake, and fountains create water sculptures. Aquarena Springs also has a golf course and conference center. The original Park Hotel still stands and has been totally renovated. The hotel has a man-made swimming pool.

Submarine Theater

The San Marcos River begins in earnest just across the street from the Southwest Texas University campus where a waterfall empties into a lagoon, then winds through the campus, residential back yards and city parks. The San Marcos River is shallow, steady, clear and cold. In some places it is full of duckweed, and caladiums and tall shade trees line the banks. If you want to swim distances, try the waterfall at the head of the river, or a spot near the Clear Springs Apartment complex across the street from campus on Aquarena Springs Drive. Swimming, snorkeling, canoeing, kayaking, tubing and Scuba diving are all permitted. Plant and animal life abound as the San Marcos River is one of the world's most fertile. White-tailed deer, doves, quails, squirrels and foxes can occasionally be seen along the banks.

Sewell Park is part of the Southwest Texas University campus on the banks of the river. Named for S.M. Froggy Sewell, a math professor who liked to swim the river, this park is technically for the use of students, faculty and staff only, though

The Park Hotel on Opening Day
April 22, 1929

258

it overlaps with city parks. Students lounge in their bathing suits and study on the banks. The river is easily accessed from a concrete bank.

The San Marcos parks system consists of twelve different units, each with a unique theme such as history, sports, nature study, ecology and picnicking. The San Marcos River Walkway winds alongside the river and through three different parks, and a hiking trail extends all the way to IH35.

City Park is located behind Strahan Coliseum, on a dead-end road off of University Drive. City Park features eight acres of park land with picnic tables and grills, a playground and basketball courts. Concrete steps lead down to the river's edge for swimming, and there is excellent shade along the banks. City Park is a popular point of origin for tubing excursions. Most people float to the dam at Rio Vista Park and take a river taxi back to the starting point. The entire trip is about an hour and a half. About 23 miles of the San Marcos River are suitable for tubing, beginning at City Park and ending at CR 199. The river is virtually pollution free, scenic, and has a constant temperature. Tubes can be rented from the Lion's Club in City Park ((512) 392-8255) which provides a river taxi to pick you up at the end of your trip.

The next access point is at **Juan Veramendi Plaza** on C.M. Allen Parkway behind the Chamber of Commerce. The river here is clear and has reeds that sway like mermaid hair. Lots of people just park, take their tubes right down to the water and jump in. The banks are grassy and dotted with picnic sites with grills, basketball and tennis courts, concessions, and information about the endangered species living in the San Marcos River. Catalpa, oak and pecan trees offer great shade along the banks. The park is lush and green, with sloping banks that lead to concrete landing areas for sunbathing and ladders for climbing in and out of the water.

Rio Vista Park, on Cheatham Street north of C.M. Allen Parkway, is the largest park in the chain and has a municipal swimming pool. The pool is L-shaped and has a separate, circular wading pool with a fountain. The main pool has a low diving board. Rio Vista Pool is fairly new, built in 1974. There is a nice bathhouse, and grassy areas surround the pool. The park has covered pavilions, tennis courts, picnic sites, a playground, a jogging trail, volleyball, and access to the river under tall cypress trees.

Open 1:00-6:00 P.M. every day.
Thursday is family night.
Admission for kids under 14 is 50¢, $1.00 for adults.
    Kids under seven must have an adult with

Rio Vista Pool

McAllister Park is an old Girl Scout Camp, just west of IH35 and C.M. Allen Parkway. It's a woodsy and shady park with the river cutting through it. There is tubing over a short dam into a shallow area. There are picnic tables as well as a restaurant and bar next door.

Cheatham Street Dam, near Hopkins and Cheatham streets, has free tubing and swimming below the dam. A few picnic tables have been set up under good shade trees. A restaurant and bar are located next door.

Cheatham Street Dam

Children's Park also has an Olympic-size pool. The best feature of the park is a giant playscape completely designed by children. It is quite a feat of imagination. There are also tennis and basketball courts, and soccer, baseball, softball and football fields.

Ramon Macias Park is the closest park to IH35, and has tennis courts and baseball fields.

SAN SABA RIVER

San Saba Chamber of Commerce
County Courthouse
San Saba, Texas 78677
(915) 372-5141
http://www.texas-on-line.com/graphic/sansaba.htm#parks

S an Saba was settled by Anglos in 1839. The city is bordered on the north and east by the Colorado River, and the San Saba River bisects it. San Saba County has more than 500 miles of running streams, more than any other city in Texas. Brine Springs supported the C.S.A. Salt Works on the Colorado River. Brine Springs was used as an infirmary and health resort, and increased operations during the Civil War for the men, Calvary horses and mule teams. To pump the brine from the springs a horse operated a lift that filled troughs on a forty-five-foot high scaffold. Cedar boughs placed in the troughs concentrated the brine, which filtered into iron kettles and boiled a bushel of salt out of fifty bushels of brine.

Pecan trees abound and San Saba is famous for this crop..

Mill Pond Park

Off of U.S. 190 on South Thomas Stewart Drive.

Open 7:00 A.M.-11:00 P.M.

Before Mill Pond Park became a municipal park, it was the first waterworks in San Saba. In 1875, Guy Risien built a rock and brush dam across Mill Creek to operate a hydraulic dam that he used to water his own garden and provide water to a few neighbors. Most of the original dam still stands. Risien installed a water wheel, a valve and piston pump, and three-inch water mains. Risien also helped the county keep water troughs at the courthouse full. Risien later sold his waterworks to John H. Brown, who built a gristmill. Later the city water system housed its machinery there. Mill Pond still provides water to the residents of San Saba.

Today, Mill Pond Park is a lovely park with a spring-fed lake and a man-made swimming pool. A waterfall cascades over rocks into ferns, moss, canna and caladiums. The water flows under a bridge then winds through the park. There are picnic sites with grills. The ideal spot is the table next to the waterfall, with the sound of the rushing water and the beautiful flowers. It is an idyllic spot for a picnic, a marriage proposal, or a romantic date.

Seven-million gallons of water pump through the lake daily. The pond water looks like Hancock Springs, with tiny bubbles rising to the surface. The water is so clear you can see the water plants deep down. Ducks and geese paddle by, and many tributaries meander through the park. The seventy-one acre park also has baseball fields, a group pavilion, tennis courts, a playground, basketball courts, a running track and nature trails. The city has received a grant from Texas Parks and Wildlife to expand and renovate the park to add more hiking trails, a sandy beach, and more camping spaces.

Mill Pond Park

The municipal swimming pool is located within Mill Pond Park and is beautifully landscaped. A semi-shallow end slopes toward the deep end. There is a separate, rectangular wading pool and a large bathhouse. The pool is surrounded by a wooden deck and concrete.

Risien Park

On the eastern edge of the city on U.S. 190.

7:00 A.M.-10:00 P.M.

Risien Park was a gift from E.E. Risien and the LCRA to the people of San Saba in 1987. The park is bordered by the San Saba River. A section of the river has been cemented in for swimming. The water is slightly chalky. A rope swing provides fun in the deep end. A bench overlooks the pool and there are stairs leading down to water. Upstream there is a small dam with a waterfall leading into a wide pool.

262

The park has picnic tables with grills, a playground, a pavilion, a golf course, and volleyball courts. Pecan trees are everywhere and provide terrific shade. The park has picturesque footbridges and low rolling hills. A horseshoe-shaped amphitheater has been cut into a hillside, and a creek runs through it. There is one bench (!) for spectators.

Risien Park

WIMBERLEY

Wimberley Chamber of Commerce
Post Office Box 12
Wimberley, Texas 78676
(512) 847-2201
http://www.lone-star.net/mall/txtrails/wimberly.htm

Wimberley is a picturesque village which lies between Cypress Creek and the Blanco River, and which has developed into an artistic, resort and retire-ment community with quaint antique shops and eateries. The Blanco River and Cypress Creek are clean and crisp and wonderful for swimming. Green meadows and the scenic Hill Country surround Wimberley, and abundant deer frequent these swimming holes. There are many private resorts and camps in Wimberley that have swimming facilities. I have only included the most popular ones here. The town is named for Pleasant Wimberley who ran a gristmill in the 1870s.

Cypress Creek springs from Jacob's Well, a twenty-eight-foot deep swimming hole so clear you can see the bottom. It is famous for an underground cave structure that Scuba divers have attempted to explore, but several divers have not survived. Attempts to block off the cave have failed but diving is still prohibited. Jacob's Well is located on private property. From FM 12 take Jacob's Well Road (182) to Woodcreed Resort Park about five miles north-northwest of Wimberley.

Blue Hole

Blue Hole Management Ltd.
Post Office Box 331
Wimberley, Texas 78676
(512) 847-9127

Located just south of town off of FM 3237.

If you just want to check out Blue Hole, you can purchase a trial membership for the day for $5. If you want to continue using the hole on a day use basis, you may purchase the day use membership for $1.00 per person (in addition to membership), or $8 per vehicle for up to five people (plus membership). If you find yourself coming more often than that, purchase a weekly or seasonal membership. A membership includes five people at any one time.

Camping fees work the same as the memberships plus day use fees. Rustic camping is $10 per vehicle plus membership. RV hookup camping is $11 nightly for water and electricity, $2.00 for air-conditioning, and $1.00 for sewer.

Reservations are available and deposits are required. On major holidays you must stay for at least three days. Small dogs up to twenty-two pounds are allowed in the camping area. Campsites have one picnic table each but no grills. Rest rooms and showers are available. No lifeguards are on duty. No radios are allowed. Minors must be accompanied by an adult or must sign a release form.

COURTESY OF TEXAS DEPARTMENT OF TRANSPORTATION

Blue Hole

Blue Hole has been in operation since 1928 when Frank J. Dobie's family opened their land to the public for access to the fabulous swimming hole on Cypress Creek. The Dobies charged five cents a carload. World War II soldiers used to cool off in Blue Hole while on leave from San Antonio. It has remained extremely popular to this day. Blue Hole is now privately owned 'to protect it'. Although the rules are somewhat strict, the swimming hole is still fabulous, and well worth protecting. Simply a deep portion of Cypress Creek, Blue Hole has a gravel bottom. Depths range from ankle deep to 13 feet. Blue Hole is aptly named because the crystal clear blue water is very cold, about 65-68°F. It's your traditional, old-fashioned swimming hole with a rope swing, tree ladders, and giant cypress trees providing shade. The swimming area is about 300 meters long. Watercress, live oaks, and cedar trees form a private fence, and large limestone boulders are nice places to sunbathe. Blue Hole is a little tucked away, but it fills up fast because it's so small.

Old FM 12 Bridge

This natural swimming hole on the Blanco River is just east of downtown Wimberley. You can park on the east side of the river and walk down to the water.

There is an access point on either side of the bridge. Respect private property, as the land around the bridge is privately owned. The Old FM 12 Bridge is popular with locals who don't have riverfront property. This swimming spot has rocky shores and banks of trees. The river here is fairly wide and shallow, and the water is cold!

Old FM 12 Bridge

MORE STATE PARKS

OVERVIEW OF STATE PARKS

Texas Parks and Wildlife Department
4200 Smith School Road
Austin, Texas 78744-3291
(800) 792-1112 for facility information
http://www.tpwd.state.tx.us

Reservations:
TPWD Reservation Center
Post Office Box 17488
Austin, Texas 78760-7488
(512) 389-8900 (9:00 A.M.-6:00 P.M., Monday through Friday)
(512) 389-8915 for TDD
(512) 389-8910 to cancel reservations

State parks will charge a day use fee if you plan on swimming for the day. If you're also interested in camping overnight and using the other amenities, the entry fees below will apply and you can swim as often as you want during your stay.

For overnight camping, advance reservations are required by calling the Central Reservation Center. Call at least two days in advance of your arrival.

Entry fees per person range from $1-5. Children under 12 are admitted free. There is a new Conservation Passport option: For $50 annually you get the Gold Passport which gives unlimited park entry to passengers travelling in the same vehicle. For $25 you can get the Silver Passport which allows carloads of visitors at certain times but is not unlimited. Youth Group Annual Entrance permits are available for $100 to nonprofit groups for up to fifty people.

Most parks are open year-round. Day use parks are open 8:00 A.M.-5:00 P.M.

The Texas State Park system began in 1921 when Mrs. Isabella Neff, mother of Governor Pat Neff, donated six acres of land on the Leon River in Coryell County to the state. The park system's holdings have grown to include over one million acres and 132 parks. Many of the parks have structures built by the Civilian

Conservation Corps during the Depression. Although still functional, many of these buildings are in need of restoration, which the park system is slowly and methodically doing. Parks are generally accessible to people with disabilities. TPWD is currently retrofitting its parks to meet the Americans with Disability Act standards.

Only a few state parks, such as Bastrop and Lockhart, have man-made swimming pools. Most others have natural swimming holes or access to rivers where swimming is allowed.

STATE PARK RULES

Fires are allowed in grills only
Gathering firewood is prohibited
Fireworks are not allowed
Pets must be on a leash
No nudity, alcohol or metal detectors
Minors must be accompanied by an adult
Quiet time is from 10:00 P.M.-6:00 A.M.
Dispose of wastes properly
Do not remove or disturb any plant, animals or historical sites

BASTROP STATE PARK

Post Office Box 518
Bastrop, Texas 78602-0518
(512) 321-2101
(512) 389-8900 for reservations
http://www.tpwd.state.tx.us/park/bastrop/bastrop.htm

Bastrop Chamber of Commerce
927 Main Street
Bastrop, Texas 78602
(512) 321-2419

Located at Loop 150 and TX 71, one mile east of TX 21 and 71. Open year-round.

The first thing you will notice about Bastrop State Park is the smell of pine trees, the only ones you'll find in the entire Central Texas area. Located 80 miles west of the main pine belt of Texas, these pines were probably a small part of a vast, prehistoric pine forest. As land masses gradually arose through glacier activity, most of the trees moved to the east. Local conditions in Bastrop have kept the 'Lost Pines' intact. One of the first records of the trees was made in 1807 by Zebulon Pike, of Pike's Peak fame. These 'Loblolly' pines are an integral part of Bastrop County's industry, with local lumber shipped all over Texas.

Bastrop State Park was built in 1939 by the Civilian Conservation Corps as part of the New Deal. The City of Bastrop donated 2,100 acres to the State of Texas, and then an additional 1,450 acres in 1979. Park amenities were built using local materials, such as pine and limestone.

Bastrop was the first settlement of Stephen Austin's 'little colony'. Located on the El Camino Real, Mina (Mee-nah), as it was then known, was founded in 1829 on the banks of the Colorado River. The town was named after Francisco Xavier Mina, a Spanish Revolutionary war martyr. But Mina faded into history in 1837, when Felipe Enrique Nering Bogel, also known as the 'Baron de Bastrop' rolled into town. Bastrop had been a land commissioner in Austin and was appointed Commissioner of the Colonies by the Mexican government. Bastrop turned out to be a complete fraud, but the name stuck. Bastrop was considered as the site of the new capital, but lost to Austin by one vote.

273

Swimming in the park's lake is prohibited, but during the summer a freshwater, man-made pool is open. The pool is shaped like a football with a shallow wading pool on each end. The deep end sports a diving platform. There is a large bathhouse, picnic tables, and a payphone. The pool area is grassy and shaded by pines. Lifeguards are on duty.

> The pool is open noon to 6:45 P.M. during the summer and closed on Tuesdays. Ages 13 and over are $2.50, 12 and under are $1.50.

The park also has an amphitheater and a large meeting and dining hall, which would be ideal for wedding receptions or family reunions. The park consists of 3,500 acres of quiet, rolling park land shaded by the Lost Pines. Camping facilities ranging from tents to cabins and trailer hookups are available. There are also picnic tables, a golf course, nature studies, and hiking and interpretive trails. Bicycles are not allowed on the trails because of erosion problems. The park also has rest rooms and hot showers, and concessions. Primitive camping is permitted in the back of the park along the Lost Pines Trail.

The park headquarters has souvenirs, ice, firewood, and maps. Bastrop State Park is completely wheelchair-accessible.

Scenic Park Road 1C connects Bastrop State Park with Buescher State Park 15 miles east in Smithville. The tour is beautiful, hilly, and thick with trees. If you're just passing through and want to get a feel for the parks, this is the way to do it.

Bastrop State Park

BUESCHER STATE PARK

(pronounced 'Bisher')
Post Office Box 75
Smithville, Texas 78957
(512) 237-2241
http://www.tpwd.state.tx.us/park/buescher/buescher.htm

FM 153 off of TX 71 in Bastrop, 3 miles north via TX 71/95 and FM 2104. Scenic Park Road 1C connects with Bastrop State Park 15 miles to the west. Open year-round.

There are a few pines here as in Bastrop, but Buescher State Park is more Texas-like with scrubby brush and oaks dripping with Spanish moss. Manmade Lake Buescher is quite scenic and is surrounded by sixty-five picnic tables with grills. Buescher State Park was built by the Civilian Conservation Corps between 1933 and 1937. Swimming is allowed in the twenty-five-acre lake but is at your own risk. The park has 1,016 acres of hilly, peaceful land. Camping facilities and rest rooms with showers are available by reservation. Concessions are readily available. A nature study program includes 7.7 miles of hiking trails. A group pavilion and recreation hall are both made of stone and timber from the park. Wildlife abounds and includes squirrels, deer, raccoons, possums, bobcats, rabbits, armadillos and ducks. The park is wheelchair-accessible.

Lake Buescher

LOCKHART STATE PARK

RR 3, Box 69
Lockhart, Texas 78644-9716
(512) 398-3479
http://www.tpwd.state.tx.us/park/lockhart/lockhart.htm

Four miles southwest of Lockhart on U.S. 183 and FM 20

Europeans settled Lockhart in 1820. In 1830, a few cabins and a trading post were built northeast of downtown. Lockhart still has a wealth of historical buildings, such as Kreuz's Store, famous for its barbecue. The Caldwell County Museum, which used to be the jail, dates from the 1850s. The museum is a castle-like structure with turrets.

A small, but picturesque municipal park can be found off of City Park Road (U.S. 183) along the shores of Plum Creek. Plum Creek, which was named for abundant wild plums growing along the banks, runs through town. A historical marker detailing an Indian attack has been erected in the park.

Lockhart used to be known as Lockhart Springs, and a few natural springs still flow under the ferns in City Park. Storey Springs is also still flowing, but is now used for the minnow tanks at Matt's Bait and Supply Store on 310 North Commerce Street. Sam Houston spoke there in 1857.

Lockhart State Park is 263 acres and has fine swimming in a large, man-made, rectangular pool ($1.00 admission). Pool depths range from three to twelve feet and a separate wading pool is about two feet deep. The pool is easily spotted just past the entrance to the park and has a bathhouse of brick and beam. There are some grassy areas but very little shade. Lockhart State Park has mildly rolling hills covered with huisache and oak trees. Patrons can also enjoy picnicking, a nine-hole golf course, a recreation hall overlooking the valley, camping, concessions, volleyball, an amphitheater, a playground, and basketball courts. Pets are permitted on leashes.

Lockhart State Park Swimming Pool

PALMETTO STATE PARK

Route 5, Box 201
Gonzales, Texas 78629
(830) 672-3266
http://www.tpwd.state.tx.us/park/palmetto/palmetto.htm

About one hour and fifteen minutes from Austin. Take U.S. 183 south through Luling about seven miles to FM 2091 or Park Road 11.

Like a walk through prehistoric times, Palmetto State Park is characterized by dwarf palmetto plants and other tropical plants, most of which can't be found anywhere else in Texas. This area is known as the Ottine Swamp which is unique and unlike any other landscape in this region.

Two artesian wells create sulfurous swimming holes. Oxbow Lake also has a swimming dock, but the water is rather murky, swampy, and reedy. Swimming is at your own risk. Palmetto State Park does not have the best swimming, but it is a sight to be seen for sure. Canoes and paddleboats are also allowed on Oxbow Lake.

Palmetto State Park is 268 acres and has camping, boating, picnicking, a playground, and great birdwatching, with over 240 species recorded in the park land. Most of the structures in the park were built by the Civilian Conservation Corps in the 1930s. There is a one-mile interpretive trail encircling tiny Oxbow Lake and another along the San Marcos River. Pets are allowed on leash.

Palmetto State Park

WATER THEME PARKS

SCHLITTERBAHN

The hottest, coolest time in Texas

400 North Liberty Street
New Braunfels, Texas 78130
(830) 625-2351
http://www.schlitterbahn.com

Schlitterbahn means 'slippery road' in German, but here in Texas it is inarguably the world's greatest water theme park and resort. Open since 1979, Schlitterbahn was ranked America's Most Popular Water Park in 1995 by Amusement Business. It also was voted Best Water Park for the third consecutive year by Inside Track, a now defunct magazine for amusement park fans. Located on the spring-fed Comal River, Schlitterbahn is a sixty-five-acre water park with over thirty rides, five different theme areas, nine tube chutes, and seventeen water slides. Other attractions include the Boogie Bahn surfing ride, a family wave pool, three regular swimming pools, five giant hot tubs, and six kiddie parks with pint-sized rides. If all that isn't enough for you, they offer water and sand volleyball, and restaurants and bars for the grownups. Add to that such thrill rides as an uphill watercoaster, tunnel slides through sheer darkness, a family tubing area, a sandy beach, picnic facilities and concessions, and you're ready for a full day, or several days, of family fun.

Schlitterbahn is divided into six sections:

Wave Fest: Enjoy the Banzai Pipeline, twin four-story-high tunnel slides; the Tunnel Tube Chute is a float through caves; the Congo River is a slow, lazy

Schlitterbahn's Blastenhoff

281

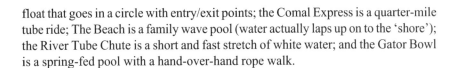

float that goes in a circle with entry/exit points; the Comal Express is a quarter-mile tube ride; The Beach is a family wave pool (water actually laps up on to the 'shore'); the River Tube Chute is a short and fast stretch of white water; and the Gator Bowl is a spring-fed pool with a hand-over-hand rope walk.

Kinderlund: Hansel and Gretel's Great Adventure is a 'forest' of fairy tale creatures with soft foam slides; the Cliffhanger is a tube chute that ends in a waterfall drop; Der Bahn is a triple racing speed slide; Polywog Pond is a water fantasy land with spraying mushrooms and swinging bridges; and the Tadpool is a shallow pool with tiny slides shaped like water critters.

Slidenplatz: the Castle Slides are the park's original tube rides, originating 60 feet up from a replica of the Bergfried Tower in Braunfels, Germany; Schlittercoaster is a toboggan ride down the roof of the three-story souvenir shop; Double Loop Slides are body flumes that twist through the trees; and the Whitewater Tube Chute has waterfalls and rapids.

Das Lagune: the Raging River is the longest tube chute in the world and takes forty-five minutes to get through; the Soda Straws are twisting tube body slides; the Lagoon is a huge activity pool with volleyball and more; The Lagoon Kiddie Park has soft slides; and the Hillside Tube Chute has eight hundred feet of rapids.

Surfenburg: This is the best place for families as it offers a variety of thrills, from high-speed watercoasters to gentle tubing rivers. Boogie Bahn is a simulated surfing ride. Ride the endless wave until you wipe out. The Dragon Blaster is a mild watercoaster which takes a two-man raft, and the Family Blaster takes a group of people through a series of twists and turns. Both of these rides were short and sweet, although the lines and the wait were quite long; the Kristal Cove is an activity pool with logs to cross; Squirt'n Sliden is another kid area with a pirate ship, submarine and more to climb on; the Kristal River is an endless, swift river which encircles the Surfenburg area and can be tubed or swum. Giant floating logs and alligators (fake!) enliven the experience. There is a sandy beach where you can build sandcastles. Surfenburg also sports an 'aquatic bar' where you sit submerged in the water on foam bar stools and order alcoholic drinks, soft drinks and snacks from a circular bar. Can this get any better? Yes...

Schlitterbahn expanded in 1996 with the addition of a four-acre section called Blastenhoff. Blastenhoff is close to the main park, but you must take a free shuttle to get to and from it. Blastenhoff contains the latest thrill rides, including the Master Blaster, a six-story, 1,000-foot long watercoaster. It's the tallest, steepest, uphill watercoaster in the world. Usually sporting a long line, the brief, exhilarating ride is worth the wait. The Wolfpack is a downhill family raft ride that drops 675 feet through curves and plunges; the Black Knight is a twin raft ride through complete darkness that plunges five stories; The Torrent is a swift-moving, wave-producing river with occasional rapids; it's much more thrilling than the Kristal River and is not for the faint at heart or inexperienced swimmers as the water is quite deep. Unfortunately, this is where my friend lost his glasses because the waves were so strong and sneak up from behind. Blastenhoff also offers a concrete beach, a more grown-up version of the wave pool and a hot tub.

Schlitterbahn fronts the Comal River with grassy areas and play-grounds, picnic grounds and tall shade trees. The Comal River flows through the park and its cool water is circulated through several of the rides. Some rides even empty into the river. The attractions are on the cutting edge, but the park is surrounded by natural beauty. Thankfully, Schlitterbahn does not have that giant, corporate theme park feel, although it can be quite crowded. The whole park is dripping wet and covered in Astroturf. Water is spraying and sloshing out of the rides, so you never really dry off. This is a good thing in the peak of summer.

Tips: Reduced price admission is an option in the afternoon, but I found that it didn't give us enough time to do the whole park. If you've never been, I recommend going for a full day and narrowing down your favorites for a later, reduced-price day. The park is usually packed to the gills and the lines for some of the higher thrill rides can last upwards of an hour. Early and late summer will have lower attendance, and from June to August, Sundays and Mondays are less crowded. Do the Blastenhoff and Surfenburg areas first and beat the lines. The signage was a little confusing; for instance, you'd see a ride that looked interesting but the entrance was difficult to find. Parking was free but extremely limited. Schlitterbahn is located right next to the New Braunfels city parks such as Prince Solms, so the area is already crowded, yet the town of New Braunfels remains quaint and beautiful. There was plenty of 'carnival' food to choose from, such as funnel cakes, corn on the cob, ice cream, sodas, hot dogs, etc., and lots of shade and grass and picnic areas to enjoy it in. The staff is wonderful, friendly and helpful. Award-winning, nationally certified lifeguards are on duty at all times and are focused and effective. Wear sunscreen; drink plenty of fluids; bring something waterproof and compact that you can carry your money and valuables in. Or, get Splash Cash, a plastic bracelet you purchase and wear with tabs in different denominations which can be torn off and used in the park as money. Lockers are available but are expensive. The large size was $5 plus a $2.00 deposit, with the deposit refundable for a souvenir or cash. If you wear glasses, strap them to your head. I couldn't believe the number of items that came in to the lost and found just for one day. The staff will do their best to return your stuff, but sometimes things just don't turn up. Don't chance it—go prepared. Lots of people went barefoot but the concrete can get hot and wear on your feet, so you might take sandals that can be strapped on tight and not fly off while you're on a ride. Life jackets are free, and signs are well posted about the ride levels (1-4). There is truly something for everyone at Schlitterbahn, and it seems like they've thought of everything. They also have a gift shop with souvenirs, film, etc. Changing facilities, ATM machines, and drinking fountains are available.

Accommodations: Choose from over two hundred rooms at Schlitterbahn-at-the-Bahn or Schlitterbahn-at-the-Rapids. Accommodations range from basic motel rooms to rooms with whirlpools, condominiums, and cottage homes. The resort rooms are adjacent to the park. Resort guests receive a discount on park admission. The resort is also open year-round.

Schlitterbahn is open weekends from late April, then daily from May through August and weekends in September. The park has in/out privileges by wearing a wristband.

Schlitterbahn is a family-oriented park. Thong suits are not permitted, nor is profanity. Picnics are welcome but glass and alcohol are prohibited.

Prices are $23.99 for adults; ages three to eleven $19.99; adult admission after 3:30 is $16.99; ages three to eleven $13.99; The park also offers two-day passes for $37.99 for adults; ages three to eleven $29.99; Season passes are $96.99 for adults and $63.99 for kids. Season passes can be purchased over the phone by credit card or while you wait at the main gate. Special group prices and catering for 15 to 5,000 people are also available. Senior discounts apply. Call for rates.

SEAWORLD SAN ANTONIO'S LOST LAGOON

10500 SeaWorld Drive
San Antonio, Texas 78251-3002
(210) 523-3611
www.seaworld.com

Adults $31.95 plus tax, kids (3-11) $21.95 plus tax

Open March through October, with varying hours

From Loop 410, exit at Highway 151 west

SeaWorld San Antonio's Lost Lagoon is a waterpark within a park of more than 25 major attractions. Lost Lagoon is a five-acre water park with slides and water rides located within 250-acre SeaWorld San Antonio proper, where you can see numerous marine exhibits. The admission price includes both features. SeaWorld San Antonio opened in 1988 and is constantly adding new features. The park has something new every summer, it seems. SeaWorld San Antonio is an Anheuser-Busch Adventure Park dedicated to conservation and education about animals. You will get to meet Shamu, the killer whale, dolphins, sea lions and walruses. There is also an aquarium and high-speed thrills such as The Great White and The Steel Eel rollercoasters.

SeaWorld San Antonio has done a good job with Lost Lagoon, making it feel like a tropical resort. There are palm-lined beaches, an aviary filled with birds and more than a dozen real alligators in a natural habitat. A wave pool generates three-foot waves. Lil' Gators Lagoon is designed especially for small children; don't worry, there are no real alligators here! A forty-foot tower with twisting slides is for the bigger kids, as is the five-story high Sky Tubin' slide. Adults aren't left out and have their own activity pool with small slides and waterfalls. Since the park is relatively small, there is a limit to the number of people allowed in at any given time, but it can still get crowded.

A gift shop has souvenirs, and food is available at the Eats Beach Grill. Changing rooms have showers. There is an additional charge for parking and for locker rental.

The inspiration for Lost Lagoon was Cyrus 'Buck' Simmons, a fictional Texas tycoon who made a fortune selling soap. He and fifty-three of his friends set out in the Caribbean on his yacht, the Castaway. Tropical storm Tess destroyed the boat but the crew and passengers made it to Lost Lagoon, an uncharted island. They took their luggage, two jars of pickles, a tin of sardines, and 224 crates and forty-nine steel drums of soap, which allowed them to thrive. Sound familiar?

Lost Lagoon at SeaWorld San Antonio

SPLASHTOWN SAN ANTONIO

(There are two Splashtown Water Parks in Texas: one in Houston and one in San Antonio. They are not affiliated with one another.)

3600 North IH35
San Antonio, Texas 78219
(210) 227-1100
www.splashtownsa.com

Open April through September. Hours vary.

General Admission: $19.99
Under 48 inches $14.99
After 5:00 P.M., all guests $11.99
Spectator $5.99
Under 2 and over 65 are free
Group Rates: 15-199, $9; 200-499, $8.50; over 500, $8
Season Pass: Family of three $99; additional members $33
Individual: $36; Child $25; Locker $30

Three minutes north of downtown San Antonio on IH35 at the Splashtown Exit.

Splashtown San Antonio is an eighteen-acre water park located just off of IH35. It is accessible and manageable. Kids and adults will both find plenty to do. Splashtown has over twenty-five rides and attractions just for kids, plus another twenty-five rides for bigger kids and adults. The park is just the right size with enough attractions to keep it interesting, but not overwhelm. It never seems to get too crowded, and it is easily navigated.

Splashtown has the largest wave pool in the Southwest which generates nice waves and breaks onto a concrete shore. A lazy river called Siesta del Rio encircles the

287

The Serpentine

park. A newly remodeled kid's activity pool called Crystal Falls has a man-made mountain with short body slides. For the more daring, try the Radical Rampage, a near vertical drop from three stories up. A milder ride is one of four enclosed tubes called The Hydras, or the Double Dipper, which hosts a variety of slides from corkscrew turns to steep drops from five stories up. Another slide with three twisting tubes is the Serpentine. Grab a friend and ride the Lonestar Luge, a bobsled ride that starts seven stories up and then drops the length of two football fields. If you're really brave, try the Starflight, a five-story double tube that descends in total darkness, or a scaled-down version called Starflight, Jr. for the kids. If you're a landlubber, Splashtown has sand and water volleyball courts and basketball courts. On certain occasions, they also have bikini and karaoke contests, and Dive-In Movies.

A gift shop sells souvenirs and supplies. Concessions are available from several vendors throughout the park. There are no coolers or ice chests allowed in the park, but a picnic area is located in the parking lot. Parking is plentiful and free, and lifejackets are provided. You can bring your own tubes, or use one of Splashtown's free of charge. Lockers are available for rent for $3.00.

Siesta del Rio

Radical Rampage

SPLASHTOWN HOUSTON

The Most Amazing Water Adventure on the Planet

IH 45 and Spring at the Louetta Road exit
Houston, Texas 77383
(281) 355-3300
www.splashtown.com
splashtown@aol.com

Open weekends mid-April through mid-May,
then full-time through Labor Day
Gates open at 10:00 A.M.

Season pass $39.99 individual, $114.99 family of three
General admission $19.99
People under 48 inches $13.99
Kids under 3 free

Although they are not affiliated, Splashtown Houston has a lot in common with Splashtown San Antonio. The layout and types of rides are comparable, though each has its unique features. The best characteristic of Splashtown Houston is that it is set in a woodsy area outside of the city, and the Guadalupe River flows through the park creating a cool, lazy river. The park has a Victorian theme with brick walkways, antique lampposts, lush landscaping, and building facades like an old village.

Splashtown Houston is home to the Waterworks Factory, a collection of water attractions. With forty rides spread out over fifty acres, there is something for everyone at Splashtown Houston. Try The Big Spin, a spinning disk full of water. The Texas Freefall is a sheer drop from eight stories up. Several tube slides such as the Zoom Flume, the Shotgun, and the Blue Beast provide hours of fun and variety.

289

COURTESY OF SPLASHTOWN HOUSTON

For the kids there is Treehouse Island, a fantasy playground, and Kids Kountry, a whole acre of pint-sized rides. The Wild Wave Pool is Texas's largest, and the lazy river is refreshingly cool.

Entertainment such as music concerts are held throughout the summer. A video arcade is an air-conditioned diversion. Fourteen different restaurants and shops have refreshments and food. A gift shop sells souvenirs and supplies. There are lockers and tubes available for rent, and changing rooms have showers.

COURTESY OF SPLASHTOWN HOUSTON

SUMMERFUN USA

1410 Old Waco Road
Belton, Texas 76513
(254) 939-0366

Monday 1:30-7:00 P.M.
Tuesday-Sunday 11:00 A.M.-7:00 P.M.
Half-day begins at 3:00 P.M.

General admission: Adult $13, Children3-12, $10, Half-day $9,
Sit and watch $5, Mondays, everyone is $8.

Groups: 15-100 people $8 each; 101-150 people $7.50 each.
Season passes: Adults $80, Children $55, military discounts;
Family Passes: Two adults, one child $205; one adult, two
children $180; two adults, two children $240; add one adult,
$60, add one child $45.

Private parties (after hours) are $400 an hour with a minimum
of two hours. Kids under age 2 are free. The water volleyball
pool is also available for private parties at $25 per hour, with a
two-hour minimum. Lifeguards are not available for the volleyball
pool.

---

*Take IH35 to Belton, exit 294B. Go west on 6th Avenue, then go east on FM 817
to Heritage Park. Summerfun USA is 1.6 miles from exit 294B.*

O pened in 1989, Summerfun USA is a small, 4.6-acre park, but has plenty of fun packed into it. Located on the shores of the Leon River, this is a family-oriented water park with a 'Texas-sized' swimming pool. Giant lily pads and tree logs drift in the pool when you want to rest on them. Hanging hoops challenge everyone to swing their way across the water. A giant mushroom

fountain in the center makes a great shower. The main pool connects with a shallow splash pool full of activities for kids, including a giant frog where you can slide down the tongue. For the bigger kids, there are three giant water slides starting forty feet up which take you through nine hundred feet of twists and turns. Two of the slides are experienced on your back and empty into the main pool. The third is designed for an innertube and empties into a lazy river. The lazy river has a forty-foot stretch of rapids to keep you from falling asleep.

Summerfun USA also has a snack bar and concessions, which can be enjoyed in shaded picnic areas next to the pool or from a shaded wooden deck on the banks of the Leon River. In neighboring Heritage Park, you will also find plenty of parking, water and sand volleyball, an arcade, horseshoe pits, a jogging trail, softball fields, and picnic tables with grills.

I visited this park on Memorial Day, but never had more than a two to three minute wait on the slides. Summerfun USA has a nice, low key, family feel to it, yet provides all-day entertainment.

292

ADVENTURE BAY

A splash of family fun

13602 Beechnut (at the corner of Eldridge)
Houston, Texas 77083
(281) 498-SWIM (7946)
www.adventurebay.com

> 10:00 A.M.-7:00 P.M. Monday through Thursday
> 10:00 A.M.-8:00 P.M. Friday and Saturday
> Sundays 11:00 A.M.-7:00 P.M.
> $16.99 for adults, under 3 free,
> under 48 inches $12.99
> Season passes available

Adventure Bay is the newest water park in Houston and is especially geared toward families with small children. The twelve-acre park is designed so that you can see your kids at all times and not lose track of them. Attractions include a lazy river called the Rio Lento, and Paradise Bay, a large wave pool. Pirates' Cove activity pool is geared toward the younger set and offers hours of fun. Kids will also enjoy small slides and face painting. The bigger kids will enjoy the Master Blaster raging river, and high-thrill slides such as the Lost Falls and Rio Rapids. Special events with musicals and dinner occur throughout the summer. You may bring your own food and drink into the park, but alcohol, glass, and cooking equipment are prohibited. Adventure Bay also has concessions for sale. There is plenty of natural shade. Parking is free. Lockers are available.

COURTESY OF ADVENTURE BAY

Adventure Bay

293

THE WAVE POOL

Max Starcke Park East
Seguin, Texas

Seguin Parks Department (830) 401-2480
Sequin Chamber of Commerce (800) 580-PECAN
(see also Max Starcke Park)

The Wave Pool is located within Max Starcke Park, south of the courthouse on the east side of Austin Street (Business TX 123) in Seguin. To get there from Austin, take IH35 to TX 123 in San Marcos. Seguin is about 45 miles southeast of Austin.

Opened in 1991, The Wave Pool is like no other swimming experience. At a cost of $1.3 million, and funded by Texas Parks and Wildlife, it re placed the city's municipal pool which had been in use since 1937. The 15,000 square-foot pool is five feet at the deepest end and slopes to a shallow end where you can enjoy gentle waves lapping at your ankles; a little further in you can act out your "From Here to Eternity" fantasies as the waves crash over you. A bell clangs and signals that the waves are imminent. People scramble from their towels and rush into the water, the kids screaming with anticipation. The water begins to churn and three to four-foot waves appear. The waves are strong and seem wild, but they also feel very safe and managed. Powered by three fans which are controlled by a computer, the wave machine produces eight different patterns. Each pattern runs for ten minutes, then the water is calm for another fifteen minutes. The waves are strongest at the deep end where they are generated. Here you can create your own rollercoaster by riding down the backs of waves which boost you high enough to see the parking lot, then plunge beneath the water line. Be careful of this because you can plunge so quickly and with such force that you can easily bang your extremities on the concrete. The waves break about half-way down the pool where you can surf the whitewash to the shore or tube the crests. The water clears out for the most part in between wave sessions and you can quietly drift away in your innertube; then the bell goes off and everybody charges back to the water. The pool is not very large and seems like it would get crowded fast, but is well worth the trip. The Wave Pool has all the fun of the ocean without the unpredictability of nature.

The Wave Pool

There is a separate kidney-shaped wading pool with a mushroom fountain and a floating sea monster, but it does not produce waves.

The pool is well-staffed by youths. Lifeguards are on duty and are extremely focused while the waves are running. They take frequent breaks and turns watching the pool.

The pool provides dressing rooms with showers, changing stalls and bathrooms. Shade is provided by towering pecan trees (what else?), but the pecan leaves tend to fall into the pool and can be a nuisance. Tubes are free, but are available on a first come, first served basis. Concessions include drinks, corn dogs, nachos, candy, chips, and Frito pie. The day I went they were blaring Top 40 music. Garland and LaPorte have similar pools.

Max Starcke Park (see page 237) is on the banks of the Guadalupe River and is filled with oak and pecan trees and picnic tables. The park also has a playground, golf course, volleyball and basketball courts, horseshoe pits, and a picturesque waterfall at an old power plant. While in Seguin, view the world's largest pecan nut behind the courthouse, or pick your own pecans in nearby orchards.

The pool is open from Memorial Day to Labor Day, Monday through Saturday, noon-6:00 P.M. and Sunday 1:00 P.M.-6:00 P.M. There is a small snack bar but no food or drinks are allowed in the pool area. Admission is $3.00 for kids four to eleven, and $4.00 for adults. Kids under 4 and seniors over 59 are free. The pool holds up to six hundred people and is available for private parties. The cost for three hours is $300. The pool is also open Tuesdays in July from 6:30-8:30 P.M. for Dip and Dine Family Night. Cost is $4.00 per person and picnic baskets are allowed. What a great way to spend time with the family and beat the heat!

The area in Caldwell County from Luling to Schulenberg to Austin was rife with mineral wells and health spas in the late-nineteenth century, so it is fitting that the aquatic recreation tradition should continue. The town was named for Colonel Juan N. Seguine of the Mexican Army.

Wading Pool

OVERVIEW OF SIX FLAGS
www.sixflags.com

After visiting Disneyland in the late 1950s, Angus G. Wynne, Jr., a Texas oil man, decided to build a new theme park that was bigger than Disneyland, had more rides, and was affordable and close to home. Along with Hollywood director Randall Duell, he opened his first park, Six Flags Over Texas in 1961. The park was divided into themed 'lands' representing each nation which had flown a flag over Texas. The park was a huge success.

Six Flags is now the second largest theme park chain in America with twelve parks across the country. It is owned by Time Warner, so you'll find lots of Warner Brothers and DC Comics characters roaming around, including Batman.

Six Flags wants you to be safe. Drink lots of water and wear and re-apply sunscreen. The parks prohibit glass, alcohol, grills, fires, pets, firearms, weapons and thong suits. No denim or clothing with metal buttons are permitted on the water slides because they can catch. Shoes and shirts are required. Some rides have height restrictions. Sometimes rides close for electrical or rain storms. Rainchecks are issued if the rides will be closed more than an hour.

Parks usually have a variety of concessions and gift shops. Life vests, stroller and wheelchair rentals are available. First aid stations look out for you, and conveniences such as lockers for rent, cash machines, diaper stations, and a kennel are usually available. Six Flags accepts all major credit cards. If you have foreign currency you can exchange it there.

In addition to the water parks, there are other major attractions, concerts, festivals, and special events. In some cases, the ticket price includes admission to the water park. In other cases, separate admission is required.

SIX FLAGS WATERWORLD

Loop 610 at 9001 Kirby Drive across from the Astrodome
Houston, Texas
(713) 799-1234
http://www.sixflags.com/houston/nonflash.cfm

Fees: Adults $16.99
Over age 54 or under 48 inches $12.99
Under age 2 is free
Disabled adult $13.99, disabled child $11.99
$30.99 ticket is also good for Astroworld
Discounts for groups
Open daily May-September

Waterworld is adjacent to Six Flags Astroworld. You can take a tram to heart of the waterpark or walk about seven minutes to get there. The main attraction is the Adventure Rivers of Texas, a 400-foot long tube ride from sixty feet in the air with four different chutes that drop you through a variety of twists and turns, then plunges into a pool. One of the chutes, The Pipeline, is enclosed, while the other three are open. The Tsunami, Hurricane and Typhoon are fairly similar to each other. The Run-A-Way River is an inner tube ride that falls through five tiered levels of pools, chutes and rapids. It is actually a fairly gentle ride. If you want high thrills, The Edge is a steep, 82-foot plunging slide experienced lying on your back. I was not brave enough

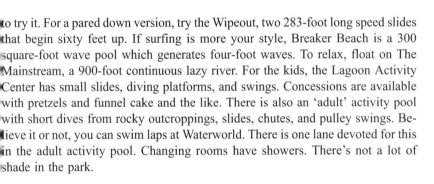

to try it. For a pared down version, try the Wipeout, two 283-foot long speed slides that begin sixty feet up. If surfing is more your style, Breaker Beach is a 300 square-foot wave pool which generates four-foot waves. To relax, float on The Mainstream, a 900-foot continuous lazy river. For the kids, the Lagoon Activity Center has small slides, diving platforms, and swings. Concessions are available with pretzels and funnel cake and the like. There is also an 'adult' activity pool with short dives from rocky outcroppings, slides, chutes, and pulley swings. Believe it or not, you can swim laps at Waterworld. There is one lane devoted for this in the adult activity pool. Changing rooms have showers. There's not a lot of shade in the park.

You could conceivably spend all day at Waterworld, but most of the features can be experienced in a few hours. I found that the mornings were the least crowded, with an average wait time of two to three minutes in line. In the afternoon, the hot folks from Astroworld started to arrive. Waterworld charges a fee for parking ($5) and to rent tubes ($5 plus $1.00 deposit) and lockers ($5 plus $1.00 deposit), so the total price wound up being about twice the regular admission. However, life jackets are free. Ice chests and coolers are not allowed, nor is outside food or beverage. A picnic area is located in the parking lot; however, it only accommodates about three to four families.

SIX FLAGS HURRICANE HARBOR
(Formerly known as Wet & Wild)

1800 East Lamar
Arlington, Texas 76006
(817) 265-3356
http://www.sixflags.com/hurricaneharbordallas/nonflash.cfm

Open May through September.

General Admission: Over 48 inches $25.85
Under 48 inches $12.92, under age 2 free, over 65 $12.92
Group Rates: Under 48 inches $17
Over 48 inches $19.93

From IH 30 between Dallas and Fort Worth, take TX 360 north or TX 157 north to Lamar Boulevard. Hurricane Harbor is across the street from Six Flags Theme Park.

Hurricane Harbor is Texas's second-largest water park at nearly fifty acres with ten different theme areas. The park seems to have everything and is evidence of an imagination run wild. Attractions range from low-speed, shallow areas suitable for leisure and children, to moderate thrill rides with water depths up to forty-eight inches, to aggressive rides which require rider control and strong swimming skills, to high-speed attractions with extreme heights, speeds, enclosed spaces and deep water. The Black Hole is a futuristic ride through 500 feet of twisting tubes filled with water and accompanied by spaceship sounds. The Kamikaze is a slide that plunges from 60 feet up down a 300-foot speedway. The Sea Wolf is the tallest, fastest ride anywhere. The Caribbean Chaos and Atlantic Panic rush you wildly through thousands of gallons of water. The Blue Raider twists and turns through torrents of water and flooded tunnels. There are twenty-six slides in all, a surfing lagoon, a lazy river, and a giant kids' play pool. There is a wave machine producing ocean-sized waves, a bubble machine, a water trolley, rain tunnels, waterfalls, and whirlpools.

Lockers, tubes, and life vests are available for rent. Hurricane Harbor has picnic areas and concessions for sale. If water isn't your thing, you can play horseshoes, enjoy basketball courts, water and sand volleyball courts, an arcade, a sky coaster, miniature golf, batting cages, and laser tag. Lifeguards are on duty and a first aid station can handle emergencies.

While you're in Arlington, check out the:

RIVER LEGACY PARKS

703 NW Green Oaks Boulevard
(817) 860-6752

Open Tuesday through Saturday 9:00 A.M.-5:00 P.M.

The park is free but the science center charges admission.

Located on the Trinity River, this lovely park has hike and bike trails, nature trails, scenic river overviews, and picnic areas. The Living Science Center features terrariums, aquariums, maps of Texas rivers, and a simulated raft ride.

SIX FLAGS FIESTA, TEXAS

17000 IH 10 West
Off Loop 10 and Loop 1604 outside of San Antonio
(210) 697-5050
http://www.sixflags.com/sanantonio/nonflash.cfm

Open daily in the summer; and weekends in the spring and fall
Closed December -February
Admission $32.31; over 55 $21.54
Under 48 inches $16.15
Parking $5.00

Fiesta, Texas was an independently owned theme park until Six Flags bought it several years ago and began adding attractions, including a water park. The 200-acre theme park is located in a former rock quarry surrounded by 100-foot cliffs. The Ol' Waterin' Hole is a water park within the main theme park. It features fourteen attractions, including eight slides and chutes which rival any roller coaster. Choose from The Pipeline, The Mineshaft or The Twister, totally enclosed pipes which loop completely upside down. The Blowout is for solitary rides open to the sky, and The Triple Dipper lets you and your sweetheart go down side by side. The Six Chuter and Texas Tumble let whole families go down together in an inflatable raft.

In this area you can also float leisurely on a lazy river around the park. The water does all the work for you! There are several shallow pools with areas for sun-bathers, miniature waterfalls, fountains, etc. There are lifeguards on duty in the massive kiddie pools. You can play sand volleyball if you get waterlogged.

You will get wet on other rides in the park, too, and sometimes even spectators get wet. There are floating rides that you can wear your street clothes on, but you will still get wet. Wear something light with pockets, and pack lightly. Hats and sunglasses can fly off on some of the rides, as I learned when I lost my wallet (and my lunch!) on the Joker's Revenge. The staff was very helpful in my panicked state, and my wallet was safe and secure in their lost and found.

The major drawback of The Ol' Waterin' Hole is the lack of space for changing in and out of bathing suits. Streetwear is not permitted inside the swimming area, and any type of denim clothing and buttons are prohibited. Thong bathing suits are not allowed. Your only option for storing your clothing and belongings is to rent a locker for a nominal charge (quarters only). You will receive a key to the locker which you will have no place to put, so packing a rubber keychain bracelet or other device for storing tiny valuables comes in very handy. There are no changing rooms or showers, only bathrooms. Long waits in line can also be expected with the most popular attractions, sometimes up to an hour.

COMING SOON

So where is Austin's water theme park? I have often wondered that myself, Austin being the young, hip, recreation-loving city that it is. As this book goes to press, word is out that a water theme park may be built south of Georgetown and just east of IH35 as early as spring of 2000. The park would have seven thrill rides. Stay tuned!

HEALTH CLUBS

CRENSHAW ATHLETIC CLUB

5000 Fairview Drive
Austin, Texas 78731
(512) 453-5551
http://austin.citysearch.com/E/V/AUSTX/0001/44/40/

Crenshaw Athletic Club has a forty-foot pool that is primarily used for lessons and water fitness, and lap-swimming times are limited. The club also has a weight room, an indoor jogging track, cardiovascular machines, and a sauna and steam room. A single full membership is $50, plus $42.50 monthly dues and a yearly insurance assessment of $15. A double full membership is $100 plus $74 monthly dues and a yearly insurance assessment of $20. Lap swim times are Monday, Wednesday and Friday 6:00-7:30 A.M., 1:30-3:00 P.M., and 7:00-9:00 P.M. Lap swimming on Tuesdays and Thursdays is 6:00-7:00 A.M. and 7:00-9:00 P.M.

THE HILLS FITNESS CENTER

4615 Bee Caves Road
Austin, Texas 78746
(512) 327-4881

Monday through Thursday 5:30 A.M.-10:00 P.M.
Friday 5:30 A.M.-8:00 P.M.
Saturday 7:00 A.M.-7:00 P.M.
Sunday 10:00 A.M.-6:00 P.M.

Memberships begin at $200-$350 annually

The Hills has been a very popular fitness center with lots of amenities since it opened in 1980. The eleven-acre campus is located in a wooded but accessible area of Westlake Hills.

The Hills has indoor and outdoor pools. Both are twenty-five meters and are open year-round. The water is heated when necessary. The Hills has private swim lessons and one-on- one training, water aerobics, water walking, and other water exercise programs. Staff aquatic specialist Terri Mitchell can design a program especially for your needs. They also have 'Pseudo Swim Team' for 8 to 15-year olds which meets Tuesdays and Thursdays from 5:00-5:45 P.M. An Adult Swim Team for all skill levels meets at 6:00 A.M. and 6:00 P.M. There are no lifeguards on duty. Kids under 13 must be with a parent and are not allowed in the whirl-pools, saunas or steam rooms. The indoor pool has a splash lane for family swim-ming. The outdoor pool is for adult lap swim only. The Hills also has yoga, massage, facials and manicures, karate, and dance and aerobics classes. They have free weights and a walking/running trail. You can finish off your work-out in their own café and pur-chase fitness gear in the store.

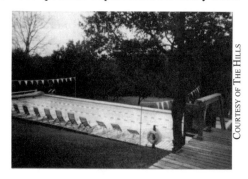

COURTESY OF THE HILLS

NORTHWEST FITNESS CENTERS

10700 Anderson Mill Road
Austin, Texas 78750
(512) 258-1800

and

8127 Mesa Drive
Austin, Texas 78759
(512) 345-8800

B oth Northwest Fitness Centers have fifty-foot indoor, heated pools. Three lanes are dedicated for lap swimming. Members can also use the rest of the club's amenities.

There is a one-time enrollment fee of $60. Memberships for individuals are based on the number of months you sign up for. A 36-month membership is $35 per month; a 24-month membership is $40 per month; and a 12-month membership is $45 per month.

Interested parties are encouraged to visit the facilities and take a tour.

YMCA

North Park Family Branch
9616 North Lamar, Suite 130 @ Rutland
Austin, Texas 78753
(512) 973-9622

Southwest Family Branch
6219 Oakclaire @ U.S. 290 West
Austin, Texas 78735
(512) 891-9622

Town Lake Branch
1100 West Cesar Chavez @ North Lamar
Austin, Texas 78703
(512) 476-6705

The YMCA is a traditional favorite for health club memberships. The facilities have so many amenities that it's impossible to get bored, and they are well-maintained and state-of-the-art.

Each of the Austin locations has a swimming pool, but they vary in size. The Town Lake Branch has a good-size pool plus a small wading pool, Oak Hill has a small pool and a whirlpool, and North Lamar has a small indoor pool. Hours for lap swimming vary, and there is usually more than one activity going on in the pool at any given time. The Y allows a maximum of eight people per lane at a time, which in my opinion is way too crowded. Swim lessons are offered in small classes which emphasize safety,

Town Lake YMCA

endurance, lifesaving and developing strokes. Classes begin at six months old and up. The YMCA also has synchronized swimming, stroke and arthritis clinics, aqua fitness, a swim team, private lessons, and lifeguard training. You can rent the pool for a private party. Other amenities include a sauna and steam room, lockers, and showers. The Y also has weights, aerobics, sport teams, and much more. The YMCA is a family-oriented recreational facility for kids and seniors and everyone in between.

Membership costs vary by location. At Town Lake, there is a $150 joining fee then $528 per year for individuals and $720 for families. The other two branches have a $99 joining fee and $480 annual fee for individuals and $660 for a family.

The YMCA will soon build a facility in East Austin at FM 969 and U.S. 183 on the site of a former landfill. The land was donated by IBM. The recreational facility is part of a twenty-year development plan for the area. The 123-acre facility will include a three-mile hike and in-line skate trail, picnic areas, a gymnasium, a swimming pool, and soccer and baseball fields and basketball and tennis courts.

North Lamar YMCA

GHOST POOLS

GHOST POOLS

For those of you for whom existing pools are not enough, you may want to explore some 'ghost' pools, or pools that no longer exist.

The City of Austin had a few swimming pools in the early days of the Parks and Recreation Department that have since been demolished. East Avenue Pool was located at East Avenue (now IH 35) and East 21 Street. It was seventy-five by thirty-six feet and three to eight feet deep. Perry Pool was located at Big Bend and Parkcrest, and Lott Pool was at Olive and Curve streets. Lott Pool was leased by the city along with sixty-nine acres of park. These pools saw their demise in the 1950s.

Cedar Park had Garner Pool and Riviera Springs Pool, but they have been closed since 1989.

Many of Austin's original pools were springs that have since gone dry. Seiders Springs, an Artesian well between 34th and 38th streets along Shoal Creek, is a part of the Shoal Creek Greenbelt. A man named Gideon White lived there from 1839 to 1842. Sometimes the springs are referred to as Cedars Springs. They must have flowed strongly, because they were recommended for the capital city's water supply. From 1847 to 1865, Army camps stayed there, and then from 1871 to 1896 it was a popular bathhouse operated by Ed Seiders. Tubs were cut from the rocky hillside and filled with hot water naturally from the springs. Seiders Springs is still operated inside Pease Park at 1300 West 34th Street. Seiders Springs is ac-

Seiders Springs Today

tually two springs, and the only active ebb and flow spring left in Texas. Now surrounded by hospitals, roads and office buildings, Seiders Springs no longer flows like it used to, but does steadily trickle. "Those delightful baths at Seiders Springs add beauty and youth and freshen old age. Baths always ready with careful attendants." Austin Democratic Statesman, July 2, 1882.

Durham Springs, located at 6th and Nueces streets on Shoal Creek, was a labor camp in 1839. Two swimming holes called Blue Hole and Cat Hole near 29th Street, and Split Rock near Wooldridge Drive were popular swimming holes way back when. There was also a place the children referred to as 'Keep Out' near the

317

Dobie property on Waller Creek. The Artesian Bath House at 5th and San Jacinto streets had hot and cold baths in "pure white sulphur water." The bathhouse was replaced by a sanitarium, commonplace in those days.

Santa Monica Springs was a very popular spot before Lake Travis covered it up. It had been in use for thousands of years as evidenced by numerous tools found around the springs. Early settlers also used the springs for its medicinal value and even bottled the water and sold it to people around the country. William Radam, an early Austinite, had malaria and lived in East Austin on thirty acres. He swore by the spring water and concocted an elaborate cure-all from the water by baking it in an oven.

medicinal springs, high in minerals, at the state capi-drilled on the grounds in 1858 produced water high and sulphur. The well was covered during the Civil War, then built over by the capitol building of 1880. Another well was drilled in 1890, and a fountain surrounds it southeast of the front steps. According to an 1893 article in the Austin American Statesman, "It is quite the fad now to take morning rides and walks to the well in the capitol yard. Each morning we see crowds of twos, threes and fours winding their way to and from the grounds and many are the little flirtations." People still come and take jugs full of the water away for a cure-all. The formula amounts to ingesting Epsom salts.

Although this book does not include the many San Antonio springs, San Pedro Springs deserves a word. San Pedro Springs has been used by people for 10,000 years. Giant tiger and mastodon bones have been found there. Father Isidro Espinosa named it in 1709 saying, "It was full of taps or sluices of water, the earth being terraced." San Pedro Springs was a stop on the El Camino Real. The surrounding park is the second-oldest park in the country (Boston Commons was first). In 1718, San Pedro Springs was selected to be the site of the mission that eventually became the Alamo. The springs are San Antonio's sole source of water; they have dried up and are the subject of much controversy. The city is planning a major renovation of the park, including replacing the current swimming pool with a lake.

SWIMMING SCHOOLS AND CAMPS

AQUATIC STUDIES CAMP

EARDC
248 Freeman Building
Southwest Texas University
San Marcos, Texas 78666
(512) 245-2329

If you're looking for something different for your kids to do in the summer, the Aquatic Studies Camp combines education and fun. For the budding biologist or environmentalist, or just for kids who like aquatic sports, this camp lets kids explore two unique aquatic habitats right in their own back yards, so to speak: the Edwards Aquifer and the San Marcos and Blanco rivers. Kids learn about the origins of the Colorado River and its ground water system, and the unique creatures that make the aquifer their home. Offered in nine one-week sessions starting in June and continuing through the start of school in August, the kids spend a solid week at the camp which is located on the Southwest Texas University campus in San Marcos. In the morning, they have educational activities such as water quality monitoring and aquatic biology. The afternoons are spent in aquatic recreation, such as tubing on the San Marcos River, Scuba diving at Aquarena Springs, rafting on the Guadalupe River near New Braunfels, or taking a day trip to beautiful Landa Park. Kids even get to spend a fun-filled day at SeaWorld in San Antonio, and then go swimming in the San Marcos River. If only this camp was offered for adults!

All camp activities are supervised by professional staff and faculty of SWTU. Scuba is taught by certified divers. Each camp is limited to twenty-six kids. Reservations are made with a $100 deposit, and camps begin and end on Saturday afternoons. Ages 9 to 15. $450 includes room, board, instruction and all activities.

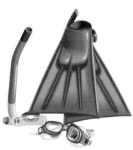

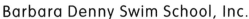

Barbara Denny Swim School, Inc.
4301 County Road 272
Leander, Texas 78641
(512) 259-4545

About seven miles from RR 620 in Austin.

Barbara Denny offers seasonal swim lessons from May to August in small group classes or private lessons. Parent and toddler classes are offered in day and evening sessions. Barbara Denny has been teaching since 1958 and is a member of the NSSA. She specializes in gentle, positive instruction. There is a shady patio for parents to watch lessons, and the pool is heated. The pool is available for party rental. Swim items are for sale, such as goggles, toys and exercise objects, kickboards, masks, shampoo, etc.

Register toddlers in early April for May classes; all other ages and abilities call the last week of April for May classes. Register by phone and give the age, skill level and dates.

Age 3 and under $95 for nine lessons. Age four and up $85 for nine lessons. Private one-on-one lesson for forty minutes is $30, or twenty minutes for $15 and a two-lesson minimum.

Crenshaw Athletic Club
5000 Fairview Drive
Austin, Texas 78731
(512) 453-5551

Morning or afternoon classes are offered for boys and girls ages 3 to 10 at four skill levels, Monday through Thursday from May to August. Terms last two to three weeks, and prices range from $65 to $90 for each term.

Sycamore Child's Place
5500 Bee Caves Road
West Lake Hills
(512) 327-0369

Summer lessons for kids only.

Barton Creek Country Club
8712 Barton Club Drive
Austin, Texas 78735
(512) 329-4000

Kirsten and Bridget Weiss and Doug Dickenson teach year-round swimming programs to build confidence and increase health. Kirsten and Bridget Weiss have twenty-five years of experience teaching and coaching. Lessons are taught indoors in warm water.

Two-week sessions for $77 include group swimming lessons with a four-to-one student-teacher ratio. There are classes to prepare youths ages 5 to 17 for swim teams, parent-toddler classes, and adult group classes. Private and semi-private lessons are also available for newborns to adults. An hour-long session costs $40-60.

Young Gymnastics Clubhouse and Sportsplex
709 North Cuernavaca Drive
Austin, Texas 78733
(512) 263-7813

Young Gymnastics has a summer camp which includes swimming and swimming lessons among other activities, such as arts and crafts, nature walks and gymnastics. Week-long sessions are held between June and July. Each session is $50, and you have a choice between morning or afternoon blocks. Kids can also be registered for extended hours or entire summers. For swimming lessons independent of, or in addition to, the other summer camp activities, classes are divided into two ability levels. Tuition is $60 per session. Classes are held Tuesdays and Thursdays with beginners at 3:15 P.M. and novices at 4:00 P.M. Novices must be able to swim fifteen feet on their front and back to be in the class.

EVENTS

SWIMATHON

Community Relations, Building 5
Austin State School
Post Office Box 1269
2203 West 35th Street
Austin, Texas 78767-1269
(512) 371-6048

S wimathon is an annual fund-raising event organized by the Austin State School to benefit its residents. The Austin State School is a residential and vocational training facility serving nearly 450 adults with developmental disabilities or hearing-impairments. The school was established in 1917 and is the oldest residential facility in Texas. The campus sits on nearly 100 acres in the heart of Austin and is covered with beautiful live oak trees. The school receives state and federal funding for the basics, but they rely on other resources to provide a higher quality of life for the residents. Swimathon has raised funds in the past to build an indoor swimming pool (the illustrious Aquadome), a chapel, and a small guest house. Other benefits have included trips to sports and cultural events. Future plans include a recreation center and campus beautification. All donations are tax-deductible.

Swimathon is open to the public and all ages and abilities are welcome. Participants garner pledges for every lap they swim. It usually takes place on a Saturday in July from 8:00-10:00 A.M. The event is held at the larger City of Austin municipal pools: Northwest, Deep Eddy, Garrison and Walnut Creek. To participate, take the following steps:

COURTESY OF AUSTIN STATE SCHOOL

Register through the Austin State School. Indicate a preference for times and pools. Secure pledges. There is a $25 minimum. Ask your friends, family, co-workers and neighbors to sponsor you per lap or with a flat cash donation. Ask your employer if they have a matching gift program. Pledges can then be mailed or hand-delivered to Community Relations, or brought to the pool the day of the event. You can also bring pledges to the victory party. The week before the event, pick up a packet containing a T-shirt, confirmations of pool times and lane reservations, also from Community Relations or at the pool on the day of the event. Swim! Go to your designated pool where volunteers, well-wishers and other swimmers cheer you on. Attend a party at the State School's Aquadome with entertainment, refreshments, and awards for those who raise the most money.

The State School provides well for swimmers with a T-shirt, goggles, sport bottle, and other goodies. The event is a lot of fun and the cause is worthwhile. For lap swimmers, it is easy to incorporate the event into their regular routine and help out the State School at the same time. The camaraderie is supportive, and school residents often participate, inspiring the rest of us. And what better way to spend an already sweltering July morning than going for a swim?

COURTESY OF AUSTIN STATE SCHOOL

SWIM-A-CROSS

Red Cross
2218 Pershing Drive
Austin, Texas 78723
(512) 928-4271

A fund-raising event, now in its eleventh year, is sponsored by the American Red Cross, the City of Austin and some area businesses. The proceeds benefit the swim team program and promote aquatic fitness. This event takes place at several swim team sites simultaneously in the middle of June. Donations help purchase equipment and provide scholarships for swim instruction. Supporting this event helps keep program costs down.

BARTON SPRINGS DIVING CHAMPIONSHIP

The Barton Springs Diving Championship sounds much more formal than it actually is. Held annually in July, amateur divers enter in categories such as Most Traditional, Most Original, and Best Splash. There are four age categories: Youth (13 and under), 14 to 23, 24 to 39, and 40 and over. Participants can also enter as three-person teams with members from each age group. The team members must first perform as individuals and then place into teams. Registration is $8 for youth, $12 for adults and $10 per team. You can register at the Springs or at one of their sponsors, or other city pools. Call the City of Austin Aquatics office for more specific information on that year's event. The fee includes a T-shirt commemorating the event and pool admission to Barton Springs.

Celebrity judges such as local comedians, musicians, athletes, newscasters, and politicians rank the competitors by holding up numbered cards accompanied by cheers or boos from the spectators. A trophy is awarded to the first place winner. Second and third place winners get medallions and ribbons. The winners in each category then square off with each other. The Grand Champion gets a silver trophy cup which is anointed with water from the Springs, then put on display in the gift shop for a year. An exhibition by the Texas Diving Team is given during the day. Live music is provided between events, and other activities such as face painting are offered for the kids. It is quite entertaining to watch the competition because there is a lot of silliness and fun. Nick Alvarado, the reigning champion, is a big guy. He has been known to dress up as Elvis for some dives. He refers to his unique brand of diving as 'heavyweight diving'. Other participants dress up in costumes such as the UT Tower, Captain Splash, and others. The contest is probably twenty-five percent serious diving, seventy-five percent fun. Anyone can enter or watch. If you just want to watch, you will pay the regular Springs admission price. Proceeds from the event go toward a charity or scholarships for children to learn aquatics skills such as swimming, diving and lifesaving.

Captain Splash prepares for his dive...

...the illustrious judges
cast their votes...

...awards are presented.

SPLASH PARTIES

Splash Parties, in my opinion, are the greatest thing since sliced bread. Catch them every Saturday night from June through August at the City of Austin Municipal Pools. Movies are shown on a screen which is mounted on the side of a truck and wheeled in for the event. The sound is amplified, but is still hard to hear over the chattering and splashing. Jim Maloy of Feature Film Service rents sixteen milli-meter projectors to the city. Maloy used to show films in Zilker Park from 1977-94, then got the idea to show them at the pools. A cartoon usually pre-cedes the movie, and the night I went it was a Texas-themed 'toon with Deep in the Heart of Texas sounding every few minutes, and everybody clap-

ping along. The movies are generally geared toward families, such as The Lion King, Pocahontas, and The Creature From the Black Lagoon in 3-D. The pools are open from 8:00-11:00 P.M. with the movie beginning at 9:00 P.M. or dusk. Admission is $2.00 for adults and 75¢ for children 12-17, 50¢ for kids 11 and

under. The event is sponsored by Aqua Chlor Commercial Pool Service and the Parks and Recreation Department and Aquatics office. You can watch the movie while floating in the pool, or even while swimming laps if the pool permits it. Re-freshments, beyond the usual vending ma-chine fare, are available. You can even bring your own cooler and picnic, but leave the glass at home. Most people bring floats and watch the movie from the water. You could also sit on the grass, but you'll have to struggle to see over the literal sea of bodies. Splash Parties must be a lifeguard's worst nightmare, because the scene is chaotic and noisy; however, they maintain their cool and focus. Unlike a traditional indoor theater, people are splashing around and jumping in and out of the water. Don't even try to follow the movie's plot because the noise level is high. During "The Creature" the kids would all start screaming whenever the monster appeared. The pool closes to the general public at about 7:45 P.M. and clears everybody out. Then they re-open and charge movie admission (even if you were just there fifteen minutes ago). Splash Parties are a great bargain, a lot of fun, and a wholly unique experience.

RIVERFEST

http://www.lcra.org

Riverfest, a relatively new event, is a festival of activities occurring every weekend in the spring. The activities are held in twenty different communities in eleven counties along the Colorado River from the pecan orchards of San Saba to Bay City on the Gulf of Mexico. 1997 marked the grand opening of the Colorado River Trail, a driving tour that connects communities and parks along the 500-mile Lower Colorado River Valley. New parks have been completed and access to the river is easier than ever. Experience everything from arts and crafts, dances, car shows, live music and entertainment, historical re-enactments of pioneer days, a poker run, bed races, air shows, demolition derbies, gunfighter shoot-outs, river parades with floats, antique and flea markets, duck races, celebrity tube races, canoe races, and many other outdoor family fun events. Of course, you can swim in any number of water ways along the trail. Riverfest is a great way to "pool-hop" from one city to another. It provides such diverse activities that anyone is bound to have fun, even if they aren't interested in swimming.

ORGANIZATIONS

There are many organizations in Central Texas that work to preserve, protect and promote our waterways. Volunteering is a great way to enjoy your community's natural resources while learning about them. Below is a sampling of some of the worthwhile groups in this area.

AUSTIN METROPOLITAN TRAILS COUNCIL
c/o The Trust for Public Land
700 San Antonio Street
Austin, Texas 78701
(512) 478-4644
amtc@juno.com

What do Austin's hike and bike trails have to do with swimming pools? Simple: they connect the pools like a connect-the-dots. You need only hike a short ways on one of Austin's numerous trails to appreciate just how many pools there are. If you find yourself sweating the summer heat, relief is just around the corner. When you feel refreshed, get back on that trail and hike over to the next pool. In fact, Austin was voted "Trail Town USA" by the American Hiking Society in 1996.

The Austin Metropolitan Trails Council is a local education group committed to the development of a comprehensive, regional trail system. AMTC supports greenway proposals that provide commuting and recreational travel alternatives, protect natural resources, promote community and improve the quality of life around Austin. The AMTC is hoping for city funding to develop six trails: Walnut Creek would create a link between MoPac, IH35 and the Colorado River. The entire trail would be fifteen miles long. AMTC would also like to improve the Bull Creek trail along Spicewood Springs and Loop 360. Improvements are underway on the Shoal Creek trail and plans are underway to build a Bouldin Creek trail linking that neighborhood to the Town Lake trail. A Blunn Creek trail would connect Big and Little Stacy Parks to the Blunn Creek Preserve. AMTC would also like to see the Colorado River Park developed. AMTC meets monthly to plan creek cleanups and build and maintain trails along area creeks and rivers. They need volunteers and public support! AMTC's grand vision includes a system of trails connecting Buda to Georgetown and the Highland Lakes to Manor.

If you enjoy Austin's hike and bike trails as much as you love the pools that dot them, support AMTC's vision for the future.

BARTON SPRINGS-EDWARDS AQUIFER CONSERVATION DISTRICT
1124-A Regal Row
Austin, Texas 78748
(512) 282-8441

Created by the Texas Legislature in 1987 to conserve, protect, and enhance ground-water resources of the Barton Springs segment of the Edwards Aquifer, the BSEACD also oversees water well permitting and registration, monitors the aquifer, controls pollution, educates the public, and assists with conservation planning and research.

FRIENDS OF THE COLORADO RIVER FOUNDATION
Post Office Box 220
Austin, Texas 78767-0220
(512) 473-3282

The Friends of the Colorado River Foundation is a nonprofit organization made up of over 700 volunteers who promote public awareness of the river's assets and encourage responsibility in using its resources. They sponsor river and land clean-ups and environmental education, such as teaching high school students to monitor water quality in their communities. The program was put to the test when Smithville High School students identified a change in water quality at Gazely Creek. An investigation detected a malfunction at a wastewater facility nearby, and the rapid response stopped the problem within 15 minutes. FCRF is the sponsor of Riverfest and Camp Chautauqua, and also provides hazardous waste collection from rural areas to avoid contamination of the river.

Membership and volunteer hours are the sole support for FCRF, and donations are 100% tax-deductible.

Friend level is $15 or more, and you'll receive a decal and newsletter.
River Champion is $50 or more, and you'll receive maps and information.
River Trustee is $500 or more, and you'll get a lapel pin and guided tours.

HILL COUNTRY FOUNDATION
Post Office Box 685075
Austin, Texas 78768-5075
(512) 478-5743

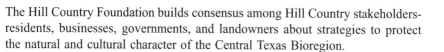

The Hill Country Foundation builds consensus among Hill Country stakeholders-residents, businesses, governments, and landowners about strategies to protect the natural and cultural character of the Central Texas Bioregion.

PARKS AND WILDLIFE FOUNDATION OF TEXAS
Post Office Box 15097
Dallas, Texas 75201-0097
(214) 720-1478

The Parks and Wildlife Foundation of Texas partners with Texas Parks and Wildlife Department to protect Texas's unique natural and cultural resources and to expand the potential for diverse outdoor recreation.

PROTECT LAKE TRAVIS ASSOCIATION
10801 Rush Road
Austin, Texas 78732

Protect Lake Travis Association monitors conditions affecting water quality and health of lake users, from San Angelo to Matagorda Bay. They educate the public about issues and promote lake access for all.

SAN MARCOS RIVER FOUNDATION
Post Office Box 1393
San Marcos, Texas 78666
(512) 393-3787

The San Marcos River Foundation works to preserve the natural beauty of the San Marcos River.

SAVE BARTON CREEK ASSOCIATION
Post Office Box 5923, Austin, Texas 78763
(512) 480-0055

These volunteers meet every Monday at the Filling Station (801 Barton Springs Road) from 7:00-8:30 P.M. to discuss ways to protect the quality of water flowing into Barton Creek and Springs. They research alternative land uses for the Edwards Aquifer watershed and encourage designation of that land for public use. SBCA also educates the public about Barton Creek's natural history.

SAVE OUR SPRINGS ALLIANCE
Post Office Box 684881
Austin, Texas 78768
(512) 477-2320

SOS protects the pristine water quality of the Texas Hill Country's Edwards Aquifer and springs through science, education, outreach and legal reform. The Save Our Springs Coalition is the only grassroots movement in the country to ever write, petition and pass a nonpoint source pollution prevention ordinance by citizen initiative. This occurred on August 8, 1992.

APPENDIX

BASIC WATER SAFETY

Swimming can be deceivingly dangerous. It seems preposterous that one could drown in a cup of water, but it is possible. Likewise, splashing in the shallow wading area of a busy pool seems foolproof, but accidents still happen. Water is an unpredictable element. Use common sense when hanging out at the pool, in the water and out. Always follow posted rules, and if there are none, be alert and prepared. Some basic safety tips to remember:

Never swim alone, no matter how advanced your skills are.

Never dive in shallow or murky water.

Don't run around the pool.

Children, no matter how experienced in the water, should never be left unattended at poolside.

Relax! That old adage about waiting thirty minutes after eating or drinking before swimming is not a bad idea because cramping can occur. Ten-minute rest periods every hour can help keep children from getting overexcited. The larger and busier City of Austin pools will enforce a break on the hour to do a safety check of the pool.

Nighttime swimming is prohibited in City of Austin pools, but you also should avoid swimming in natural springs and lakes after dark.

If you hear thunder or see lightning, definitely get out of the water. The City of Austin will force everyone out of the water if thunder is heard less than ten minutes apart.

Avoid hyperventilation: This can occur when a swimmer takes several deep breaths in preparation for a long swim underwater. The overdose of oxygen forces carbon dioxide out of the lungs, and the brain doesn't get the message that the swimmer needs more oxygen. The swimmer can black out underwater and drown.

Floatation devices can sometimes carry swimmers into water that is too deep for their swimming abilities. Most city pools confine floatation devices to the shallow end of the pool.

Glass and electrical appliances should not be kept around the pool.

If swimming long distances, have a spotter accompany you in a non-motorized boat, and stick to shallow water where you can stand up if you get tired.

Be especially careful if you are swimming directly below a dam. Water levels can fluctuate rapidly and sink a swimmer in seconds.

If you really want to be prepared, take a water safety course, swimming lessons, or CPR from a qualified organization.

CAPITAL METRO BUS ROUTES

(512) 474-1200 or 1-800-474-1201

Following is a list of some of the available bus routes that service swimming pools in the Greater Austin area. Bus routes and times change periodically and should always be confirmed by Capital Metro.

POOL	ROUTE
Barton Springs	Barton Hills 29 or Ben White 30
Emma Long	None
Bartholomew	Govalle 8
Deep Eddy	UT Lake Austin Shuttle
Mabel Davis	Duval 7/27
Northwest	Burnet 3/17/25
Walnut Creek	None (yet)
Balcones	Use Teleride for Central Millwood
Brentwood	Ohlen 5 or Walnut Creek 39
Canyon Vista	None
Citivan	Martin Luther King 4
Dittmar	South Central Flyer
Dottie Jordan	Colony Park 37
Dove Springs	Travis Heights 14/Dove Springs 27
Garrison	Manchaca 12/20 and Manchaca Flyer
Gillis	South Central Flyer 64/Rosewood 10
Givens	Govalle 8/East 12th 6
Govalle	Johnston 17
Kealing	East Austin Circular 208/Rosewood 2/ Chicon 21
Kennemer	Johnston 25
Martin	Chicon 21
Metz	Chicon 21
Montopolis	Airport 32/Montopolis 4
Murchison	UT Far West Shuttle/Bull Creek 19
Palm	Pecan Street Dillo/Chicon 21
Parque Zaragosa	Pecan Street Dillo/Chicon 21

Patterson	East Austin Circular 208
Ramsey	Burnet 3
Reed	Enfield 9
Rosewood	Woodrow 2
St. John's	Govalle 8/St. John's 120
Shipe	Ohlen 5/UT Intramural Field Shuttle/Duval 7
Stacy	Enfield 14
West Enfield	Enfield 9/UT Enfield Road
Bailey	Burnet 3
Clarksville	Enfield 9
Eastwoods	Red River 15
Odom	South First 10
Pan American	Pecan Street Dillo
Pease	Enfield 9
Ricky Guerrero	South Fifth 16
Little Stacy	Enfield 14
West Austin	Enfield 9
St. Edward's	Ben White 28/South Congress 13
Gregory Gym (UT)	Any UT Shuttle/Congress Dillo
Jamail Swim Center	Any UT Shuttle/Manchaca 20
Cat Hollow	Bull Creek 19

Teleride services Anderson Mill, Oak Hill and Pflugerville.

CHLORINE AND WATER QUALITY

Most pools add chlorine to the water to kill bacteria and algae. The outdoor pools are obviously well-ventilated, while the indoor pools can be permeated with chlorine fumes. Some people, myself included, are sensitive to these fumes. The spring-fed pools are a better choice in this respect because they generally have less chlorine added to them. And even though the water often looks greenish and murky, it is perfectly safe. A handful of spring-fed pools in the City of Austin system are drained and refilled at varying schedules rather than being filtered and chemically treated. Deep Eddy is spring-fed, and no chlorine is added to Barton Springs. However, the natural springs have their own set of troubles when run-off and heavy rains increase fecal coliform counts and the pools close to swimmers until the water quality is restored.

LAP SWIMMING ETIQUETTE

With the popularity of swimming in Austin, you should expect to share a lap lane. If two people want to swim, they usually split the lane in half length-wise. Try to time your swim so that you pass somewhere in the middle and avoid swimming side by side; if three people want to share the lane, they swim 'circles' by traveling in a counter-clockwise fashion and staying to the right side of the lane. Place about half a lap-length between yourself and the other swimmers. More than three swimmers in one lane is really too crowded, but sometimes unavoidable.

Be careful with fins, hand paddles, and any equipment you might be using. Swimmers sharing a lane pass very close to one another.

Enter and exit the lap lanes from the same end of the pool. Generally, you will be able to observe which end is designated by people climbing in and out.

Ask permission of the other swimmers before you enter a lap lane. Agree on whether to split the lane or swim circles. Sometimes it is difficult to get a lap swimmer's attention. I have tried waving, shouting, and swinging my legs in the water. Sometimes you will get a non-verbal consent when the other swimmer simply moves over or assumes swimming circles.

LAP DISTANCE CONVERSION CHART

Probably the most frequently asked question by lap swimmers is how many laps equal the length of one mile. While the lengths vary from pool to pool, I have tried to include all variations for the pools included in this book. A lap is equal to two lengths, or traveling the length down and back. I have rounded the number of laps to the nearest whole number. Find your pool's length and then consult the chart below.

1 mile=5,280 feet=1,760 yards

60 feet=44 laps=1 mile
(Citivan, Govalle, Kealing, Palm, Patterson, Reed, St. John's)

100 feet=26 laps=1 mile
(Deep Eddy, Gillis, Metz, Parque Zaragosa, Ramsey, Shipe, Stacy, West Enfield)

130 feet=20 laps=1 mile
(Rosewood)

25 yards=35 laps=1 mile
(Balcones, Canyon Vista, Dittmar, Dottie Jordan, Dove Springs, Kennemer, Murchison)

50 yards=17.5 laps=1 mile
(Bartholomew, Givens)

25 meters=32 laps=1 mile
(Walnut Creek, Martin, Montopolis, St. Edward's)

50 meters=16 laps= 1 mile
(Garrison, Mabel Davis, Northwest)

Barton Springs is one-eighth of a mile long, so swimming the length eight times equals one mile.

MOONTOWERS

The story of Austin's unique moon towers began in 1894 when the first of thirty-one towers was erected to light the City of Austin. Towers were used because the hilly terrain prevented other means of power from easily reaching the different neighborhoods developing in the new city. Standing at 165 feet, or seven stories tall, the towers each housed a cluster of six carbon arc lamps which illuminated the city in a 3,000-foot circle. Initially, the filaments were replaced daily by a city employee who climbed all seven stories of wrought iron. In 1923, the carbon arcs were replaced by incandescent bulbs, then again in 1936 with bulbs which were even dimmer. The carbon lamps cast a bluish glow akin to moonlight, hence the name, and the mercury vapor bulbs used today approximate the original look. While only seventeen towers remain, Austin is the only city whose original lighting towers remain in place and in modified use. The remaining towers were refurbished in 1985 and should remain standing as is for another fifty to seventy-five years. What do the moon towers have to do with swimming pools? Originally, the Colorado River fueled the lamps after the first dam and hydroelectric plant were completed. Today, several moon towers are located near city pools, and provide moonlight to swim by even on a moonless evening. A complete locator map is available from the Austin Visitors' Center. Each is a historical landmark.

Moon Towers that are near pools:

> Canterbury and Lynn (Metz/Martin)
> Leona and Pennsylvania (Kealing)
> East 13th and Coleto (Rosewood)
> Zilker Park (Barton Springs)
> Eastside Drive and Leland (Big and Little Stacy)

Zilker Park Moontower

Austin's golden dream was realized. Her electric light towers were running full blast, and what's more, they were a success. The entire city, from one end to the other, was brilliantly illuminated, and the streets which have for so many weeks been steeped in utter darkness, were as bright as day.

Austin Daily Statesman, May 4, 1895

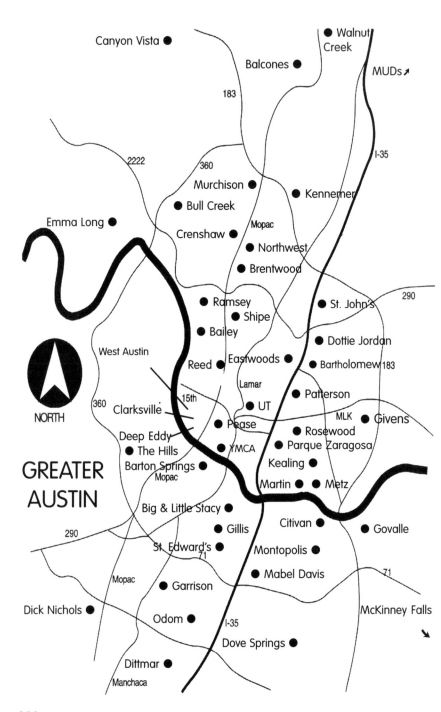

GREATER
AUSTIN

NOT TO SCALE

BIBLIOGRAPHY

The Austin American Statesman, *Deep Eddy Rats,* by Elaine Ayala, April 2, 1992; *Budget move opens pool; dry weather could close it,* by Kori Donaldson, Tuesday, June 4, 1996; *Mr. Zilker's Living Legacy,* by Patrick Beach, Saturday, June 23, 1997; *Plunging into Barton Springs,* by John T. Davis, September 28, 1997; *Springs under strain,* by Ralph Haurwitz, November 23, 1997.

The Austin Chronicle, *A Day in the Life of Barton Springs,* by,R.U. Steinberg, August 12, 1988; *Hitting the Trails,* by Nelson England, November 15, 1996; *Empire Wide and Glorious,* by Julia Austin, May 24, 1996; *Whatever Floats Your Boat,* by Robert Bryce and John Koephe, and *Hiking the Greenbelt,* by Gerald McLeod, April 17, 1992 and reprinted April 18, 1997; *Poolwatch,* Public Notice, July 11, 1996; *Not a Drop to Drink,* by Robert Bryce, July 12, 1996; *Best Bellyflop Wins!* by Mary Beth Gradziel, July 11, 1997; *It's My Pool Party and It Freaks Me Out!* by Harry Jay Knowles, July 11, 1997.

Austin Weekly, *Swimming Pool was a Wild Idea,* by J.W. West, July 19-25, 1989.

Barton Springs Eternal, Turk Pipkin and Marshall Frech, Softshoe Publishing, The Hill Country Foundation, Austin, Texas, 1993.

City Manager's Report to the City of Austin: A Historical Record of Recreation in Austin, City of Austin, Parks and Recreation Department, 1937; City of Austin Parks and Recreation Department Annual Reports: 1941; 1948; 1954; 1957-58; 1961-62; 1966-67; 1970-71; Planning Ahead for Recreation in Austin: A study of the present and future needs of the parks and recreation system in Austin, Texas, 1950-1960.

Connecticut Yankee in Texas: A Biography of Elisha Marshall Pease, Roger Allen Griffen, UT Austin Ph.D. Dissertation, 1973.

Crazy Water: The Story of Mineral Wells and Other Texas Health Resorts, by Gene Fowler, Texas Christian University Press, Fort Worth, 1991.

Cultural Resource Investigations at Hamilton Pool County Park, David G. Robinson, Austin, Texas, 1986.

Daily Democratic Statesman: 1878: (Je 6, 4:3) (Je 15, 4:2) (Je 16, 4:4) 1879: (Ag 9, 1:5) (S 13, 4:2) 1881: (Ap 16, 4:2) (My 18, 4:4) (My 27, 4:2) (Jl 20, 4:3)

(S 21, 3:1) 1882: (Jl 2, 3:5) (Jl 12, 4:2) (Ag 22, 4:3) (S 8, 4:3) (O 3, 4:3) 1883: (Jl 10, 4:4) (Jl 15, 3:3) (Jl 20, 4:3) (Jl 22, 1:7)

Damming the Colorado: The Rise of the Lower Colorado River Authority, 1933-1939, by John A. Adams, Jr., Texas A&M Press, 1990.

Drop by Drop: The Life Cycle of the Lower Colorado River, Written and edited by Quentin Martin, LCRA Corporate Communications.

Haunts of the Black Masseur: The Swimmer as Hero, by Charles Sprawson, Pantheon Books, New York, 1992.

Hill Country Oasis: Barton Springs, Barton Creek, Edwards Aquifer, Julie Martyn-Baker, Editor; Austin Parks and Recreation Department, Barton Springs Conservation District, Save Barton Springs Association, 1992.

History of Central Texas, by Mary Starr Barkley, 1970.

Ideas for Swimming Pools, Sunset Books, Edited by David E. Clark, 1981.

Lakeway: The First 25 Years and Earlier Times Around the Colorado River, Byron D. Varner, 1988.

Splash! Great Writing About Swimming, Edited by Laurel Blossom, The Ecco Press, Hopewell, New Jersey, 1996.

Springs of Texas Volume 1, by Gunnar Brune, Branch-Smith, Inc., Fort Worth, Texas, 1981.

Texas Highways, *Austin's Zilker Park: From A to Z*, by Nancy Bishop, August 1997.

Texas Monthly, *Last One In...* by Joe Nick Patowski, June, 1985.

Trail Map: Barton Creek Greenbelt, Breakthrough Publications, 1988.

Zilker Park Walking Tour Guidebook: A Recreational Visit to the Edwards Limestone, Jennifer Walker and Paul Knox, Gulf Coast Association of Geological Studies, 1994.

Historical Presentation on Deep Eddy Bathing Beach at the Texas Historical Marker Dedication, by Beverly S. Sheffield, May 16, 1992.

ABOUT THE AUTHOR

Chandra Moira Beal is a freelance writer who lives in Austin, Texas. She has published numerous articles in national publications. This is her first book. When she is not writing or swimming, Chandra stays busy with many hobbies and volunteering, promoting animal welfare and rescuing rabbits. She enjoys spending time with her best friend, Maia, and her partner, Stan. She explores the splendid aquatic resources of Central Texas every chance she gets. To read other works by this author and to learn more about Chandra, visit <www.beal-net.com/chandra>.

INDEX

A

D

E

L

ORDER FORM

Yes! Please send me _____ cop(ies) of *Splash Across Texas!*

Ship to:

Name: _____

Address: _____

City, State, Zip + 4-digit: _____

Telephone: _____

E-mail: _____

_____ books x $16.95 per book = $ _____

Shipping and Handling ($3.95 per book) + _____

Sales Tax 8.25% (Texas residents only) + _____

Grand Total $ _____

☐ Check or money order enclosed
(made payable to La Luna Publishing)

Mail to:

La Luna Publishing
Post Office Box 33189
Austin, Texas 78764-0189

Or order online at:
www.beal-net.com/chandra

Questions? Call (512) 441-6524
or e-mail laluna@onr.com